# AAAAALLLVIIINNN!:
## THE STORY OF ROSS BAGDASARIAN, SR., LIBERTY RECORDS, FORMAT FILMS AND

## THE ALVIN SHOW

### BY MARK ARNOLD

# OTHER BOOKS BY MARK ARNOLD:

*The Best of the Harveyville Fun Times!*

*Created and Produced by Total TeleVision productions* (BearManor)

*If You're Cracked, You're Happy, Part Won* (BearManor)

*If You're Cracked, You're Happy, Part Too* (BearManor)

*Mark Arnold Picks on The Beatles*

*Frozen in Ice: The Story of Walt Disney Productions* (BearManor)

*Think Pink: The Story of DePatie-Freleng* (BearManor)

*Pocket Full of Dennis the Menace* (BearManor)

*Long Title: Good Clean Fun; Examining The Monkees Songs, One By One by Michael A. Ventrella and Mark Arnold* (BearManor)

# AAAAALLLVIIINNN!:
## THE STORY OF ROSS BAGDASARIAN, SR., LIBERTY RECORDS, FORMAT FILMS AND

## THE ALVIN SHOW

Aaaaalllviiinnn!: The Story of Ross Bagdasarian, Sr.,
Liberty Records, Format Films and *The Alvin Show*

© 2019 Mark Arnold and Fun Ideas Productions

The character names and likenesses of Alvin and the Chipmunks, *The Alvin Show*, The Chipmunks, Alvin, Simon, Theodore, David Seville, Clyde Crashcup, Leonardo and The Chipettes are trademarks and © by Bagdasarian Productions, LLC.

Mr. Magoo and The Lone Ranger are © Classic Media, a division of NBCUniversal, LLC.

Looney Tunes and Merrie Melodies is © Warner Bros. Pictures, Inc.

Liberty Records is © UMe

All prominent characters mentioned in this book and the distinctive likenesses thereof are copyrighted trademarks and properties of their respective copyright holders. The images included in this book are © their respective copyright holders and are used as Fair Use to be illustrative for the text contained herein.

The material used in this book is used for historical purposes and literary criticism and review and is used by permission. It is not designed to plagiarize or in any other way infringe on the copyrights of any copyrighted materials contained herein.

First printing
All Rights Reserved.
Reproduction in whole or part without the author's permission is strictly forbidden.

Published in the USA by BearManor Media.

For information, address:
BearManor Media
P.O. Box 71426
Albany, GA 31708
bearmanormedia.com

Permission is granted to other publications or media to excerpt the contents contained herein for review purposes provided that the correct credit and copyright information is included for any materials reproduced.

Library of Congress Cataloging-in-Publication Data

Aaaaalllviiinnn!: The Story of Ross Bagdasarian, Sr., Liberty Records, Format Films and *The Alvin Show* / by Mark Arnold

Includes index.

ISBN    978-1-62933-432-5 (Paperback)
        978-1-62933-433-2 (Hardback)

Cover artwork by Jim Engel

Typesetting and layout by Darlene Swanson • van-garde.com.

Dedicated to the life and creations of Ross Bagdasarian, Sr. (1919-1972). Without him, there would not be this book or many entertained children.

Special thanks to Ross Bagdasarian, Jr., Jerry Beck, Cullen Blaine, Jamie Coville, Steve Cox, Rick Detorie, Jim Engel, Greg Ehbar, James Fanning, Dale Hale, Barry Hansen, Tim Hollis, Janice Karman, Mark Kausler, Mike Kazaleh, Bob Kurtz, Craig Marin, Jeff Missinne, Jack Roth, Lucinda Ann Sanderson, Scott Shaw!, Stu Shostak, Joe Siracusa, Danny Solazzi, Steve Stanchfield, Steve Thompson, Tralfaz, Mark Warden, Katy Wesley and Mark A. Yirkuw.

Interviews conducted by the author for this book:

Joe Siracusa - June 27, 2013
Bob Kurtz - June 29, 2017
Dale Hale - July 12, 2017

# CONTENTS

Foreword By Danny Solazzi. . . . . . . . . . . . . . . . . . . . . . . . . . ix

Introduction . . . . . . . . . . . . . . . . . . . . . . . . . . . . . . . . . . . xi

"Come On-A My House" . . . . . . . . . . . . . . . . . . . . . . . . . . . 1

Liberty Records. . . . . . . . . . . . . . . . . . . . . . . . . . . . . . . . . 29

"The Witch Doctor" And "The Chipmunk Song" . . . . . . . . . . . . 55

Format Films. . . . . . . . . . . . . . . . . . . . . . . . . . . . . . . . . .133

*The Alvin Show* . . . . . . . . . . . . . . . . . . . . . . . . . . . . . . . .183

*The Mixed-Up World Of Bagdasarian*. . . . . . . . . . . . . . . . . . .241

*Chipmunk Punk* And Beyond. . . . . . . . . . . . . . . . . . . . . . .309

Index. . . . . . . . . . . . . . . . . . . . . . . . . . . . . . . . . . . . . . .369

About the Author. . . . . . . . . . . . . . . . . . . . . . . . . . . . . . .385

# FOREWORD BY DANNY SOLAZZI OF THE CHARACTERS

When I was a kid growing up my family had *Meet The Beatles*, The Monkees self-titled first album and The Chipmunks' *Lets All Sing With The Chipmunks*, *Around The World With The Chipmunks* and *The Alvin Show*. Pretty good way to start a record collection!

The Chipmunks records were so much fun to listen to.

The covers were shiny foil. The vinyl, for the first LP was red and the songs and the skits were extremely well put together. They are still as entertaining and musical as when they first came out many years ago. I loved the three part harmonies of Alvin, Simon and Theodore and the way Dave would get annoyed at Alvin and yell at him. It seemed real to me.

Ross Bagdasarian was a great songwriter, arranger and producer. The records have a depth and are so well crafted. These are not just children's records.

When my band, The Characters, were first getting together back when we were only in our teens, our influences came from the music we grew up on: The Beatles, The Rolling Stones, The Kinks, The Monkees and so many more. I am sure that the music of Ross Bagdasarian and The Chipmunks were on that list, too!

Mark Arnold has put together a fantastic book unearthing a world of information about Ross Bagdasarian, Liberty Records, Format Films and *The Alvin Show*. The interviews and session information on the recordings shed new light on these important records.

There is a wealth of fantastic photos, behind the scenes background on *The Alvin Show* and revealing insights into the inner workings of Liberty Records.

If you love The Chipmunks, you will love this book!

— Danny

# INTRODUCTION

A FEW YEARS AGO after the publication of my TTV book, I had a conversation with cartoonist Scott Shaw! about what animation studio I should cover next. Scott said that he wanted to know more about Format Films. I flippantly answered, "Format did *The Alvin Show*, *The Lone Ranger* and then closed. The End." I was dismissive because I honestly thought that that is all they did at the time. I had no idea of Format's connection to UPA and to other studios at the time like Jay Ward, TV Spots, Pantomime Pictures, DePatie-Freleng and Warner Bros.

With this book, I plan to cover that and more. I was always a fan of Alvin and The Chipmunks as long as I remember. My mother owned and played me the original Chipmunks record, "The Chipmunk Song" and I would watch the cartoons in the early 1970s on Saturday mornings. I honestly thought they were being made at the time and not 10 years earlier and airing in primetime no less! I also didn't know that the original voice of The Chipmunks, Ross Bagdasarian, Sr., had passed away in 1972 during the time I was watching these shows originally. I also didn't know that was his name as I thought there really was a man named David Seville.

I will say it here in this intro and then refrain from speaking about it any further, but there are many who say that the Ross Bagdasarian,

Sr. version of The Chipmunks is and always will be the ONLY version of The Chipmunks to pay attention to. I don't tend to feel that strongly about it as the versions by Ross Bagdasarian, Jr. and Janice Karman have their own merit. For the sake of this book, the latter day versions will be covered in the final chapter.

That said, I realized a book solely about the Ross Bagdasarian, Sr. version of The Chipmunks would not be a complete picture without covering the man, the major record label he recorded for - Liberty, and the animation company that Ross hooked up with do to *The Alvin Show* - Format Films. This book covers it all.

One small note to the text: Ross Bagdasarian, Sr. will generally be referred to as "Bagdasarian", while his son, Ross Bagdasarian, Jr. will generally be referred to as "Ross Jr." unless in context within a quote.

— Mark Arnold

# "COME ON-A MY HOUSE"

Ross Bagdasarian, Sr. tells his story in the liner notes of his third and final solo LP called *A Summer Day's Delight*, released in 1970, "My name is Ross Bagdasarian. I was born in Fresno, California, on January 27, 1919. My home town of Fresno is an average size town, I would say. The population is around 90,000 people, and at least twice that many grapes and raisins. The people are average but the raisins are the finest you can get anywhere in the world." Although Bagdasarian claims his name is Ross, his real full name was Rostom Sipan Bagdasarian and he was 5'7" according to his son, Ross Jr. He graduated from Fresno High School in 1937.

Bagdasarian also had two older brothers: Richard Sirak Bagdasarian (1910-1966) and Harry Sisvan Bagdasarian (1915-1989).

Lucinda Ann Sanderson and Michael J. Tawney continue the story from *Mindrot* #12, "Bagdasarian came from the Armenian-American community in Fresno, where the family owned a vineyard and was associated with the Sierra Wine Company. One of Bagdasarian's first cousins was the famous playwright William Saroyan. Bagdasarian was first generation Armenian-American and could speak Armenian."

Bagdasarian continues, "I went to school in Fresno. The usual thing, grammar school, junior high school and high school. Finally, one miserable year in college and boredom really set in. I wanted to be an actor and the man in charge, they called him "Prof", said I should start by painting some walls a deep green. I told him I wanted to be an actor and then I quit. Before I forget, I want to say that in 1927, I became famous with my family. I skipped the third grade.

"The name Bagdasarian is, needless to say, Armenian and my father, also needless to say, was a grape grower. I worked in the grapes, if I worked at all, and at the age of 16, while driving a truckload of grapes from the vineyard to the packing house, I wrote my first song. It was called "Nuts To You." Some smart alec I knew claimed that it wasn't what you would call a "ballad." Now that I look back I guess he was right. It was a song thought. It had words and it had music and when I sang it, it had spirit, but I guess it wasn't a ballad.

"After I quit college, I decided that if I was going to be an actor the thing to do was to go to a place where they did some acting. They didn't do much acting in Fresno. It was a good place to stay and learn to pick grapes but I wanted to act so I went to New York. This was in 1939 and I was 20 years old. I went straight to the Theatre Guild and after three days I got in to see Theresa Helburn. She was one of the directors of the guild. She asked me some pretty important questions about my background in the theatre and I gave her some pretty important answers, the most important of which was that I was the best natural born actor she had ever seen. I got the part of the singing Greek newsboy in *The Time Of Your Life* and every night I came out and sang "When Irish Eyes Are Smiling" in addition to the six or seven lines that I had with Eddie Dowling. I didn't exactly steal the show with my performance, but two weeks later I was given the part of the pinball way and on the road. During that summer, I was the assistant stage manager for a show called *Love's Old Sweet Song*. The show closed in three weeks, just in time for me to go on the road with *The Time Of Your Life*."

Bagdasarian doesn't mention that his mother Verna "Verkin" Saroyan passed away on April 21, 1941, at the age of 50. She was born in Turkey in 1891. Nor does Bagdasarian mention that he got married to his wife, Armen, in 1946.

Bagdasarian continues, "It was during this period that I drove back to Fresno with Bill Saroyan and while we were in New Mexico I started singing a song that I had been thinking about. It was called "Come On-a My House." Saroyan liked it and helped me finished it." The song was first performed in an off-Broadway production of *The Son*, and cousin William Saroyan (1908-1981) and Bagdasarian recorded their own version with lengthy spoken-word passages. They released the single on Coral Records as "Come On-a My House" / "Oh, Beauty". Their version didn't chart.

It was then covered by fellow Armenian singer Kay Armen (real name Armenuhi Manoogian) (1915-2011) in 1951 with the Ray Charles Singers and the John Gart Orchestra for Federal Records. There are some sources that say Armen was related to Bagdasarian and Saroyan as another cousin, but other than an Armenian background, a blood relation is not confirmed. Armen (last name) certainly was not the same Armen (first name) who was Bagdasarian's wife as some sources have stated, nor was the song necessarily written for Armen.

It wasn't until Rosemary Clooney (1982-2002) recorded it later on in 1951 for Columbia Records that it became a major hit. Clooney recorded it upon the recommendation of Mitch Miller (1911-2010).

Son Ross Jr. appeared on episode #82-34 of the long-running *Dr. Demento Show* starring Barry Hansen (1941-   ) on August 22, 1982. It was one of the first times he publicly talked at length about his father and his creations, "Back in 1950, he came to Los Angeles with a song called "Come On-a My House" and everyone in the town told him that he'd never be able to make it in the business, but one day Mitch Miller insisted that Rosemary Clooney sing the song and that was my dad's first song and his first success, and after that he figured, "This is a snap!"

"His cousin was Bill Saroyan. They went way back when Bill had written one of his biggest plays *The Time of Your Life*, my dad was actually in that play in New York at the age of 19, so they went way back. Then there were some other hits. There was 'Hey Brother, Pour the Wine' for Dean Martin (1917-1995). Then there were some really dry times for him. He did a song that was an instrumental that you would probably not remember the title to. It's titled "Armen's Theme", but you hear it in every elevator that has musak."

Lawrence Lee and Barry Gifford elaborate this early success for Bagdasarian in their book, *Saroyan: A Biography*, "Ross sent a copy of the song to Mitch Miller, then a powerful artist-and-repertory executive with Columbia Records.

Rosemary Clooney comments, "Mitch had a demonstration record of it, and he heard it one day and wanted to record it the next, and he was absolutely sure that it was going to be a huge success for me.

"Now, the fact that it was an Armenian folk song, he wanted an accent. I don't know how to do an Armenian accent, so I used what I laughingly called an Italian accent because that was the band I sang with, an Italian band, Tony Pastor.

"It is a strange piece of material, but it took off like a house afire. It was one whole summer. That was the one that Mitch Miller called the sales department and said, 'Ship 300,000 on consignment,' and if he does that, everybody listens. And they did it.

"I went to Florida for a week and came back, and at that time on Broadway, there were four big record stores, and they had loudspeakers on the outside and they'd be playing the top records they were selling. I came back from Florida and drove down from La Guardia, down Broadway, with my head stuck out of the cab, and listened to myself for the first time on Broadway, just out of these record stores."

The book continues, "The record sold 900,000 copies almost instantaneously, and it was the inescapable soundtrack to the summer of 1951."

"Ross and I have made about $15,000 apiece out of the song so far," Saroyan said that summer. He and Ross had a small office in Beverly Hills where they dealt with the business aspects of their sudden success and tried to extend it by converting other Armenian material in the same vein. "What we do with these songs is, we just grab them. If they ain't in the public domain, why, we sort of ease them over into the public domain," and all the material was based on Near Eastern themes. "Oh, Beauty" had been "Akh, Yavroos" in the original Armenian, and like the others and despite its merit, failed to replicate the success of "Come On-a My House", with its recitation of delights, including the most Armenian of produce items, the pomegranate."

Enid Fife comments in her article "David Seville: Brings Alvin to TV" from the October 1961 *TV Radio Mirror*, "Two things saved him for show business: The first, of course, is talent. The second, being the cousin of playwright William Saroyan. "Through Bill, I got to play the pinball maniac (type casting, if there ever was any) in his *Time of Your Life* hit on Broadway. Then came the war."

*Mindrot* adds, "In 1956, Bagdasarian adopted the pseudonym of David Seville, probably because he wanted the public to know him by a more American-sounding name and because he wanted to be known by a surname which was shorter and easier to remember."

Ross Jr. on *Dr. Demento* adds, "Ross Bagdasarian is not only a very difficult name to pronounce, but it also goes on longer than most labels did. So the record company at that time said, 'Ross, please, this is too difficult for anyone to pronounce, could you shorten it up?' And when he was in the army, he had been in Spain and loved the city of Seville and they were thinking that if they ever had another child and it was a boy, they would name it David. He put the two together and the next day he was known as David Seville."

Marty Winters in "Ross Bagdasarian: The Man Who Would Be Chipmunk King" from *Cool and Strange Music* #18, August-November 2000 continues, "In the meantime, Uncle Sam had other plans. Bagdasarian was drafted and spent four years as an Air Force control tower operator, during which time he was sanctioned in Europe spending some memorable time near Seville, Spain. By the time he was discharged from the service he had decided to get back to his roots and try his hand at grape growing. According to Bagdasarian, he "was looking for a good clean kind of existence," so in 1945, he headed back to central California and the vineyards."

Bagdasarian continues, "Right after the show closed I was called into the Army and spent the next four years in the Air Force as a control tower operator. I visited nearly all the European capitals while with the Air Force and I did my job well, although I did nothing heroic except the time I kept Sam Williams from going into an off-limits joint and thereby saved him a painful trip to the medics."

*TV Radio Mirror* elaborates, "After four years in the Air Corps, Ross returned to Fresno, met a local lovely named Armen, and settled down to raising a family and grapes—with the customary by-products of wine and raisins. He had three lean years, then, in 1949, produced a real bumper crop. Alas, it was then he discovered the bottom had fallen out of the grape market. 'That's when I decided grapes were for the birds. I took my wife, two children, $200 and an unpublished song, "Come On-a My House", and headed for Hollywood.'

"Ross had composed this song almost ten years before, with the help of cousin Saroyan, when they were driving from New York to Fresno after the closing of Bill's play. Both had forgotten about it until Ross came across the manuscript while packing."

Bagdasarian agrees, "I got out of the Army I went right back to Fresno. A man gets confused after spending four years in the Army. I went back to the grapes because I was looking for a good clean kind of existence and I figured that the vineyards were the answer. I met and married a wonderful girl and just by way of showing off to her I branched out for myself and leased sixty acres of land, all grapes, in order to make a small fortune and prove to her that her choice had been a wise one. I worked hard with the grapes and when harvest time rolled around I had the prettiest sixty acres of grapes anyone had ever seen. The market dropped before we started and we had to give the grapes away. I guess she thought I was all right though because we're still married.

"Upon her insistence - her name is Armen by the way - we came to Los Angeles with two children and an unpublished song called "Come On-a My House". I spent the next year and half whistling, singing and stomping out the words and music of the song to anyone who would listen. Dave Barbour and Peggy Lee said it was the wrong time of year for a song like that. Frankie Laine said there was no use in trying to get a song like that recorded because dialect stuff just wouldn't get it. It went with many others until somehow Rosemary Clooney made a record of it and things finally popped loose."

*Cool and Strange Music* elaborates, "Bagdasarian's songwriting career spanned decades and his most famous contribution to American pop culture - The Chipmunks - have been enjoyed by three generations of children the world over. His first million seller "Come On-a My House" is a classic pop tune that still sounds fresh today. Over 40 years after it was recorded, Bagdasarian's rise from grape-grower to million-selling songwriter and television mogul is nothing short of miraculous and a perfect example of the American Dream come true."

Bagdasarian followed up his first Coral Records single with "The Girl with the Tambourine" / "He Says Mm-Hmm", this time released under his own name at the end of 1951 to no success.

By November 1953, Bagdasarian switched labels to Mercury and released "Let's Have a Merry, Merry Christmas" / "Hey Brother, Pour the Wine". The A-side is a silly novelty record with whiny vocals and sound effects, but is significant as it is Bagdasarian's first released Christmas song. A portent of things to come. The B-side did nothing for Bagdasarian with its ethnic sounding ditty, but found success with another cover version.

Ross Jr. explains on *Demento*, "By 1954, he had scored another minor hit with his vineyard inspired "Hey, Brother, Pour the Wine", as recorded by Dean Martin. He had previously recorded his own version of the same song as the B-side of a Christmas single he made for Mercury Records in 1953, as well as a couple of singles for Coral Records including his version of "Come On-a My House" in 1951.

"While working at Mercury, Bagdasarian also appeared on an EP that featured himself and fellow Mercury recording artists Vic Damone and Georgia Gibbs doing their interpretations of songs from the 1953 hit Broadway musical *Kismet*. Bagdasarian sang "Not Since Nineveh" and "Zubbediya", two tunes that easily lent themselves to his humorous approach. He wouldn't find real success in the music industry until he joined Liberty Records in 1956."

David Edwards and Mike Callahan, in their "Liberty Records Story" from 2001 discusses when Bagdasarian joined the label, "It was around this same time that Ross Bagdasarian, Sr. joined the label, "Bagdasarian had been a songwriter of some success when Liberty signed him in 1955. He first recorded under the name "Alfi and Harry". His follow-up single was under his own name, but it disappeared without a trace. A quick reverting to Alfi and Harry didn't do much either. Seeking a simpler pseudonym, Bagdasarian then recorded the instrumental "Armen's Theme" under the name David Seville.

"He soon shifted to novelty records, with a few chart successes within the next few years such as "Gotta Get to Your House", "The Bird On My Head", "Little Brass Band", and "Judy".

*Cool and Strange Music* continues, "Bagdasarian was friends with pianist Mark McIntyre, father of Liberty recording artists Patience and Prudence, and had been instrumental in bringing their talents to the attention of label executives. As a result, he soon found himself recording under the name of Alfi and Harry (with Mark McIntyre as the woeful pianist, Harry) and a series of novelty singles were issued which featured Bagdasarian adding monologue over what were essentially instrumentals.

"The Trouble With Harry" / "A Little Beauty" came out in December 1955 and is probably the most successful of the bunch, rising to #44 on the US charts. It features Bagdasarian's Alfi (short for Alfred, as in Hitchcock?) berating the heavy-handed pianist Harry, eventually firing him by song's end. Probably not so coincidentally, the song title is the same as the Hitchcock film released earlier in the year."

The B-side "A Little Beauty" is a silly song written by Bagdasarian where he literally asks on the record if it is a hit or a miss.

*Cool and Strange Music* continues, "Other Alfi and Harry singles included "Persian On Excursion" / "Word Game Song" from April 1956 and "Safari" / "Closing Time" from April 1957 - all penned by Bagdasarian. After a follow-up single in 1956 under his own name "The Bold and the Brave" / "See a Teardrop Fall", which didn't crack the charts, Bagdasarian issued a series of singles under what would become his most famous pseudonym - David Seville. The instrumental "Armen's Theme", named for his wife, was released by Bagdasarian under the David Seville name and became a #42 hit in November 1956. Interestingly, it would make the charts again in 1963, also on Liberty, but this time as a vocal recorded by Bobby Vee and retitled "Yesterday and You.""

A version of "Armen's Theme" was released on all four of Bagdasarian's solo albums. The B-side was called "Carousel in Rome" and it is a standard but effective accordion instrumental reminiscent of the "Third Man Theme", but written by Bagdasarian. Bagdasarian would go on to cover the "Third Man Theme" and both would appear on Bagdasarian's first LP *The Music of David Seville*.

"The Donkey and the Schoolboy" / "The Gift" was released next in February 1957, both written by Bagdasarian and both appearing on *The Music of David Seville* album. "Donkey" is a whistling instrumental tune and "Gift" is a slow song with simple guitar, that was also covered by Mike Secrest. "Donkey" also appeared on Bagdasarian's second album *Witch Doctor*.

"More Seville singles followed including "Gotta Get to Your House" (June 1957), which was a kind of answer song to his earlier "Come On-a My House", and an LP - *The Music of David Seville* came out in 1957 as well. The record even included liner notes written by his famous cousin and songwriting partner, Saroyan. Still, the name David Seville was hardly a household name, and as luck would have it, Liberty Records was only treading water financially, in spite of having such great artists as Julie London, Martin Denny and Eddie Cochran on its roster, the label had not been able to score a huge hit. All that would change in 1958 and Bagdasarian would be the man responsible."

"Gotta Get To Your House" / "Camel Rock" reached #77 on the charts and sported a picture sleeve, the first for a Bagdasarian-recorded single. "Gotta" is a tinkly piano tune with spoken phrases and humor ("eyes...house" and "She ain't home?") The song appears on three of the four Bagdasarian albums. "Camel" is another whistling instrumental like "The Donkey and the Schoolboy" with an ethnic-sounding guitar and drums. It too appears on the first two of the four Bagdasarian solo albums.

The final three Seville singles before the explosion of "Witch Doctor" include "Cecilia" / "Pretty Dark Eyes" in September 1957; "Bagdad Express' / 'Starlight, Starbright" November 1957 and "Bonjour Tristesse" / "Dance From Bonjour Tristesse" in February 1958. Here's some information on each:

"Cecilia" is a cover version sang well and "Pretty Dark Eyes" features Ernie Freeman on piano accompanied by accordion and guitar and is an instrumental except for the title shouted multiple times. Both songs appear on *The Music of David Seville* and on *Witch Doctor* LPs.

"Bagdad Express" sounds like an instrumental version of "Come On-a My House" and "Starlight" features female singers and a chorus. Neither song ever appeared on an album.

"Bonjour Tristesse" is an instrumental featuring cymbals and trumpet and "Dance From Bonjour Tristesse" is an instrumental featuring mandolin and trumpets. Again, neither song ever appeared on an album.

*The Music of David Seville* needed more songs to fill out the album, so Bagdasarian recorded covers of "Amapola", "Third Man Theme", "Willow Weep for Me" and "Goofus". All are instrumentals featuring basic guitar, drums, piano, sometimes chimes and a tube and other percussion. Strangely, none of the Alfi and Harry tracks were used for the album, nor were any songs Bagdasarian recorded for Coral or Mercury.

Bagdasarian adds, "I kept writing songs and also started to do parts in pictures. The songs, in addition to "House" are "Oh, Beauty", "He Says 'Mm-Hmm'", "The Girl with the Tambourine", "What's the Use", "Dot's Nice, Don'-a Fight", "Y-y-y-yup" and "Shepherd Boy", all published and all recorded. Hot Dog! The pictures have been seven in number, the best of which have been the last two. By best I mean I had featured parts in both of them. I don't think they will win any awards either here or abroad. And I'm pretty sure I won't either. Anyway, the names of the pictures are *Destination Gobi* for 20th Century Fox, and *Alaska Seas* for Paramount." It is unknown as to whether Bagdasarian recorded proper versions of "What's the Use", "Dot's Nice, Don'-a Fight", "Y-y-y-yup" and "Shepherd Boy", but demos may exist.

Marlene Dietrich (1901-1992) and Rosemary Clooney recorded "Dot's Nice" as a hopeful hit follow-up to "Come On-a My House". Comedian Jerry Lewis (1926-2017) recorded "Y-y-y-yup" making Bagdasarian one person to compose a song for both Dean Martin (1917-1995) and Jerry Lewis. Louis Prima (1910-1978) and Keely Smith (1928-2017) recorded "Shepherd Boy" and Johnny Ray (1927-1990) sang "What's the Use". The latter two have middle eastern sounding orchestration.

*Mindrot* continues, "In the 1950s, Bagdasarian established himself as a songwriter, but he was surely one of the most paradoxical songwriters of all time. He could neither read nor write music or play any instrument in the acceptable sense. The music he made was transcribed onto music paper by professional musicians. Yet in spite of his unconventional methods, Bagdasarian's career was a success story as glorious as anyone could wish.

"Bagdasarian was fascinated with sound. Any kind of sound he could produce on any kind of instrument or any kind of vocal sound. And since he worked constantly with tape recorders, he inevitably considered the the kinds of sounds one could make by recording something at a slow speed and then playing it back twice as fast. Of course, this had already been done in animated cartoons and on children's records. But under Bagdasarian, the "sped-up voice" achieved a level of popularity it had never known before and which it has not known since."

*TV Radio Mirror* elaborates, "Anyone who thinks my songs are nuts," says Bagdasarian, "is only half right. Raisins had just as much to do with the success of my musical concoctions." In these words, the composer of such weirdies as "Witch Doctor" and "The Chipmunk Song" refers to the fact that he was born in the grape (and raisin) country of Fresno, California. His father was in the vineyard business and, for a while, it looked as though Ross would follow in his dad's footsteps."

*Cool and Strange Music* continues by discussing Bagdasarian's various acting roles, "Never one to put all his eggs in one basket, though, Bagdasarian continued to pursue acting roles and worked in film throughout the 1950s. He had parts in several B-movies and some features as well, including *Destination Gobi* (1953), *The Proud and Profane* (1956), *The Devil's Hairpin* (1957) and *The Deep Six* (1958). One of his most interesting roles was in the 1954 classic by Alfred

Hitchcock, *Rear Window*, where he played the part of (What else?) the songwriter, one of the characters living across the courtyard from James Stewart."

*TV Radio Mirror* adds, "But you don't get rich on one song, so I kept acting," Ross explains. His movie parts got bigger, better. He appeared in *The Proud and Profane*, Hitchcock's *Rear Window*, and *The Deep Six*. He kept writing songs, too—among them, "Hey, Brother, Pour the Wine", "What's the Use" and "Gotta Get to Your House."

In the years leading up to The Chipmunks, Bagdasarian would make his initial mark as not only a songwriter, but also as a bitplayer in a number of Hollywood movies. Many of these parts were uncredited and he seldom had speaking lines, but the combination of songwriting and publishing and these parts, helped sustain the family during the years after he signed up with Liberty Records, but before he hit paydirt with "Witch Doctor" and "The Chipmunk Song".

The film roles Ross, Sr. tackled, included *The Greatest Show on Earth* (1952) as Spectator (uncredited); *Viva Zapata!* (1952) as Officer (uncredited); *The Stars Are Singing* (1953) as Song Promoter (uncredited); *Destination Gobi* (1953) as Paul Sabatello; *The Girls of Pleasure Island* (1953) as Marine (uncredited); *Stalag 17* (1953) as Singing Prisoner of War (uncredited); *Alaska Seas* (1954) as Joe, Jim's crewman; *Rear Window* (1954) as Songwriter; *Kismet* (1955) as Fevvol (uncredited); *Hot Blood* (1956) as Gas Station Attendant (uncredited); *The Proud and Profane* (1956) as Louie; *Three Violent People* (1956) as Asuncion Ortega; *The Devil's Hairpin* (1957) as Tani Ritter; and *The Deep Six* (1958) as Pvt. Aaron Slobodjian.

Bagdasarian concludes, "That's pretty much the story. I'm delighted with the whole cockeyed thing because if it hadn't been cockeyed, none of the good things would have happened and I might still be driving a truckload of grapes to the packing house, trying to improve on the lyric of "Nuts To You.""

Bagdasarian doesn't discuss his home life much in interviews, but he married Armenouhi Kulhanjian (1/13/27-11/11/91) in 1946, and eventually they had three children: Carol Askine Bagdasarian (born July 4, 1947), who became an actress; Ross Dickran Bagdasarian, Jr, (born May 6, 1949) who ended up focusing on The Chipmunks in their later incarnations; and Adam Serak Bagdasarian (born March 25, 1954), who became a published author.

During Bagdasarian's lifetime, the children pretty much did their own things and didn't really participate much with their father's work; Ross Jr. proudly proclaiming in many interviews to preferring the Little League to his dad's music. After his death in 1972, Ross Jr. took it upon himself to continue the legacy of his father and to revitalize Alvin and The Chipmunks, and started making appearances on various shows.

Some of the earliest photos that publicly exist of Bagdasarian appear in the 1936 Owl Yearbook from Fresno High School:

Bagdasarian (far left) appeared at cousin William Saroyan's wedding from the book Sayoran: A Biography. From left to right: Ross and Armen Bagdasarian, William Saroyan, Archbishop Calfayan, Carol Saroyan, Araks and Manuel Tolegian. (Photo courtesy of Adam Saroyan.)

Bagdasarian's first song was "Come On-a My House", co-written with his cousin, the author William Saroyan. Singer Kay Armen was the first to cover the song in 1951; then Rosemary Clooney had a break-out hit with it later in the year. It was Bagdasarian's first major success. These are the sheet music covers.

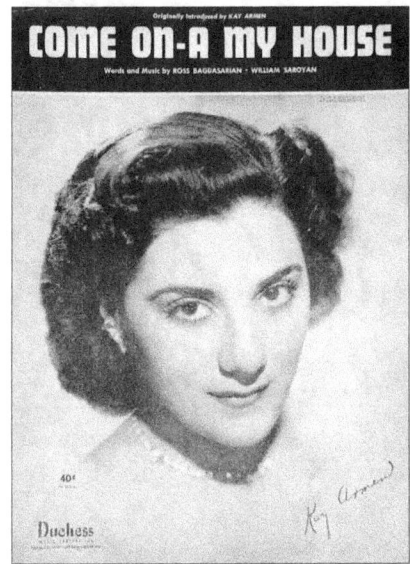

**Come On-a My House Kay Armen sheet music**

**Come On-a My House Rosemary Clooney sheet music**

William Saroyan, Bagdasarian, and George Cates around the time of "Come On-a My House" (1951).

Bagdasarian appears with Rosemary Clooney in The Stars Are Singing (1953).

Sheet music for "Hey Brother, Pour the Wine", a hit for singer Dean Martin in 1954 after Bagdasarian wrote and recorded it in 1953.

Bagdasarian performed two songs on this "Kismet" EP from 1953: "Not Since Nineveh" and "Zubbediya".

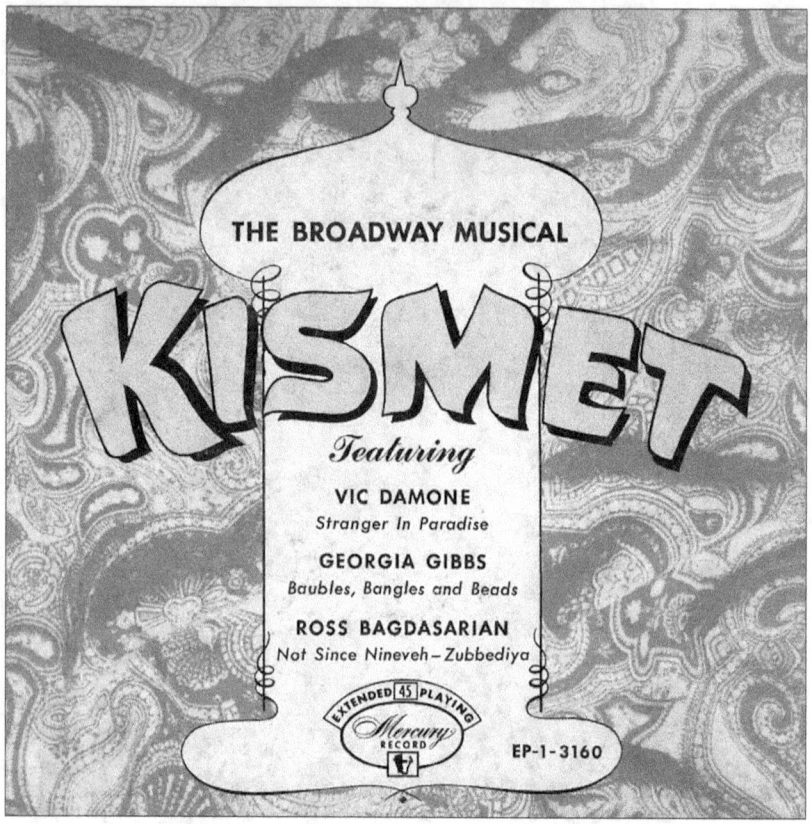

Kismet picture sleeve

Bagdasarian's first published Christmas song from 1953, recorded for Mercury Records.

*Let's Have a Merry Merry Christmas* sheet music

Bagdasarian signed on with Liberty Records in late 1955 and had a long and fruitful relationship ship that lasted 15 years. "Armen's Theme" from December 1956 was the first to carry the David Seville name.

Bagdasarian's first 45 picture sleeve: "Gotta Get to Your House" b/w "Camel Rock" (1957) and sheet music.

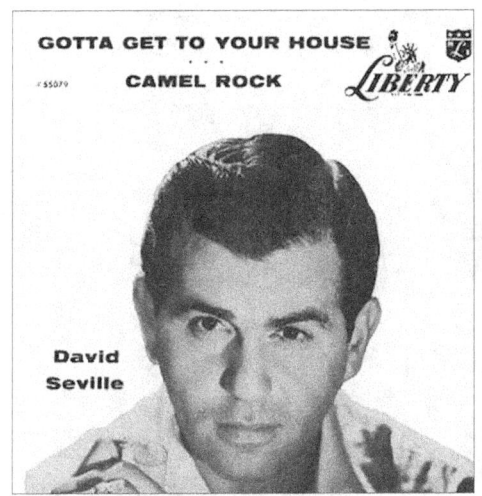 

The first LP: *The Music of David Seville* (1957).

Early photos of Bagdasarian circa 1952.

Bagdasarian with director Alfred Hitchcock on this set and in *Rear Window*.

## Bagdasarian in *Destination Gobi*:

Bagdasarian in *The Deep Six*:

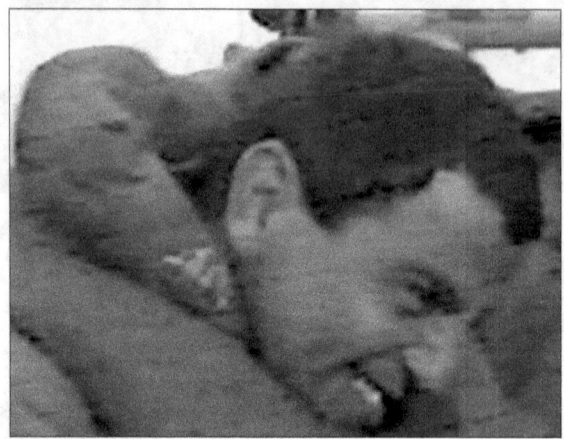

# LIBERTY RECORDS

In David Edwards and Mike Callahan's *The Liberty Records Story*, they described the origins of the label that became the primary home for the majority of Bagdasarian's records, with and without The Chipmunks. Here are some edited highlights of their story and short bios of other major artists that appeared on the label over the years:

"Liberty Records was founded in 1955 by Simon Waronker (1915-2005) in Hollywood, California. Si was born in 1915 in a poor section of Los Angeles. When he was five, his father started him playing the violin. He was a child prodigy, starting high school at eleven and graduating at thirteen. Si got a scholarship to study violin in Philadelphia and then France. He ended up in Germany during the rise of Hitler. After barely escaping from a Nazi youth gang that was pursuing him because he was Jewish, he returned to the United States. Back in Los Angeles, he worked for 20th Century Fox from 1939 until 1955, playing musical scores for movies.

"In 1955, his cousin, Herb Newman, called and suggested they go into the record business. After much thought and discussions with Alfred and Lionel Newman at 20th Century Fox, Si Waronker gave up his highly paid job to start a record company. By this time Si made up his mind, however, Herb Newman had backed out of the deal and formed his own record company called Era, so Waronker was on his own. The first releases on the label were lush orchestral recordings by Lionel Newman (1916-1989). The numbering system for the singles started with the 55000 series, probably just the year the label was established followed by some zeros, but it ran sequentially for 16 years. The first single was Lionel Newman's "The Girl Upstairs".

Here are brief stories of many of the major Liberty Records signings:

One of Liberty's first signings was Julie London (1926-2000). Originally, Waronker wanted to sign Bobby Troup (1918-1999), who was a jazz artist signed to another label. Troup encouraged Liberty to sign his girlfriend instead. London's first hit was a version of "Cry Me a River". London had a series of successful albums for Liberty and eventually Troup did record for the label as well.

In 1956, a new signing proved successful with a #4 hit version of "Tonight You Belong to Me". The artists were Patience (1942-   ) and Prudence McIntyre (1945-   ), who were the daughters of Mark McIntyre, an orchestra leader who encouraged them to record for the label. They recorded at least six other singles and had an additional hit with "Gonna Get Along Without Ya Now", which hit #11 on the charts.

A little known soundtrack music writer for Universal Studios who was providing incidental music to various motion pictures during the 1950s was signed next in 1956. He recorded many albums for Liberty, but as he became enormously successful by the end of the decade, Henry Mancini (1924-1994) departed the label in 1959 for RCA, and soon became a movie music composing legend. After Mancini's departure, Liberty reissued the albums he recorded for the label multiple times to cash-in on this worldwide success.

Poet Rod McKuen (1933-2015) also signed to Liberty in 1956 and recorded an unsuccessful album, and even Gracie Fields (1898-

1979) signed to the label for a brief time. She's best known today for her song "Sing As We Go", which was plagiarized by the Monty Python team in 1980 as "Sit On My Face".

When rock and roll began to have mainstream success, Liberty was quick to sign Eddie Cochran (1938-1960), who soon had a hit with "Sittin' in the Balcony" in 1957. Cochran followed this hit with "C'mon Everybody", "Twenty Flight Rock" and "Summertime Blues", which has become a rock and roll anthem, recorded by numerous others including The Who and Blue Cheer. Cochran continued to have success and appeared in the film *The Girl Can't Help it* before his life was tragically cut short in 1960 at the age of 21, when he died in an automobile accident in England, while on tour. He is considered an influential legend of many rockers that have followed.

R&B artists Billy Ward (1921-2002) and the Dominoes were signed next to Liberty in 1957. The group formed in 1950 and featured Clyde McPhatter (1932-1972) as lead singer. However, by the time they signed, McPhatter had left and was replaced by Jackie Wilson (1934-1984). Wilson too, had left just prior to their Liberty signing and so did not achieve much success except with the old pop standards "Stardust" and "Deep Purple".

Comedian Jerry Colonna (1904-1986) also signed to the label in 1957 and recorded *Let's All Sing With Jerry Colonna*, which turned out to be a flop, but the album title must have caught the ear of Ross Bagdasarian. It is a highly collectible record today and somewhat difficult to find, but prices have decreased dramatically as Colonna is now basically forgotten except for the role of the March Hare in Disney's *Alice in Wonderland*.

Liberty started to flounder until 1958 and almost went out of business. After signing Ross Bagdasarian in 1955, he had a pair of hits with "Witch Doctor" as David Seville and "The Chipmunk Song" as The Chipmunks featuring David Seville, that basically saved the label from extinction. More on this incredible success next chapter.

Liberty's next major success came in the form of an unexpected hit called "Quiet Village" by bandleader Martin Denny (1911-2005) in 1959. Denny had recorded all sort of jungle sound effects to a basic rhythm track and started a whole new genre and a line of seemingly endless albums featuring Denny's exotic music. Interestingly, the song "Quiet Village" was originally recorded in mono for the Liberty album *Exotica*. After the song became a huge hit, it was re-recorded in stereo for stereo album release.

Occasionally, as with Henry Mancini, artists did not have success with Liberty, but achieved their greatest success after leaving the label. This was the case with Texas DJ Willie Nelson (1934-    ). He signed on to Liberty in 1961 and recorded such songs as "The Part Where I Cry", "Hello Walls", "Crazy" and "Funny How Time Slips Away". Many of the songs from this period of 1961-1964 have become country standards, but at the time, they were mostly ignored. Nelson had somewhat greater success with RCA in the late 1960s, before he broke out in the 1970s as a country superstar.

During this 1959-61 period, Liberty also signed bandleaders Si Zentner (1917-2000), Felix Slatkin (1915-1963), and the inimitable Spike Jones (1911-1965). Jones had middling success with Liberty with both comedic and straight albums, but were mostly lightweight affairs in comparison to his RCA classics during the 1940s and 1950s.

Bobby Vee (1943-2016) became the most consistent hit maker for Liberty as the 1960s began. He had top hits with "Devil or Angel", the Carole King (1942-   ) and Gerry Goffin (1939-2014) tune "Take Good Care of My Baby", which made #1 in 1961. Vee had a long list of hits into the late 1960s and issued over 20 albums on Liberty.

Johnny Burnette (1934-1964) wrote several hits for Ricky Nelson (1940-1985) and in 1960, signed to Liberty as a pop singer. Burnette had a handful of hits for Liberty, including "Dreamin'" and "You're Sixteen", and issued six albums. Unfortunately, he drowned in a boating accident in 1964.

Other artists signed to Liberty in the 1960s include Walter Brennan (1894-1974), Gene McDaniels (1935-2011), Garry Miles (Buzz Cason) (1939-    ), Buddy Knox (1933-1999), Timi Yuro (1940-2004), Vikki Carr (1940-    ), Ernie Freeman (1922-1981), Ed Townsend (1929-2003), Nick Noble (1926-2012), Gary Paxton (1939-2016), Dick (1944-2003) and Dee Dee, the Johnny Mann (1928-2014) Singers, Van McCoy (1940-1979), Matt Monro (1930-1985), Billy Strange (1930-2012), the post-Buddy Holly Crickets, Eddie Heywood (1915-1989), the Mar-Kets, and P.J. Proby (1938-    ). Even football star Roosevelt Grier (1932-    ) made several singles for Liberty.

Liberty's next successes were with The Rivingtons, a high-energy rock and roll/R&B group who had hits "Papa Oom Mow Mow" and "The Bird Is the Word". These became the basis for the classic by the Trashmen, "Surfin' Bird".

Liberty signed singing duo Jan Berry (1941-2004) and Dean Torrence (1940-    ) to their first contract with a major label in 1962. The duo had hits dating back to 1958 for Arwin Records. Surf and hot rod music were just gaining popularity, with their friends, The Beach Boys, having the most success. Jan and Dean jumped on the fad and in the summer of 1963 had a #1 hit with "Surf City". The song was written for them by Beach Boy leader Brian Wilson (1942-    ). Several hits followed, including "Drag City", "Dead Man's Curve" and

"The Little Old Lady From Pasadena". The hits lasted for Liberty well into 1966. Unfortunately, on April 19, 1966, Jan Berry was involved in a very serious automobile accident which pretty much ended the duo's career for quite a number of years.

Edwards and Callahan continue from their "Liberty Records Story" essay as to what happened during Liberty's later years, "By 1963, the Vice President of Liberty, Al Bennett, was responsible for the business side of things, and also much of the success of the company. In the 1962-63 time period, Bennett was approached by Avnet (an electronics company) about buying Liberty. Si Waronker was in poor health, so he and Bennett agreed to sell the company to Avnet for 12 million dollars.

"Si Waronker cashed out of the company, leaving Bennett in control of day-to-day operations. Liberty started losing money after the Avnet sale. After two years in the red, Avnet wanted out. During this period, Avnet bought out another Los Angeles label, Imperial, which also gave Liberty control of the catalogs of Aladdin and Minit. Avnet then sold the whole company, including Imperial, Dolton, Aladdin, and Minit, back to Al Bennett for eight million dollars!

"In 1965, Liberty began to augment their roster with some of the talent that would be the mainstay of the label for the next few years. They signed comedian Jerry Lewis' son Gary Lewis (1946-   ) and his group the Playboys, who proved to be a lot more talented than the dismissal that being a star's son usually warranted. Other acts like the T-Bones, Gants, Del Shannon (1934-1990), and Ken Dodd (1927-2018) all had chart hits, but most of the chart action for the post-Avnet Liberty was going on at Imperial, which had been turned into a rock and roll hit machine."

Lewis had quite a few hits for Liberty including "This Diamond

Ring", "Count Me In" and "Everybody Loves a Clown" until military service took Lewis out of the game during 1967-1968. By the time he resumed his career, it was over.

In 1966, Liberty formed the Sunset label was formed as a budget subsidiary. They issued albums of previously released Liberty and Imperial material including some of The Chipmunks. It continued until the early 1970s.

Then in 1968, insurance conglomerate Transamerica Corporation, purchased Liberty Records (along with Imperial, Sunset and the rest) for 38 million dollars and combined it with another of their record labels, United Artists, but they didn't have a clue about running a record label or company. After six months, Al Bennett was fired, the company rapidly declined and by 1972, the Liberty name had disappeared.

Edwards and Callahan adds, "Artists such as Bobby Vee, Gary Lewis, and Jan and Dean, who had been the hot product of the mid 60s, were in decline in the charts, and Transamerica didn't come up with replacements that they could promote effectively. They shut down Dolton, Imperial and Minit and transferred their artists to Liberty, but they still couldn't maintain the chart presence to make it work. Although Transamerica called it "consolidating," the company was in effect imploding."

It was during this time that Ross Bagdasarian took a stab at another label, recording a one-off single for Dot Records, but Bagdasarian soon continued with Liberty until 1970, when he effectively retired.

New artists signed in the late 1960s and early 1970s included Canned Heat ("On the Road Again"), the Nitty Gritty Dirt Band, Ike (1931-2007) and Tina Turner (1939-   ), Bobby Womack (1944-2014), and Sugarloaf ("Green-Eyed Lady").

Edwards and Callahan continue, "Although these artists had modest success on Liberty, most had bigger hits later with other labels. Finally, with the 1971 single "Tongue In Cheek" by Sugarloaf, Transamerica shifted all new singles and albums to the United Artists label, along with the Liberty artists. For all intents and purposes, it was over for Liberty, although the Liberty catalog continued to be used for reissues well into the 1970s. A few Chipmunks and David Seville reissues came out on the United Artists label from 1973-1976.

"In 1978, the United Artists labels, including the Liberty masters, were sold to Artie Mogull and Jerry Rubinstein. They borrowed the money for the purchase from EMI, the parent company of the Capitol label. Mogull and Rubinstein were not successful, and in February 1979, EMI foreclosed on them.

"EMI/Capitol has since reactivated the Liberty name several times. In the late 1970s, it was used to reissue the Liberty and Imperial catalogs. In 1980, Capitol reestablished the imprint as a country label, primarily featuring Kenny Rogers (1938-   ). When Rogers left EMI for RCA in 1983, Liberty wasn't long for the world, and EMI discontinued the label in 1984.

In 1992, EMI announced that they were renaming their Capitol-Nashville division. The new label was... Liberty Records! The biggest artist for the 1990s incarnation of Liberty was Garth Brooks (1962-   )."

The Liberty Records catalog today is owned by the Capitol Records unit of Universal Music Group also known as UMe.

Liberty president Al Bennett and founder Si Waronker, the namesakes for The Chipmunks' Alvin and Simon; Theodore was named after engineer Ted Keep.

The headquarters of Liberty Records in the 1950s and 1960s.

An article from the *Corpus Christi Caller Times* from November 18, 1956 about Liberty Records recording artists Patience and Prudence.

Various ads featuring Liberty Records first hit recording star Julie London.

Julie London Liberty Ad

Julie London Cry Me A River Liberty Record ad 1

Julie London Cry Me A River Liberty Record ad 2

Inner sleeve advertising various Liberty Records over the years.

A Liberty Records *Billboard* ad from 1961.

A Liberty Records *Billboard* ad from April 16, 1966.

A Liberty Records ad from June 17, 1967 soliciting new talent.

A Liberty Records ad from *Cash Box* in 1968.

The Imperial Records logo. A couple Ross Bagdasarian releases came out on Imperial.

# Liberty Records recording artists:

## Patience and Prudence

Eddie Cochran

Bobby Vee

Julie London, Martin Denny, Si Zentner

Johnny Burnette, Gene McDaniels, Timi Yuro, Jan & Dean, Gary Lewis & The Playboys

Jan & Dean in *Billboard* on February 20, 1965.

Matt Monro in *Billboard* on February 20, 1965.

Ad for the Nitty Gritty Dirt Band.

An ad for Sugarloaf.

# "THE WITCH DOCTOR" AND "THE CHIPMUNK SONG"

EDWARDS AND CALLAHAN CONTINUE from their Liberty Records story, "Minor hits would have ensured Seville a brief but forgettable career if not for a bit of innovation that landed him on the top of the charts. In 1958 he got the idea of speeding up the tape of the human voice to create funny voices, and he had a number one record with the classic "Witch Doctor". He followed that up with "The Chipmunk Song" in late 1958, and then a long running series of albums and singles by Chipmunks "Alvin, Simon and Theodore." The Chipmunks were wryly named for Liberty executives Alvin Bennett, Simon Waronker, and Theodore Keep."

Most of these minor hits were compiled into Bagdasarian's first LP collection, *The Music of David Seville* (1957), still a fascinating look at the music by the man pre-Chipmunks and "Witch Doctor", although long out of print and never officially released onto CD. Bagdasarian now needed a hit and fast.

Ross Jr. continues the story as told in the *Still Squeaky After All These years* booklet, "In 1958, my family was down to our last $200. Being a gambler at heart, my dad did what any other prudent person would do. He took $190 of it and bought the latest state-of-the-art tape recorder, one that allowed him to change tape speeds.

As he tried to decide what to write about, he spotted a book on his desk, *Duel With the Witch Doctor*. In a burst of creative energy, fueled mostly by sheer panic, he wrote "Witch Doctor" - a song about a guy who's hopelessly in love and goes to see a Witch Doctor for advice:

> "I told the Witch Doctor I was in love with you
> I told the Witch Doctor I was in love with you
> And then the Witch Doctor, he told me what to do
> He said that "OO EE OO AH AH
> Ting Tang Walla Walla Bing Bang
> OO EE OO AH AH
> Ting Tang Walla Walla Bing Bang"

"Once he finished the song, he needed a voice for the Witch Doctor, something really different. He remembered experimenting with a piano sound a few years earlier. He had recorded the piano at half speed and then played it back at normal speed. He decided to try this technique for the voice of the Witch Doctor. Once he finished the song, he called me brother, sister and me into his den as he always did. We would tell him if we liked the song - we generally did - and then we'd ask him if we could go back out and play, but "Witch Doctor", with that crazy voice, was different. We loved it, and asked to hear it over and over!

Shana Alexander, from her article "Alvin! Composer's Yells at Son Inspire Another Chipmunk Hit", from *Life* magazine, March 23, 1959 elaborates, "Most remarkable of all, he can neither read nor write music or play any musical instrument in the accepted sense of the word. What he lacks in musical techniques is amply made up by his amazing virtuosity on the tape recorder.

"Bagdasarian is extremely fond of unusual sounds. Two winters ago, at his home in Van Nuys, California, Bagdasarian was fooling around with the tape machine in his den, barking and woofing and hissing sounds into the microphone while tinkling with one finger on the piano, "Oooh...Eee..Oooh...Ahhh...Ahhh..."

"The other members of his household paid no attention to the weird noises. Daddy often spent his free hours like this. Flipping the tape recorder switch back and forth from full speed to half speed, Bagdasarian experimented with various vocal experimented with various vocal effects. "Ting...Tang..." He mouthed slowly while the tape was moving at half speed. Then, remembering an uncle who once moved to the state of Washington, he uttered the words, "Walla Walla". This was topped off with an exuberant "Bing Bang!" He flipped the switch to full speed and played it all back. Both doors to his study flew open and his wife, his children and a startled cleaning woman appeared.

"What was *that*?" cried his wife. "Play that again, Daddy!" the children shrieked.

"This was the genesis of Bagdasarian's hit song, "Witch Doctor". It was a simple exercise in pairing Bagdasarian's normal voice - "I told the Witch Doctor I fell in love with you." - with the medicine man's tinny reply - "Oooh Eee Oooh Ahhh Ahhh", made by speeding up Bagdasarian's recorded voice. "Witch Doctor" is basically a simple duet."

Lucinda Ann Sanderson and Michael J. Tawney continue from "Alvin and the Chipmunks: Ross Bagdasarian Remembered", *Mindrot* #12, November 1, 1978, "His first song employing the sped-up voice was "Witch Doctor". In this hit, David Seville sings of "his friend the Witch Doctor" who "told him what to say" in order to impress a girl. What the Witch Doctor told him to say was just some nonsense syllables, but the public ate it up. The Witch Doctor's voice is Bagdasarian's own voice played twice as fast, which makes it easy to believe he is supposed to be a Pygmy Witch Doctor, but the main reason the Witch Doctor was given the speeded voice was to make him sound different from Bagdasarian's natural voice.

Marty Winters in "Ross Bagdasarian: The Man Who Would Be Chipmunk King" from *Cool and Strange Music* #18, August-November 2000, adds, "In his musical approach, Bagdasarian was by nature, experimental, and by the late 1950s, he had bought his own tape recorder. While playing around with it one day, he was struck by the quality of his voice when recorded at half speed and then played back at normal speed. The technique gave his singing a funny, high-pitched sound, similar to the effect of breathing helium and was an immediate success with his family, especially his young children. Sensing he was onto something and inspired by the title of a book he owned, *Duel With the Witch Doctor*, Bagdasarian wrote what would become one of the classic novelty songs of all time: "Witch Doctor".

Bagdasarian himself has been quoted as saying: "Every time I write a song I keep a mental picture of a housewife with her hands in soapy water, listening to the radio. I try to figure out how to get her hands out of the dishwater to turn up the volume to hear my song.

"While the tape was moving at half speed, I said 'ting tang' and then I remembered an uncle who had moved to the state of Washington, and I sputtered 'walla walla' topped off with a resounding 'bing bang'."

Ross Jr. from the *Still Squeaky* booklet continues, "Now he had to convince his record company, Liberty Records, to release it. Unfortunately, they didn't share our enthusiasm. The good news was that Liberty was about to go out of business and a pop pointed out to them, they really had nothing to lose. If the song was a flop, they would still go out of business, but if it was a hit… "Witch Doctor" was released 24 hours later."

Enid Fife in "David Seville: Brings Alvin to TV" from *TV Radio Mirror*, October 1961 adds, "For some time, he had been casting about for a wacky novelty number. One afternoon in January, 1958, he glanced up from his desk and saw a book entitled *Duel with the Witch Doctor*. Ross says. "Since many of the top records at that time had the craziest sort of lyrics. I figured it might be fun to have the Witch Doctor give advice to the lovelorn in his own gibberish." Having recorded the orchestra track, he spent two months trying to get a "Witch Doctor's voice." One day, he sang the words at half-speed into his tape-recorder, then played it back at normal speed. Before the first "wallah-wallah-bing" had sounded. Armen and children were in the room, fascinated and tickled. Ross knew he'd struck gold. At Liberty Records, president Si Waronker flipped over the piece. It sold close to two million."

Winters in *Cool and Strange Music* continues, "He was able to quickly sell the idea to Liberty executive Sy Waronker, who had worked with Bagdasarian since his first recordings with Liberty, but label president Al Bennett was skeptical. One of Bennett's first duties at the company had been to meet with distributors around the country and reassure them that Liberty was financially sound and that unsold records could be returned. It was hard to imagine for Bennett that a song with a chorus of "Ooh-eee-ooh-ahh-ahh! Ting-tang-walla-walla-bing-bang!" would be a hit at all, let alone save the company from bankruptcy. Luckily, 1958 was a time when rock 'n' roll novelty records were selling like hotcakes. Before long, radio stations around the country were playing "Witch Doctor" and millions of Americans were singing along with the goofy lyrics.

"Witch Doctor" by David Seville quickly sold over a million copies, and rose to number one on the national charts for two weeks. The first of three novelty records to top the charts in 1958, and the first of two by Bagdasarian. It was another first as well, being the first national chart-topping hit for Liberty, and was featured on Seville's second Liberty Album *The Witch Doctor Presents David Seville ... and Friends*, also issued in 1958. Liberty was finally in the black and Bagdasarian found himself in the spotlight."

Ross Jr. in the *Still Squeaky* booklet concludes, "The song quickly went to number one, selling more than a million records. Being eight years old, I didn't have much understanding of the importance of the number one million-selling thing. What I did understand, however, was that it meant we could have our own swimming pool. I loved "Witch Doctor"!"

"Witch Doctor's" B-side was a song called "Don't Whistle at Me Baby" which was written by Bagdasarian and Si Waronker and is kind of guitar-rockish. It also appears on the *Witch Doctor* album. "Witch Doctor" stayed at #1 for three weeks starting April 28, 1958, and ended up being the #4 song for 1958. It was remade a few times with The Chipmunks in succeeding years.

"Witch Doctor" was nominated for a Grammy for Best Children's Recording, but lost to (what else?) "The Chipmunk Song". Bagdasarian performed the song on his first appearance on *The Ed Sullivan Show* on May 4, 1958. Although there were a few technical difficulties in matching Bagasarian's hand movements with that of the cameraman's camera image tweaking, the performance is bright and spirited with a "damsel in distress" wearing a pith helmet making appropriate facial expressions. He also performed it on his final *Sullivan Show* appearance with The Chipmunks on September 25, 1960.

Fortunes changed for the Bagdasarians with "Witch Doctor", and fortune would change permanently with a certain single release of November 18, 1958, but first Bagdasarian had a few modestly successful singles under his David Seville name before that major second breakthrough including a song called "The Bird On My Head", in which the speeded voice represents a bird.

"Actually, not all of the songs of this era which employ the speeded voice are songs by Bagdasarian. Another songwriter composed something called "Purple People Eater" which was just as popular. In this song, the speeded voice was supposed to be that of a creature from another planet. But it was unquestionably Bagdasarian who capitalized upon the speeded voice in the most spectacular way."

"The Bird On My Head" / "Hey There Moon" was a minor hit at #34 for Bagdasarian in June 1958. "The Bird On My Head" is also on the *Witch Doctor* LP. "Hey There Moon" is a straight doo-wop and is not on the album.

Bagdasarian performed "Bird" (as well as "Witch Doctor") on *The Dick Clark Beech-Nut Show* (not *American Bandstand*) with a bird puppet designed by puppeteer Morey Bunin (1910-1997) in July 12, 1958. Bunin went on to design The Chipmunks puppets when Bagdasarian appeared on *The Ed Sullivan Show* in 1959 and 1960. Amazingly, *American Bandstand* later gave "The Chipmunk Song" its lowest rating - a 35 - on its Rate-a-Record segment, yet it sold a million copies by year's end.

An online comment by Rhett Bryson on his "Great Foodini" page about Bunin's work with Bagdasarian says, "Morey Bunin collaborated with David Seville to produce the puppets of Alvin and the Chipmunks. Morey had made a large puppet of a duck with articulated head and mouth to sit on the head of singer David Seville when he appeared in 1958 on Dick Clark's show singing "The Bird On My Head". He also made a Witch Doctor puppet to accompany the singing of that bigger Seville hit."

Morey Bunin of *Foodini* fame created and performed them. An episode of PBS's *Antiques Roadshow* from 2014 confirms this, where The Chipmunks puppets were appraised at $10,000 insurance. The puppets are currently owned by Bunin's son and daughter-in-law, Rachel, who appears on the episode.

But Bunin wasn't the only one to create Chipmunks puppets for Bagdasarian. Before Bunin created his Chipmunk puppets, former Looney Tunes animator and director Bob Clampett (1913-1984) designed and performed his versions on *The Ed Sullivan Show* in 1958 and *This Is Your Life* in 1959. After leaving Looney Tunes, Clampett created puppets for his own *Time For Beany* (1949-1955). In 1962, Clampett returned to animation with *Matty's Funnies with Beany and Cecil*.

Two more records were released by David Seville before Bagdasarian hit paydirt again at the end of the year: "Little Brass Band" / "Take Five" which made it to #78 in August 1958 and the non-charting "The Mountain" / "Mr. Grape" in October 1958.

"Little Brass Band" has lyrics about musical instruments with a sound similar to "Witch Doctor" and is also on the *Witch Doctor* album. "Take Five" is too, but is a Bagdasarian and Mark McIntyre original, not the Dave Brubeck classic.

To fill out the *Witch Doctor* album along with repeats of "Gotta Get to Your House", "Pretty Dark Eyes", "Cecilia", "Goofus", "The Donkey and the Schoolboy", "Camel Rock" and "The Gift" and the single tracks already mentioned, there was "Dinah", a fast song sang in accent with a marimba and a piano that is kind of tuneless, and "I Can't Give You Anything But Love" which is a cover.

Not on the album are "The Mountain" with flute, guitar and bongos, written by Bagdasarian and McIntyre that sounds a lot like "Japanese Banana", and "Mr. Grape" a Bagdasarian original instrumental with sax, flutes and piano.

October 31, 1958 was the date Bagdasarian recorded the game-changing record of his career, that was released on November 17, 1958.

Ross Jr. continues, "One hit song can't save a record company for long. A few months later Liberty was running low on cash and asked pop to write another one of those novelty things. This was in the summer of 1958. My brother, who was now five, kept asking pop if it was Christmas yet. It wasn't that he was particularly religious, he just knew that you got lots of presents at Christmas time and he couldn't wait. Translating that youthful exuberance, pop wrote:

"Christmas, Christmas time is near
Time for toys and time for cheer
We've been good, but we can't last
Hurry Christmas, hurry fast."

"Pop had loved the voice of the "Witch Doctor", but wanted to marry that voice with personalities. However, he hadn't decided if they should be singing reindeer, potato bugs or God knows what else. While he was driving his car to Yosemite, and thinking about singing gophers, ostriches and butterflies - a tiny chipmunk dashed in front of his 4000-pound car. The chipmunk stood on its hind legs, daring my dad to pass. Pop loved the audacity of that chipmunk. He knew he had found his star."

Ross Jr. continues from the *Dr. Demento* radio show in 1982, "In 1958, about nine months after he wrote the "Witch Doctor". He had just finished writing the "Witch Doctor" and he wanted to use that sped-up sound for some characters and didn't know whether they should be singing alligators or reindeer or elephants and he was driving along near the Sequoias and one day a chipmunk actually jumped out on the road and dared he and his 4000 pound car to drive by and as he picked himself out of the road there after laughing hysterically at this little chipmunk, he figured it's going to be three singing chipmunks. The record sold 4½ million copies in seven weeks. The amazing thing about it is the record company there was running out of labels."

Returning to the *Still Squeaky* booklet, Ross Jr. adds, "The record company initially printed the labels on green backgrounds, but is sold so quickly that they ran out of green and switched to black. Ran out of black and switched to blue. Ran out of color and switched to plain white. Some days they sold as many as 550,000 records! Liberty tried valiantly to keep up with the unprecedented demand. When they ran out of trucks to deliver the records, they used vans. When they ran out of vans, they used station wagons. By the end, they used everything but Cub Scouts pulling little red wagons!

"My dad was a wonderful singer. His voice was rich and strong and reassuring. It could strike fear in you or make you laugh or feel safer than anywhere else in the world. His talent made David Seville much more interesting because you know Dave could sing as well as The Chipmunks. Maybe not as high, but definitely as well.

"His Christmas song became "The Chipmunk Song". Alvin, the smallest one, embodied the spunk of that Yosemite chipmunk. Simon became the logical, brainy one, and Theodore just giggled. Pop felt that a human character was needed to act as a straight man for The Chipmunks. His own name, Ross Bagdasarian, was out of the question. It was too ethnic and too long to fit on a 45, so it became David

Seville (the city in Spain where he had been stationed during World War II), and The Chipmunks.

"When pop finished "The Chipmunk Song", my brother, sister and I were once again summoned to the den for our opinion. We immediately loved it. Part of it was the way The Chipmunks sang. Part of it was listening to them talk, which made them seem real, but our favorite part was hearing Alvin talk back to our dad, something we never did.

"Although the song's success meant many new perks from my third grade classmates, like free milk and Twinkies, I was most excited about pop appearing on *The Ed Sullivan Show*. This meant I could stay up until 8:30!

"One of the things Ed Sullivan loved about my dad was that used less time than he was allotted. Performers coveted each second on *The Sullivan Show* like gold because of its huge audience and influence. Nonetheless, if pop was given time for two songs, but only felt he could deliver one good performance, he told Ed to give the extra time to someone else. That may be one of reasons Ed invited him back six times.

"Although everyone in the country now knew what The Chipmunks sounded like, no one knew what they looked like. The Chipmunks appeared as puppets. They were a tremendous success. From the beginning, Dave and Alvin were the draw. They were the musical equivalent of Desi Arnaz and Lucille Ball. Instead of "Lucy, you have some 'splaining to do," it became "Alvinnnnn!!!!!"

"When the dust settled in mid-January 1959, "The Chipmunk Song" had sold four and a half million records in seven weeks, an all-time record in the music business.

"A few months later pop received two Grammy awards, one for

the Best Selling Children's Record, and the other for Best Comedy Performance.

"By 1959, The Chipmunks had become a cottage industry. Even the front page of *The Wall Street Journal* heralded the squeaky-voiced trio. Soon there were Chipmunk plush dolls with harmonicas, singing greeting cards, charm bracelets, cufflinks, cigarette lighters, key chains, comic books, board games and a host of other Chipmunks paraphernalia. Pop even bought 220 acres near his hometown in Fresno and named it The Chipmunk Ranch.

"This label appeared on each box of grapes that was shipped from The Chipmunk Ranch."

The *Life* magazine article interviewed Bagdasarian and he discussed the process he did and the inspiration he had in coming up with The Chipmunks and "The Chipmunk Song", "First, having set down a melody, he recorded it with a simplified orchestra - two saxophones, four rhythm instruments - at normal speed. Then on a second tape, he recorded two pianos playing at half speed. Played back at normal speed, the pianos had a tinkly, mandolin-like sound.

"Bagdasarian made a third tape of his own normal voice at normal speed, shouting "Alvin! Stop that!" and the like. The fourth tape was Simon, the lowest voiced of the three chipmunks in the song. His lines were recorded in a normal voice at half speed, then played back at normal speed to produce a squeaky tone. By this time, the control booth at the recording studio was filling up with tape like cauldron of spaghetti, so the first four tapes were combined on a fifth.

"The sixth tape was a variation for Theodore, the laughing chipmunk: "Ha...Ha...Ha ..." spoken carefully at half speed in a tone pitch slightly higher than Simon's. The seventh was Alvin's, also at half speed and pitched highest of all. An eighth track was added for the harmonica, normal speed. Finally, one master tape combined all the others in one glorious tonal conglomeration.

"When Bagdasarian is experimenting with his tapes at home, he frequently bursts out of his den to test new songs and sounds on his children. He tried three versions of "The Chipmunk Song" - at one time it was an instrumental number "In a Village Park" - before he and his family agreed that this was it.

"When he does not want to be disturbed, Bagdasarian closes the doors of his den, and no one is allowed to enter. This is the strictest rule of the household. It means nothing, however, to four-year-old Adam. The other children, like chipmunks Theodore and Simon, are well-behaved, but Adam comes in whenever he has something to say. He opens the door softly and, before the father can finish muttering, "Adam, you know you're not supposed to come in here," the son is off.

> "Son: I made a Valentine for you in school today.
> "Father: Adam, I told you not...
> "Son: But I didn't bring it home because it's not finished yet.
> "Father: (mounting irritation) Adam, didn't you hear me?
> "Son: You see I only made the Valen today.
> "Father: (trembling) Shut up, Adam...
> "Son: I'm making the tine tomorrow.
> "Father: (full volume) A-A-A-A-A-DAM!

"The routine seldom varies. The son's lines change: "There are plates and spoons, and there are clocks. Some clocks say 8:30. Some clocks say 11:15." But the father's agonized replies are always substantially the same.

"Not only was the character of Alvin, the truculent chipmunk, patterned after the Bagdasarian Adam, but the final bellow on the records, the famous "Alvin!" is a true-to-life noise in every respect - save volume. All the Bagdasarians think Daddy modulates his voice a bit on the records."

*Teen Magazine* in January 1960 also featured an article on David Seville and also interviewed Bagdasarian, "Here's a TEEN-VUE into the life of a recording dynamo who hit pay dirt with a cat called the Witch Doctor, then came back with a group of furry little beasts called The Chipmunks.

"Almost nothing ever happens to David Seville, unless of course you count the times he thinks he's a chipmunk or a songwriter named Ross Bagdasarian. It's very confusing being three people at once, especially if you're a father and have a five-year-old son who also reminds you of a chipmunk. You see, actually it's very simple, Ross Bagdasarian is a nice, talented guy who records songs, and Alvin is a chipmunk. Now it should all be very clear, but somehow it isn't. Let's try it again.

"All of these people are one man. You see him across the page sprawled out on the floor. He's the character you hear on wax giving ever-lovin' Alvin the old raspberry whenever Alvin steps out of line. He's also the cat who whips up Alvin's hip routines for wax and his recording name is David Seville, but his real name is Ross Bagdasarian. Now, is everybody clued in?

"Meeting David Seville for the first time is quite an experience! He doesn't exactly look like a chipmunk; he doesn't talk like a chipmunk; but by his own words, he occasionally thinks like a chipmunk. His face is rugged and tanned and when he answers a question, it's obvious that he's about as sincere a guy as could live in Movietown. He'd make a first-rate dad for any guy or gal, even if he does bug Alvin a little too much.

"According to my father," Seville admits, "I *am* Alvin. When I was young I was always a kind of rebellious character and would never go along with the family kind of work which was always farming. I think Alvin's me, basically. I also think he's all kids who just won't take what is said to them as being the last word. Alvin's any child or grownup who rebels against the rules that demand 'you must start at the bottom.' Alvin doesn't believe in that. He believes that you start at the top and if you can't make it there, you go to the bottom. There's a little Alvin in all of us. There sure is a great deal in me, and in Adam, my son, age five."

"Listening to a guy like this talk makes you believe Alvin is really around somewhere, but since this can't be the straight scoop, you begin asking where and how did Alvin come to be?

"Well, it was this way," Seville answers, "In September of 1958, I decided to try for a Christmas novelty song. I thought of a melody on my way to work, and I went right to the studio and whistled it into a tape machine, so that it wouldn't be forgotten. Since I can't read or write music, I whistle into tape machines.

"Then I wrote the words and decided that the singers should be animals or maybe even insects. I don't know why, but that's what I decided. I recorded the song with the half speed little voices (my own) and sang an introduction in my normal speed voice.

"When I finished the first recording, the voices sounded like butterflies or - or mice - or rabbits - but most of all, they sounded like chipmunks. The brass of Liberty Records listened with me and we all agreed that something was missing.

"Everybody liked the melody, so I wrote a new lyric and called the song "In a Village Park". A quartet sang -- nothing! The more I listened to "In a Village Park", the more I could hear the chipmunks singing "Christmas, Christmas time is near, time for toys and time for cheer,"

So, I recorded it again, this time with no words, as an instrumental. This, too, was nowhere. I decided against doing anything further and gave up the whole project, but the project wouldn't give me up.

"By the end of November, the chipmunks in my head were driving me crazy, so I decided to try it again, but this time to give the chipmunks some kind of identity. I gave them names and had a conversation with them. The record was finally finished after three months and four versions.

"All I can say is that I love Witch Doctors, Chipmunks, and - most of all - tape machines.

"Now that we're acquainted with Alvin's birth, let's get back to his hard-hearted master, David Seville. Smilingly, he admits being a bit of a goof-off in his high school days. "In high school, I was all in the plays and was singing in all of the operettas. I was a real, wild noisemaker.

"His eyes light up as he remembers, "If my grades weren't as good, and very often they weren't, the principal couldn't do too much about it because I was the lead in the play. I'd always say, "I can't do anything about my grades because I've got to spend all my time learning lines." In this way, I bluffed my way a little.

"Recalling those meetings with the principal reminded David of something. "You know," he questioned, "I think the reason kids do like Alvin is because I, as David Seville, resemble the high school principal or the teacher who says, "Now you've got to do this my way," and Alvin says, "Drop dead. I'll do it my own way," and he winds up doing it much better than I had in mind in the first place. I think teens understand Alvin especially well.

"David Seville has a keen interest in anything that has to do with teenagers. He has a 12-year-old daughter who is constantly bugging him about wanting to be a teen, so in self defense, he must keep up on teenage activities. About Dick Clark, Seville has deep admiration. "I respect and admire the guy. He's a very bright young man and I like the fact that whenever any of the kids appear on his shows - they wear ties and they're well-mannered. I think Dick is showing the teenager that being a teen doesn't mean you go to dinner in dirty clothes. You can be a teenager and still belong to society.

"Watching *American Bandstand* now and then, David thinks it's a well-adjusted program, but adds, "I feel kind of sorry for those girls who dance together. I think it comes out of the sad fact that no boys have asked them to dance.

"Both Fabian and Elvis rate high on Seville's list of favorites, but when questioned about Tuesday Weld, the friend to all chipmunks was stymied. "That's the sort of a day in the week to me," he replied, "I don't know who she is.

"In the dark only about Tuesday, Seville shed a lot of light about a lot of important things that mean something to teenagers everywhere. He could only add one note of caution to his full-fledged praise of teenagers and it goes something like this:

"My daughter, who is 12, recently said to me, "I can hardly wait. Next year, I will be a teenager." I tried to explain to her that this isn't something special, but that it was just an age in her life. I think she has some sort of an idea that being a teenager means she can break the windows and a few dishes and everybody will bow down and say, "That's fine, honey, you're a teenager now that makes it ok." I told her that being a teenager is a fun part of your life, but being out of the teenage years is also fun and being a pre-teen can be fun.

"I think too much emphasis is placed on teenagers as such. Teens are great and they should have all the fun they can, as I did, but everyone tends to make the term *teenager* a label. That is wrong. Being a teenager doesn't make anyone immune to all the rules that are around. I mean good rules, not stupid ones.

"The world of David Seville might be called 'zazy' by some, but after hearing him out, it's a cinch that if more adults thought along his same lines, the worlds of many teens would be a lot less 'zany' and much more fun!"

The article in *Mindrot* adds to the story, "Before 1958 was over, Bagdasarian went on to create what was to be his greatest achievement - The Three Chipmunks. Using a recording technique which enabled him to play his voice back three time simultaneously, he recorded three speeded voices which, in the finished recording, were all heard together. Bagdasarian knew he had the start of something big, but he needed a name for what he created. He decided that the three voices (all of which, remember, were his own voice) should be designated as the voices of small animals of some kind. He thought of rabbits or insects, especially butterflies. (What would *The Alvin Show* have been like if he had ultimately chosen butterflies!) His three children, Carol, Ross Jr. and Adam called the voices chipmunks. Walt Disney's Chip and Dale cartoons employed the use of speeded voices; this probably gave the children the idea for their suggestion, which their father accepted. In the history of cartoon characters, Bagdasarian's Chipmunks are unique; instead of voices being developed to fit the characters, the characters were developed to fit the voices.

"The first Chipmunk song was called "The Chipmunk Song" naturally enough, but it is really a Christmas song and is also known as "Christmas Don't Be Late". When The Chipmunks sing, their voices form a triad - that is, a chord with three notes. Simon's voice is the lowest, Theodore's is the highest, and Alvin's voice is in-between and somewhat nasal.

"In general, Chipmunk music is not hear much on the radio any more, but to the United States and the world of the late 50s and early 60s, it was a sensation. The first Chipmunk record album was followed by others and these sold in the millions. An article on Bagdasarian appeared in *Life* magazine. He appeared on *The Ed Sullivan Show* and put on a musical show with hand puppets of The Chipmunks.

"Chipmunk toys and games of all sorts soon appeared in the stores. There were dolls, hand puppets, a game called The Big Record, a bubble bath called "Soaky" molded into The Chipmunks and so forth. The Barris Company created a custom car called "Alvin's Acorn". It is shaped like an acorn and is equipped inside with a little television set and stereo, but just as Chipmunk music isn't heard much on the radio anymore, this car is not seen very often at Custom Car Shows these days."

The *TV Mirror* article adds, "No story about Seville-Bagdasarian can be complete without some mention of the chipmunks. Trying for a Christmas novelty, Ross was whistling melodies into his tape recorder (his method of remembering tunes, since he can neither read nor write music). His idea was to depict the ringers as animals or insects, "just to be different." Finally, he taped a song, the introduction in his normal speed voice, and the rest in his half-speed "little voices." His "little voices" came out, he thought, like mice or rabbits, but his children disagreed. They heard them as chipmunks.

"Still, something was missing for a real click. He spent months searching for the answer. Finally, Si Waronker and Al Bennett of Liberty, along with Mark McIntyre, a long-time friend, suggested his having an argument with the chipmunks. Thus, Simon (after

Waronker), Theodore (after engineer Ted Keep) and Alvin (after Bennett) came to fame and fortune."

*Cool and Strange Music* continues, "Most of us 30- and 40-something year old kids have been affected by Ross Bagdasarian's songs in some way. For sure, Alvin and The Chipmunks hold a special place in our childhood memories of Christmas past, and who among us doesn't instantly recall the words to "Witch Doctor" when it comes on the radio, gleefully singing along to the wacky chorus?

"Enthusiastic about the possibilities that the tape recorder allowed for manipulating sounds and voices and never one to rest on his successes, Bagdasarian wasted no time before continuing to experiment with the machine. If one voice was interesting, what about two? What about a series of voices harmonizing? Bagdasarian was convinced he could write a hit Christmas song, and had tried in 1953 with "Let's Have a Merry, Merry Christmas" on Mercury Records, but Irving Berlin's "White Christmas" had dominated holiday airplay for many years and remained the American favorite.

"Accounts vary as to the actual origins of The Chipmunks idea, and legend has it that the first Chipmunk Song was inspired by Bagdasarian's close encounter with one of the little rodents while driving in Yosemite. According to sources at Liberty Records, it evolved from a demo that Bagdasarian made for his Christmas song with a trio of female voices. Accidentally played for Waronker at the wrong speed, it seems more likely that The Chipmunks simply grew from further experiments with the tape recorder, this time with Bagdasarian singing three separate parts and carefully speeding them up to form three distinct singing voices. Whatever the actual genesis, he had hit upon a great idea again.

"Of course, the concept needed a bit of fleshing out. After recording the harmonizing Chipmunks, it became apparent that when they speeded up the tape, they didn't have as much material as they thought they had, and not nearly enough to even make a song, clocking in with something around a minute. Bagdasarian added his own voice as David Seville, in much the same role as the Alfi character he had used in his early Liberty recordings, and slowly The Chipmunks began to take shape. Each was given his own identity. Alvin's incorrigible personality was then modeled after Bagdasarian's youngest son Adam, who often invoked his father's ire and the famous shout of " Al-Viiiiinnnnnn!" was born.

"With the interplay between the characters of Seville and Alvin, they were able to add time between choruses and their dialogue was ultimately responsible for the success of the record. "The Chipmunk Song (Christmas, Don't Be Late)" quickly went to number one and stayed there for four weeks, selling over six million copies and becoming the fastest selling single ever up to that point in time. According to Liberty sources, it was selling over 600,000 copies in one day. It went on to chart around the holiday season for the next four years, becoming a perennial Christmas favorite. More importantly, it earned Bagdasarian three Grammys for the year 1958 (the very first year the awards were given) for Best Children's Recording, Best Comedy Performance and Best Engineered Record in the Novelty category. Even though it wasn't able to unseat "White Christmas" as America's most popular Christmas tune, "The Chipmunk Song" eventually did tally in at number 23 on ASCAP's list of the top 25 holiday songs of the 20th century."

Finally, Bagdasarian sums it all up, "The Chipmunk Song" was completed November 7th, but no radio station wanted to play a Christmas record before the beginning of December, so we took it to

Minneapolis, to try it out on a small, independent station that didn't have so many rules. By the time it had completed its first airplay, the station's switchboard was lit up like a you-know-what. Listeners demanded they play it over and over again, and then they called other stations and asked for it. The rest is history.

"The Chipmunk Song" was so overwhelmingly popular that it sold in stores that never before sold records; such as lingerie shops and flower stores. It was a wonderful sight to see stacks of my records piled high on a cigar store counter and selling as fast as the clerk could take the money."

Finally, an online review of "The Chipmunk Song" / "Almost Good" reads, "This is the all-time classic that started everything. Every element is established in the brief 2:17 (originally it was 1:30, before Liberty Records honcho Si Waronker made Bagdasarian add extra banter). Dave is the patriarch trying to get his protégées to produce in the recording studio. Alvin is the problem child who makes his "dad" yell at him mere seconds into the song. Simon is the smart one (his one solo line of dialogue demonstrates a fine vocabulary), and Theodore is the giggling idiot. The tune demonstrates Bagdasarian's snappy pop craftsmanship, and also sets up the formula in which Alvin's attitude cause the record to teeter towards chaos, yet stay on point just enough to end up a solid song. Finally, the record strikes a balance between appealing to children and appealing to adults, a hallmark of early Chipmunk records.

"This became a Christmas perennial because it balances the irreverence of Alvin's mischief with an overall wholesomeness, making the record appropriate for the holidays, but not too sappy. While this ostensibly is about materialism (the Chips each sing about what they want for Christmas; Alvin coveting a hula hoop), I think the vibe it really captures is the way family members interact during holidays. David Seville's turn as an exasperated father hopelessly trying to get his kids to play the part of little angels for Christmas really rings true. Alvin is really funny on this record (as is Simon, who arrogantly answers "Naturally!" when David says he was good), but I think the funniest bit here is when David says, "Alvin, you were a little flat. Watch it." Alvin keeps pushing Dave's buttons and pretending to not be listening until Dave yells, but notice that Alvin never misses a beat...he's in total control! Another really nice thing here is the accurate demonstration of the effect of one bad apple; at the end after Alvin opens the door to anarchy (they might as well put a circle around the "A" on his sweater), Simon and Theodore start acting out just as much! This record, by the way, sold six million copies, and made over $4.5 million in less than two months when it was released.

"Bagdasarian's studio wizardry didn't end with sped up nut grabbers. Naw, the B's of early Chipmunks singles had their own form of magic, under the guise of "The Music of David Seville". This B-side opens ominously with jungle bongos, then piano and reverb drenched handclaps join in. This persuasive percussion gradually turns into more of a party over its two minutes and two seconds as David enthusiastically and periodically exclaims, "Hey, that's almost good!" Self-deprecation through understatement."

Success was stellar for this record as reported in the December 8, 1958 issue of *Billboard*, "Getting back to the more strictly pop field, we have the fascinating novelty by David (Ross Bagdasarian) Seville on Liberty. This one is called "The Chipmunk Song", by The Chipmunks. Malverne Distributors mahoff, Al Hirsch, tells us this is the biggest record he's had since Frankie Laine's "Mule Train", which was back when Hirsch handled Mercury. "I've got backed up on orders like crazy," said Hirsch. "Our orders for New York now stand at about 130,000. This looks like the first million seller Christmas single in a good long time."

Then in *Billboard*'s December 15, 1958 issue, in a short article entitled, "Wonderful Figures", "Here are some of the wonderful sales figures that have pulled the singles business out of the doldrum: The Liberty Record of "The Chipmunk Song" is selling at the rate of 200,000 per day, according to sales topper Al Bennett. It is reported that 240,000 records of this Christmas novelty have been sold in New York along and many tradesters think it will reach a total of three million by the time St. Nick starts climbing down those chimneys."

Finally, in *Billboard*'s December 22, 1958 issue, they claim, "There is no longer any need to mention that "The Chipmunk Song" is one of the fastest-selling records of the year and looks toward becoming the biggest seller of 1958. Sales city by city have been astounding and it has been blaring out of radios, jukeboxes and loudspeaker systems from New York to Los Angeles every day for weeks. It looks certain to top 3,000,000, making it the biggest seller since "Hound Dog" a few years ago."

The song won three Grammy Awards in 1958: Best Comedy Performance, Best Children's Recording, and Best Engineered Record (non-classical). It was also nominated for Record of the Year. Bagdasarian appeared on *The First Annual Grammy Awards* on November 29, 1959, telecast on ABC to pick up his awards where the special was entitled *Sunday Showcase*. The excellent 2015 documentary called *The Wrecking Crew!* features a small snippet of "The Chipmunk Song", but doesn't go into any further details of who plays what on this or later Chipmunks tracks.

Bagdasarian first performed "The Chipmunk Song" live on *The Ed Sullivan Show* on December 21, 1958, with a pre-recorded tape.

He also performed the song when he appeared a second time on *The Dick Clark Beech-Nut Show* on January 3, 1959, well after Christmas. It is presumed that he used the Bob Clampett Chipmunks puppets for these appearances.

Shana Alexander discusses Bagdasarian's highly successful follow-up to "The Chipmunk Song" called "Alvin's Harmonica" which was released on February 20, 1959 and peaked at #3, "To millions of listeners, the agonized cry "Alvin!" emanating from a loudspeaker means just one thing: that man on that record is once again absolutely fed up with that singing chipmunk. But in the home of a Hollywood songwriter named Ross Bagdasarian, the same voice means something else: Bagdasarian is one again shouting at his four-year-old Adam to get out of the office. The fact that "Alvin!" sounds like "Adam!" is no coincidence. Ross Bagdasarian in the past few months has squeaked and squawked his way through two spectacular record successes. Both were inspired by the obstreperous Adam and both featured the irritating, nasal-voiced chipmunk, Alvin. One of these, "The Chipmunk Song", has already sold four million copies, and a sequel called "Alvin's Harmonica" passed the million mark after being out only five weeks.

"Though Americans have always been partial to rodents - Peter Rabbit, Mickey Mouse, Bugs Bunny - this is the first time we have elevated a chipmunk to folk hero status. It is also the first time in the annals of popular music that one man has served as writer, composer, publisher, conductor and multiple vocalist of a hit record, thereby directing all possible revenues from the song back into his own pocket. What is more, Bagdasarian does four vocal parts single-handed, or single-voiced.

"By comparison, Bagdasarian's new song, "Alvin's Harmonica", is a toccata and fugue. It took nine perfect tapes, or tracks, and three days' work from the composer's head to acetate.

"The original ending of "Alvin's Harmonica" involved Alvin's getting his nose stuck in his instrument. After dinner on the night before the actual recording of "Harmonica" was to begin, Bagdasarian suddenly ad-libbed some cha-cha-cha nonsense at the end of the song "and the kids fell on the floor laughing. I asked them if they knew what cha-cha-cha meant and they said no, but it had a funny sound, so the next day at the session, we threw it in."

Sanderson and Tawney add, "Besides singing, Alvin plays a harmonica and became famous for this in the song "Alvin's Harmonica". This song also shows Alvin's talents for getting into mischief. At one point, David Seville has to say, "Alvin, stop playing your harmonica!" David Seville often showed his displeasure with Alvin's antics simply by yelling Alvin's name in a long, drawn-out way: "Aaaaalllviiinnn!" It actually originated not with David Seville and Alvin, but with Bagdasarian and his son, Adam. When Adam was about four years old, Bagdasarian would yell at him in exactly the same way if he thought Adam was making too much noise while daddy was recording in the den. The names Adam and Alvin sound similar, so it is easy to see how this gave Bagdasarian the idea for the Alvin yell."

An online review of "Alvin's Harmonica" / "Mediocre" states, "The second chapter of the Alvin legend adds three more elements to the mythos: Alvin plays harmonica (though he really is more playing with it like a toy than playing it like Harmonicat). The Chipmunks are ladies men (Lyric: "We sure like girls, all kindsa girls, from Annie to Veronica. We like them small or fat or tall… and if we want to get a kiss we take them food or popcorn"). And we also learn that Bagdasarian has a charming but square notion of what constitutes

Rock and Roll, as demonstrated by the kids adding "cha cha cha" to the end of the song. This unsupportive, harsh tone towards Alvin, "Alright Alvin, make a fool of yourself, play your harmonica!" But you gotta feel for him when it all falls apart after Alvin's rudimentary hard skills set off a domino effect of youth music chaos. "Now look what you did, you got them all cha-cha- ing..." You know that everything is really going against Dave when he yells, "Theodore... Simon... Orchestra!" I mean, you don't have to be paranoid to feel like things aren't going right if the orchestra turns on you! Funniest moments are when Alvin annoys Dave by answering him with a talking harmonica, and then appropriately (for a foraging rodent) yells, "Ah, nuts!"

"The non-Alvin flipside is the same concept as "Almost Good", but obviously much more self-defeating and self-deprecating. No handclaps this time round, but we do get to cha-cha- cha! David hems and haws and I-don't- knows all throughout the number until he tells the band to stop as he says, "Wait a minute! I can't publish that! It's uh, mediocre!" They didn't even get to hit the two minute mark! They sounded like they were having fun, too! No, it's certainly not mediocre and David's running commentary of saying that it's mediocre actually makes the song even less so and anything but!"

There are variations on the releases of "Alvin's Harmonica" on how "Alvin's Harmonica" sounds. Like the later "Ragtime Cowboy Joe", this may be due to deficiencies in the master tapes, or adding new harmonica sounds in order to accommodate the digital format. Regardless, there are differences. It is presumed that Bagdasarian performed a version of "Alvin's Harmonica" when he appeared on *The Ed Sullivan Show* on March 8, 1959.

"Alvin's Harmonica" went gold with over 500,000 sold and

re-entered the charts in 1961 and 1962, peaking at #73 and #87, respectively.

Next, Bagdasarian as David Seville had a minor success in April 1959 with the single of "Judy" / "Maria From Madrid", which reached #86. "Judy" was later released as "The Prom" under Bagdasarian's own name. It is violin and piano instrumental with spoken word bits that was also used as background music on *The Alvin Show*. "Maria From Madrid" also appeared on *The Alvin Show* and is a piano, violin and sax instrumental, also with some talking bits.

Johnny Jason from *'Teen Magazine* remarks, "The continued success of Alvin and The Chipmunks with the subsequent hit records of "Alvin's Harmonica", "Ragtime Cowboy Joe", "Alvin's Orchestra" and the first three Chipmunks albums led to the animated series *The Alvin Show*. But before that, Ross Sr. dabbled with The Chipmunks in a variety of different guises and designs including puppets on *The Ed Sullivan Show* and *American Bandstand*\* and realistic versions of The Chipmunks featured on their early albums, on Golden Books, and in the initial comic books."

A review of "Ragtime Cowboy Joe" / "Flip Side", released later on in June 1959 and reaching #16, reads, "One this number, The Chipmunks sing about the "...high falootin' rootin' tootin'" Ragtime Cowboy Joe, punctuated by random gunfire. Party poopin' David tells Alvin to put the gun down. Is David so concerned with gun safety that he doesn't want Alvin to hurt himself? Is David anti-NRA?

---

\* *'Teen Magazine* is where the *American Bandstand* appearance rumors may have started. Through my research, it has been discovered that Bagdasarian never appeared on *Bandstand*. He did, however, appear TWICE on *The Dick Clark Beech-Nut Show* and on the Clark episode of *This is Your Life*. No one remembers Clark's primetime music show, so the names were probably confused.

Actually, he just wants Alvin to finish the song. One must truly appreciate Seville's perfectionism. The number ends with horse gallops as Alvin yells, "Hi-yo, Alvinnnn...." The flip side is called "Flip Side" because that's what it is. It's also a very exotic instrumental! Ominous jungle bongos that stay ominous. Whistling kicks off a melody that piano and, later, a vocal chant of "Doo doo doo dee doo, ree dee dee dee dee doo..." follow. And more reverb handclaps! Has a bit of a Joe Meek vibe. When I hear this, I see toucans."

"Ragtime Cowboy Joe" was written by Grant Clarke, Lewis F. Muir and Lester Abramson. The song dates back to 1912 and was recorded primarily because Liberty Records needed a quick follow-up to "Alvin's Harmonica" and cowboys were very popular on TV at the time, so the pairing was natural.

The sound effects of "Ragtime Cowboy Joe" vary from the original single to the versions released today on CD as with "Alvin's Harmonica". It is possible that the sound effects track had deteriorated and had to be replaced or replaced due to the higher sonic fidelity of the compact disc. In either case, it creates a couple sonic variations on this track.

All of this hit single activity was bound to lead to a full-length LP featuring The Chipmunks. Sanderson and Tawney continue, "The Chipmunks' first record album was called *Sing Along With The Chipmunks*. Later, the title was changed to *Let's All Sing With The Chipmunks*. Perhaps Bagdasarian felt that the first title was too close to that of the then-popular television program *Sing Along With Mitch* (Miller). Bagdasarian autographed the back of the first album, but instead of signing his own name, he signed David Seville. On the front cover of the album, The Chipmunks were drawn to look like real chipmunks. They looked more like real chipmunks than Disney's

Chip and Dale. Alvin, Simon and Theodore were shown wearing sport coats and carrying canes. The precise "family" relationship between David Seville and The Chipmunks was never made clear; David Seville is the manager and guardian of The Chipmunks."

Winters from *Cool and Strange Music* continues, "With the huge success of the first Chipmunks' record, Liberty green-lighted a series of follow-up singles as well as a full-length album, *Let's All Sing With The Chipmunks* from 1959. That LP included three more million-selling hits: "Alvin's Harmonica", which reached #3 nationally, "The Chipmunk Song" and "Ragtime Cowboy Joe" It was also the first in a string of successful Chipmunks albums that included *The Chipmunk Songbook, Christmas With The Chipmunks* and *The Chipmunks Sing The Beatles Hits*."

Before the first Chipmunks album proper, Bagdasarian as Seville and The Chipmunks appeared in two spoken word bits on the stereo test demonstration album called *Liberty Proudly Presents Stereo... the Visual Sound* in June 1959. The album had narration by Jimmy Wallington, who at times talks over the intro to the songs and sound effects. Songs include "The Notre Dame Victory March" by University Brass Band & Russ Garcia, "Sweet Someone" by The Invitations, "I Got Rhythm" by The Stanley Johnson Orchestra, "Bubble Bath" by The Spencer Hagen Orchestra, "Tiger Rag" by Jad Paul's Banjo Magic, "Stranger In Paradise" by Martin Denny", "El Cumbanchero" by The Don Swan Orchestra, "Comin' Through The Rye" by Julie London, "Caravan" by The John Buzon Trio, "Samoan Knife Dance" by Chick Floyd, "Salta Perico" by Jack Costanzo, and "Aloha Oe" by Billy Ward's Orchestra and Chorus.

Seville and The Chipmunks appear twice in brief moments between songs where he is yelling at them and chasing them from speaker to speaker trying to get Alvin and the boys back into the correct recording studio to make their next record. Engineer Ted Keep is also heard on the record. A second stereo demonstration record appeared in 1960 without Chipmunk help, narrated by Spike Jones, a recent signing.

Here is an online review of the first pre-*Alvin Show* LP that featured the earlier rabies-infested Chipmunks and later reissued with the TV show designs. *Let's All Sing With The Chipmunks* was released in 1959: "The album opens with a funny and sophisticated joke right off the back. The music starts up for "Yankee Doodle Dandy", and David asks if everyone's ready, to which Simon and Theodore respond affirmatively. Alvin isn't paying attention, so when David yells at him, Alvin snaps out of his daydream and starts mechanically singing, "Christmas, Christmas time is here!" The joke for the rest of the song is Alvin singing "spaghetti" instead of macaroni. The album balances the kiddie and the adult audiences well. "The Little Dog" and "Pop Goes the Weasel" are very much kiddie songs, with some lines left out for tykes to sing along. But "Chipmunk Fun" has lecherous Alvin talking about his love for "pretty women". Best Seville rant of the LP: "Alvin, will you get out of that tuba!" It's notable that thought the words "Rock and Roll" gets thrown around this LP, Seville's take on it is a swinging sax-heavy square Jazz Pop with a polka beat.

"The album tracks are good, but this also compiles the hot hit singles, "Alvin's Harmonica", "The Chipmunk Song" and the not as hot, but still great "Ragtime Cowboy Joe" single. All the early Chipmunk LPs came with covers printed on metallic foil covers so as to be extra shiny for the kids. The first few LPS also debuted with The Chipmunks in their more animalistic form. The original cover for this has them in Vaudeville bow ties, vests, straw hats and canes, while a cartoon Dave conducts an orchestra in tails. The Chips would quickly lose the old timey look and become contemporary kids (though their knock-off rivals, The Grasshoppers, maintained the Ragtime look for years).

"In 1961, the new designs for Alvin, Simon, Theodore and David were debuted for the TV show (they spent an extra long time developing the new look) and this LP was reissued with the new Chips and the new David on the cover, plus the caveat "Songs from *The Alvin Show*". Alvin is still crooning on one knee as in the original cover, but now his pose mimics Elvis, not Jolson. This also was available pressed in red vinyl."

This album was The Chipmunks' most successful chartwise, peaking at #4 thanks to the help of three hit singles. The album also won a Grammy for Best Children's Album in 1960. Ted Keep was the engineer, Pate/Francis & Associates did the original cover design and actual artwork and Studio Five drew the animation artwork for the reissue pressing. It was nominated for a Grammy for Best Album Created for Children.

Bagdasarian appeared on the June 24 1959 episode of *This is Your Life* saluting *American Bandstand* host Dick Clark. On it, Bagdasarian performed The Chipmunk Song" with the Chipmunk puppets that animator Bob Clampett designed and performed.

Bagdasarian also appeared on the December 13, 1959 edition of *The Ed Sullivan Show* with The Chipmunks, this time with the Bunin Chipmunks puppets instead of Clampett's. On this episode, "Yankee Doodle", "The Chipmunk Song" and "Alvin's Harmonica" were performed.

It is this appearance on *Ed Sullivan* performing "The Chipmunk Song" that usually makes it onto Christmas or Chipmunks or *Ed Sullivan* salutes or compilation videos or shows and is the most accessible clip of Bagdasarian singing and performing next to the *Ed*

*Sullivan Show* "Witch Doctor" clip from 1958.

Next was another single release. An online review of "Alvin's Orchestra" / "Copyright 1960", released in January 1960, and charting at #33 states, "Variations on a theme in the sequel department often use the "bigger is better" scenario. An orchestra is much more bombastic and chaotic than a harmonica. David develops a coronary when Alvin gets into conductor mode. David calculates the rental costs in his head and yells, "Alvin, will you cut it out? What are you going to pay this orchestra with, chestnuts?" Alvin then passive-aggressively claims not to understand a word that David is saying. "Orchestra, will you please go home?" One can see the vein in David's forehead rise and pop out. The song itself is about driving along the countryside, a difficult activity to do when one has an orchestra in tow.

"The orchestra, since they were already hired, are put to use again on David's languid piano-led B-side, "Copyright 1960". I guess this means that David just threw his hands up in defeat. Time is money and the instrumental is only one minute and 52 seconds long."

The Abnuceals Emuukha Electric Symphony Orchestra is credited as being "Alvin's Orchestra". These are the same session musicians that Frank Zappa (1940-1993) later used for his *Lumpy Gravy* album in 1967 and he gave them the eccentric name. It is presumed that Bagdasarian performed "Alvin's Orchestra" when he appeared on *The Ed Sullivan Show* on April 17, 1960, but all that is mentioned is that they did a sing-along and that Alvin gives Seville an exploding Easter basket.

The next Ross Bagdasarian release was not released at all, despite getting a Liberty Records catalog number of F-55239. The song was called "Lotta Bull", the B-side is unknown and why the song and the single remain unreleased is unknown. It may have been retitled and released later.

In April 1960, the two biggest Chipmunk hit A-sides were reissued as a double-sided hit: "The Chipmunk Song" / "Alvin's Harmonica", this time with a picture sleeve. The two sides charted yet again at #39 and #73, respectively. An internet review states, "This double A-side picture sleeve reissue is notable because The Chipmunks are still portrayed on the picture sleeve as realistic animals. Early Chipmunks records feature illustrations of rodents with anatomy that resembles a real live chipmunk. When the boys wear shoes or cowboy boots, they don't fit their oddly-shaped paws. Years later Ross Jr. said the original Chipmunks looked like things that could give you rabies. Thought there would be some variation (sometimes they wore clothes; sometimes their faces seemed more human), this was pretty consistent until 1961. Aware that the visual was limiting, Ross Sr. and the production house spent an extra long time developing a new look for the animated version of the 'Munks. A year after this record, they would be the cartoon Chips we know and love." In 1961, this single was reissued again with a new picture sleeve reflecting the new designs.

"Coming 'Round the Mountain" / "Sing a Goofy Song" was the next new single release later in April of 1960 and was The Chipmunks first miss. An online review states, "Coming Round" is a weird record that half sounds like they're doing and eclectic progressive PoMo arrangement, and half sounds like they're trying on different arrangements for size. They open as an almost creepy marching band, then the next verse they get jazzed up, then they get kind of New Orleans on the next, and then back to the marching band for the fade-out. It's a pretty novel concept, with no narrative set-up or jokes, but maybe kids wouldn't dig this as a single.

"The flip is really David Seville singing with the Chips backing him up. Then, during the instrumental break, he whispers to the boys that it's going well, but Alvin isn't paying attention and starts messing up. As the song ends, David is pleased as punch that there wasn't an argument on the record and then he makes the mistake of praising himself, which gives Alvin a chance to get back at him for calling him out for being "a little flat" back in '58." "Sing a Goofy Song" is another Bagdasarian original.

The third and final single from the album is a Chipmunks remake of "Witch Doctor" / "Swanee River", released in June 1960. An online review states, "The Chips prepare themselves for the dialect humor of their next LP with this exchange:

"David: "Boys, how would you like to do something Southern?"

"Theodore: "Like fried chicken?"
"Simon: "Or cornpone?"
"Alvin: "Or ham hocks?"
"David: "No, like "Swanee River".
"Simon: "Well, hush my mouth!"

"A nice moment is when The Chips ask David to sing "Witch Doctor": "I don't think so fellas; I made that record once." "But not with us." Then they snappily go into it, with three harmonizing Witch Doctors instead of one."

These and "Alvin's Orchestra", "Coming 'Round the Mountain" and "Sing a Goofy Song" all ended up on the second Chipmunks album, *Sing Again with The Chipmunks*, released in early 1960. The album peaked at #31. As with *Let's All Sing With The Chipmunks*, Ted Keep was the engineer, Pate/Francis & Associates did the original cover design and actual artwork and Studio Five drew the animation artwork for the reissue pressing.

The online review continues, "Though it doesn't have the power punch of having a couple of million selling singles on it, this funny platter is no sophomore slump. Prime shtick includes Alvin messing with Seville's mind by bastardizing "Home On the Range" with the line, "where the deer and the cantaloupe play." When David corrects him, Alvin responds, "Well, I'm hungry." This LP includes the bouncy Bagdasarian original "I Wish I Had a Horse", which features no mischief, but some really great rhythmic exchanges.

"This LP features the singles "Coming "Round the Mountain" and "Alvin's Orchestra", plus the prime B-side "Sing a Goofy Song". On the back cover liner notes, David writes, "The Boys (Alvin, Simon and Theodore) had a wonderful time making this record for you. As for me, I should be released from the hospital soon." The LP originally came with gold foil cover art and the realistic Chipmunks causing mischief by leaving a skate on the stairs causing David (a real life photo of Bagdasarian) to fall. The post-cartoon reissue has a drawing of David, as well as the new Chipmunks."

Bagdasarian continued with non-Chipmunks single releases with "Lazy Lovers" / "One Finger Waltz" released under his own name, Ross Bagdasarian, in July 1960. It didn't chart. An interesting thing about this release: "Lazy Lovers" is a sax, violins and drums instrumental that became "Frumpington's Song" and "One Finger Waltz" became "Crashcup's Work Theme"; both for *The Alvin Show.*

1960 was also the year of a very close Presidential race between Senator John F. Kennedy and Vice President Richard M. Nixon. Many fictional characters also threw their hats into the ring including *Mad*'s Alfred E. Neuman and Hanna-Barbera's Huckleberry Hound, so why not Alvin? The resulting single was "Alvin For President" / "Sack Time", released in August 1960, right before the elections.. An online review says, "If Alvin was running against Kennedy and

Nixon, who would you vote for? He loved the ladies like Jack, but came from a much more wholesome family. He would have certainly played dirty tricks like Dick, but likely couldn't pull off the diplomacy with China as well (check out his attitude in Japan on the *Around the World* LP). Well, all I know is, if he ran in 2000, he would have won in a landslide."

Ross Jr. adds from the *Still Squeaky* booklet: "One of my personal favorites is "Alvin For President". This 1960 hit featured some of the best interaction between David Seville and Alvin. Alvin threw his cap into the ring with Senator John F. Kennedy and Vice President Richard Nixon. Shortly after the song's release, pop got a note from then Senator John F. Kennedy, which read: "I am pleased to know that I have at least one worthy opponent."

Bagdasarian prepared Alvin's platform in *The Pittsburgh Press* on September 15, 1960, "No taxes, more money for teenagers, doubling of teacher's salaries and rotation of people instead of crops. Send the city children to the country and the country children to the city and in six months, they'll all be happy to go back where they came from." Liberty Records also gave Alvin a slogan: "Throw the Rascal In".

This song never appeared on an original Chipmunks LP, but has popped up on a few compilations since, and only made it to a paltry #95 on the charts. It was also featured on *The Alvin Show* and much later on, a floppy soundsheet record was given away in 1983 with Chipmunks toys. The B-side was not reviewed, but it is a simple non-Chipmunks piano tune similar in style to "Copyright 1960" and replete with Bagdasarian yawns. "Alvin For President" is similar in composition to "I Wish I Could Speak French" and was nominated for a Grammy for Best Comedy Performance (Musical). Apparently, Bagdasarian did not perform the song when he appeared on *The Ed*

*Sullivan Show* on September 25, 1960, his sixth and final appearance on the show. Instead, he performed "Coming 'Round the Mountain" and "Witch Doctor" with the Bunin puppets.

Next came "Rudolph the Red-Nosed Reindeer" / "Spain" in December 1960 with its online review, "The Chips drag David to the North Pole, where he's freezing, but they've promised him a surprise. And that surprise is Rudolph, who sings along with the boys in a voice that indicates his nose is red from nasal congestion, Dave, unimpressed, or on the verge of frostbite, retreats to a warm igloo before the song is over, missing Alvin's song ending bitch-and-moan fest about still wanting a hula hoop.

"On the flip, the boys are invited to sing with a Spanish orchestra led by a florid guitar. Alvin takes his time, then wails "OH, SENOR!..." one every few bars, almost randomly, as if he has no lyrics, but then just as they wind it up he breaks into a verse about a senorita, but is cut off by a heavy Spanish accent telling him, "I'm sorry, Senor Alvin, you're too late, the song is over." This is followed by dead silence. An almost dadaistic piece. This is one of the gloriously weirdest Chipmunk tunes."

*Around the World With The Chipmunks* was released late in 1960: "Possibly the funniest Chipmunks LP of all, Though the previous LP's feature the all time classic songs, this concept album is rock solid. The Chipmunks are circling the globe and, if such a thing is possible, engaging in semi-innocuous ethnic humor (Alvin in Scotland upon seeing a bagpiper: "How come the man in the dress is squeezing an octopus?").

"The absolute highlight is the amazing "Japanese Banana". I can't recall how many musicians I've heard praise this as their favorite

Chipmunk song. In it, Alvin craves a food they can't get, and to an Eastern melody decides to torture Dave with the refrain, "Can I have a Japanese banana, it would be so very nice, want a juicy Japanese banana, don't want the cherries and rice. We can see that they have so many things, and we are glad that it's so, but do they grow a Japanese banana? That's what we'd like to know." The banter between an embarrassed Dave and an indignant Alvin is some of their funniest.

"Alvin: "That's the worst banjo player I've ever heard."
"David: "That's not a banjo. It's a shamisen."
"Alvin: "That's the worst sham-i-sen player I've ever heard."

"The other great song is "I Wish I Could Speak French", in which Alvin tried to pick up a mademoiselle by musically lamenting his lack of language skills with the smooth cadence and delivery of Chevalier. It ends with her going for him, to which he responds, "Oui? Oui? Wow!"

"In Italy, a gondolier doesn't appreciate the boys singing along and chides, "Hey you-a mouse-a, pipe down!" To which Alvin responds, "Mouse! Mouse! I'm Alvin the chipmunk!" Gondolier: "Chipmunk, shmipmunk, silencio!" After another exchange, the boys (to the tune of "O Sole Mio") sing, "Oh, Gondelier-o, we are not mice, we're singing chipmunks, we told you twice!"

"When Alvin asks the bagpiper to use his "octopus", the piper responds, "Sure, laddy!" The boys then start "rocking and rolling", and Dave has the nerve to say, "You're playing in the wrong key, Alvin!" Imagine that... denigrating a child's bagpipe skills during his first attempt to play the thing!

"This record was available with an awesome foil cover, but I don't think it appeared without the cartoon Chipmunks, as many of these skits were animated in the cartoon that premiered around the time that this was on the shelves."

The reviewer is incorrect. The album was foil, but did feature the original, realistic Alvin sitting on an airplane's tail with David yelling at him from a plane window with the other Chipmunks for its original release. The reissue shows the cartoony Chipmunks riding a camel in the desert with David crazily waving a shovel nearby.

The original back cover had spot illustrations of the realistic Chipmunks in various worldwide locations, with the reissue of The Chipmunks aboard a gondola with Dave as the gondolier.

Once again, Ted Keep was the engineer, Pate/Francis & Associates did the original cover design and actual artwork and Studio Five drew the animation artwork for the reissue pressing.

The sole single from *Around the World With The Chipmunks*, their third LP. It reached #21 on the charts. "Rudolph" went on to also appear on the first *Christmas With The Chipmunks* LP.

Bagdasarian released one last single under the David Seville moniker prior to him getting seriously involved with The Chipmunks and *The Alvin Show*. It was called "Oh Judge, Your Honor, Dear Sir, Sweetheart" / "Freddy, Freddy" and released in March 1961 to no chart action. 'Oh Judge" is a novelty song used on *The Alvin Show* and "Freddy" is a silly song sung by a female chorus.

Of course, the success of "The Chipmunk Song" and its sequels prompted much competition, most with middling success, but some of the more successful competitors included "Uh Oh" by The Nutty Squirrels (#14 in 1959) and "The Happy Reindeer" by Dancer, Prancer and Nervous a.k.a. Russ Regan (#34 in 1959). There were even knock-off Chipmunks records attributed to The Chipmunks!

All this success led to the crowning achievement of Bagdasarian's Chipmunks, *The Alvin Show*! For the purposes of this new venture, Bagdasarian formed Bagdasarian Film Corporation in 1961 for the TV show and Bagdasarian Enterprises for albums, merchandise and everything else, with a small, round Bagdasarian Enterprises logo featuring The Chipmunks now appearing on everything as Bagdasarian's official stamp of approval. His music publishing company, Monarch Music, formed in 1958, also continued to exist.

Bagdasarian hired Nick Draklich (1926-1997) to run Bagdasarian Enterprises and became Executive Producer for *The Alvin Show*. Their original address was at 465 South Beverly Drive in Beverly Hills, California. Today, it's the offices of Nahai Insurance Services.

But first, a little bit about the studio that helped create the series, Format Films.

"Witch Doctor" becomes a sensation. The EP, the sheet music, the LP and another LP that has nothing to do with Bagdasarian.

*Witch Doctor* EP                    *Witch Doctor* sheet music

Witch Doctor LP                    Witch Doctor LP not Ross

Bagdasarian performs "Witch Doctor" live on *The Ed Sullivan Show* on May 4, 1958. Despite some technical difficulties, it is a fun and energetic performance.

Puppeteer Morey Bunin and his "Witch Doctor" and "Bird On My Head" puppets.

"The Bird On My Head" sheet music.

"The Bird On My Head" song index card.

```
Title:   BIRD ON MY HEAD, THE                              #J-8
Performing Rights licensed through    BMI    Date of this issue   August 1958
Writers W: )
         M: )   Ross Bagdasarian

Copyright   1958 by Monarch Music Company, Inc. - Sole
            Selling Agent: Keys-Hansen, Inc. - 119 W. 57 St.,
            New York, N.Y.
Other information:

             Recorded by:  David Seville - Liberty
```

**WARNING!** Int'l copyr't secured. All rights reserved, inc. the right of arrangement & public performance for profit. Printing, reprinting, copying or publishing by any means and methods whatsoever, by enlarging, mimeographing, or otherwise, constitutes infringement of copyright. Offenders will be prosecuted under the copyright law.

Litho'd by Tune-Dex, Inc. Box 49, N. Y. 19, N. Y. (U. S. A.) by permission of the copyright owners.

Bagdasarian singing "The Bird On My Head" on *The Dick Clark Beech-Nut Show* (not *American Bandstand*) with Bunin's Bird puppet on July 12, 1958. Dick Clark is the program's host.

"The Chipmunk Song" originally did not have a picture sleeve. This is the picture sleeve released with the single's reissue.

After the chipmunk characters were redesigned for *The Alvin Show*, "The Chipmunk Song" was reissued again with this revised picture sleeve.

"The Chipmunk Song" sheet music before and after *The Alvin Show* remodel.

Chipmunk Song sheet music 1          Chipmunk Song sheet music reissue

An ad for "The Chipmunk Song" on Liberty Records.

Bagdasarian appeared on an episode of *This Is Your Life*, honoring Dick Clark. Here, he performed "The Chipmunk Song" with puppets designed and performed by Bob Clampett on June 24, 1959. Clampett was a Warner Bros. director and transitioned to puppets with his *Time For Beany* show.

A picture sleeve for a cover version of "The Chipmunk Song". Such knock-offs were rampant once the song became a major hit.

A Disney Chip and Dale album touting them as the originals!

A "Chipmunk Song" album by The Grasshoppers touting chipmunks on the cover.

Another "Chipmunk Song" album. This one by The Bunnyhoppers.

Yet another Chipmunks rip-off LP.

Alvin and The Chipmunks inspired similar groups of animals with sped-up voices. Here are two of the most successful: The Nutty Squirrels and The Happy Reindeer.

Nutty Squirrels                 Happy Reindeer

The Chipmunks as they appeared on *The Ed Sullivan Show* on December 13, 1959. These puppets are the Morey Bunin designs.

The Morey Bunin Chipmunks and other Bunin puppets.

The Morey Bunin Chipmunks on *Antiques Roadshow* in 2014.

The two earliest Alvin dolls circa 1958-1959.

Alvin doll 1958     Alvin doll 1959

Early Chipmunks games: Acorn Hunt, Big Record, and Cross Country.

**Chipmunks Acorn Hunt Game**

Chipmunks Big Record game

Chipmunks Cross Country Game

First Chipmunks book: *The Chipmunks' Merry Christmas* with artwork by Richard Scarry.

A Chipmunks plate featuring an early design.

Chipmunks pins featuring early designs.

A Chipmunks Stuff and Lace Set.

A Chipmunks Loot Box.

A Chipmunks Paint and Crayon Set.

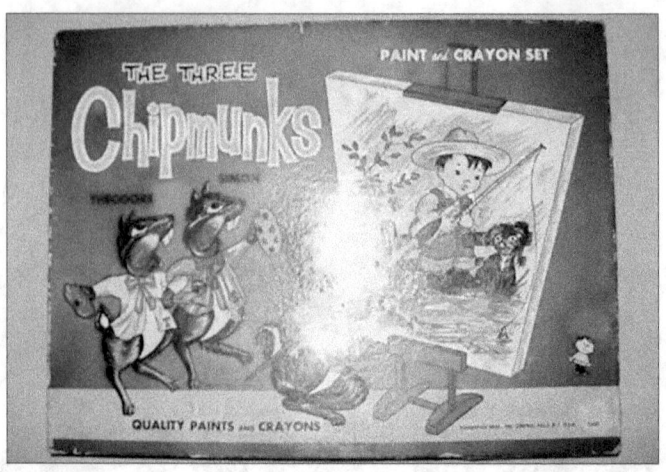

A collector's case full of various Chipmunks merchandise over the years.

As with "The Chipmunk Song", "Alvin's Harmonica" originally did not have a picture sleeve. This is the picture sleeve released with the single's reissue as the B-side to "The Chipmunk Song".

After the chipmunk characters were redesigned for *The Alvin Show*, "Alvin's Harmonica" was reissued again with this revised picture sleeve as the B-side to "The Chipmunk Song".

A picture sleeve for a cover version of "Alvin's Harmonica".

"Alvin's Harmonica" sheet music.

An ad for "Alvin's Harmonica".

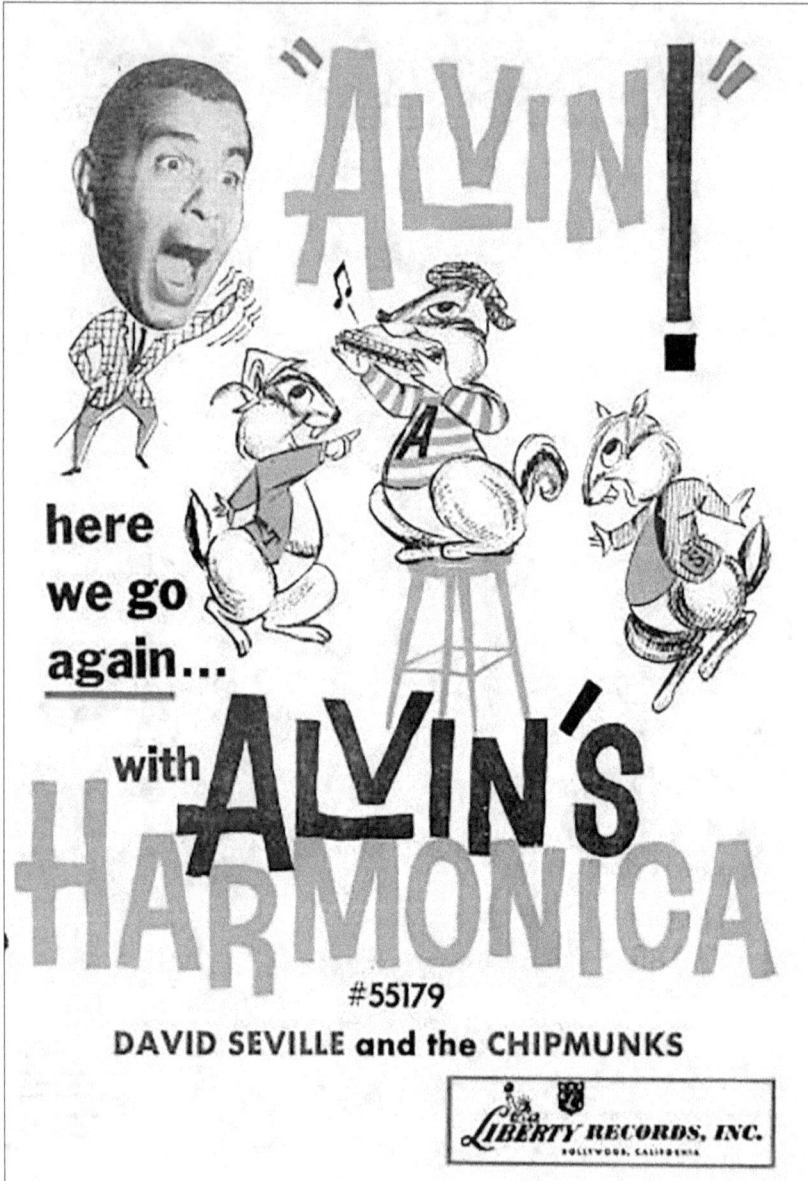

An "Alvin's Harmonica" plush doll complete with harmonica and box.

Ross Bagdasarian's autograph on an "Alvin's Harmonica" sheet music.

Bagdasarian with his three Grammys won at the first annual awards show.

Various photos of Ross Bagdasarian.

Once "Witch Doctor" and "The Chipmunk Song" were hits, people wanted to know all about the history of this magic hitmaker. Here are articles from *Burlington Free Press* (April 1, 1959), *Decatur Herald*, *Greenville News* and *Detroit Free Press* (all March 31, 1959), and *The Times* (November 20, 1960).

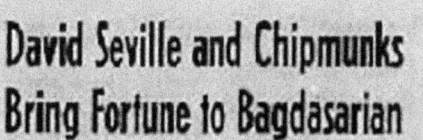

### Song Writer Hits Big Time Again
# 3 Chipmunks Make Grape Grower Hottest Item In Record Business

### AS ALVIN SAYS, 'THIS IS ALLLL RIGHT!'
# Those Chipmunks Are in the Chips

Ross, Alias David

Picture sleeve for The Chipmunks' third hit single "Ragtime Cowboy Joe".

American sheet music for "Ragtime Cowboy Joe".

An ad for "Ragtime Cowboy Joe".

"Alvin's Orchestra" picture sleeve and sheet music.

Picture sleeve for "Coming 'Round the Mountain" b/w "Sing a Goofy Song".

"Alvin For President" picture sleeve.

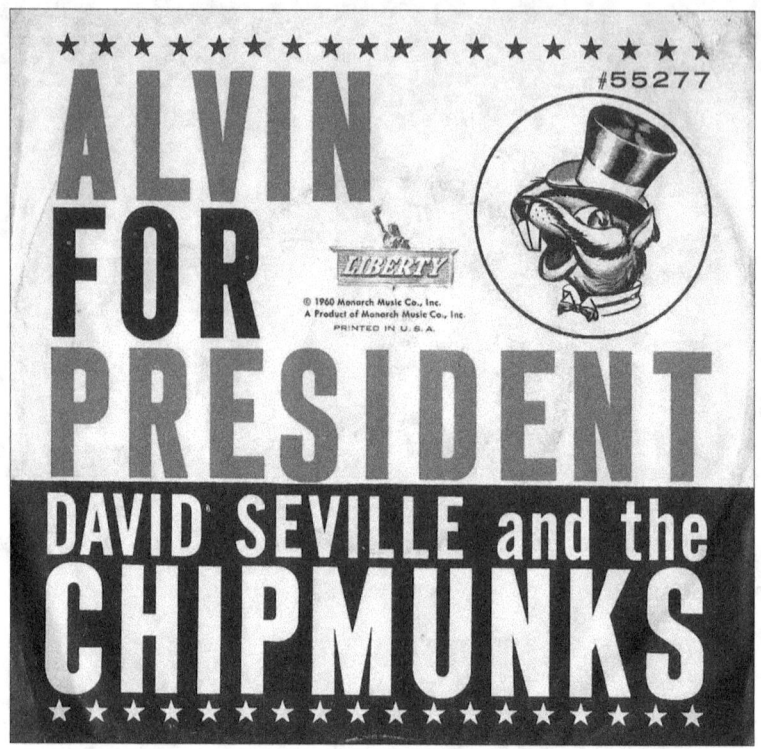

Article about "Alvin For President" from *Pittsburgh Press*, September 16, 1960.

A double-page spread ad for "Alvin For President".

An "Alvin For President" chart and pin.

"Rudolph, the Red-Nosed Reindeer" picture sleeve front and back.

 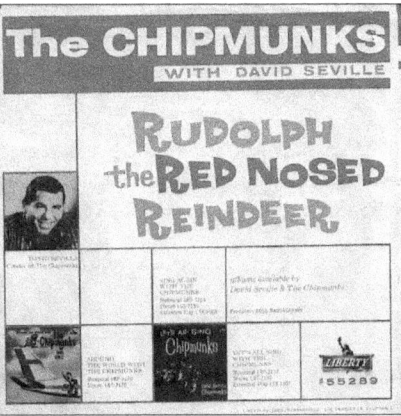

"Rudolph, the Red-Nosed Reindeer" reissue picture sleeve featuring *The Alvin Show* designs.

'Teen Magazine from January 1960 featuring Alvin on the cover.

The first Chipmunks album *Let's All Sing With The Chipmunks* original and reissue cover and song book.

The second Chipmunks album *Sing Again With The Chipmunks* original and reissue cover.

British EP with the alternate title *Sing Along With The Chipmunks*.

The third Chipmunks album *Around the World With The Chipmunks* original and reissue cover.

# FORMAT FILMS

*THE ALVIN SHOW* WAS produced by Format Films in association with Bagdasarian Productions. The antecedents of Format were UPA and Walt Disney Productions. For a complete and detailed account of the history of UPA, also known as United Productions of America, please refer to Adam Abraham's *When Magoo Flew: The Rise and Fall of Animation Studio UPA*.

In short, the origins of UPA can be traced back to the 1941 strike at Walt Disney Productions. Three men who eventually formed UPA came from Disney: Stephen Bosustow, David Hilberman, and Zachary Schwartz. None of them went on to Format, but it has been claimed that Bosustow was the inspiration for the Format character Clyde Crashcup, i.e. a man who claimed to invent things that weren't already invented.

UPA is mistakenly thought of as the originator of limited animation, but this is somewhat of a fallacy. Although UPA used arguably more stylized or simplistic designs that the typical Disney cartoon, in its heyday UPA had the same amount of movement than other cartoons. The main impetus behind UPA cartoons was its design sense. Where Disney wanted to be as close to life as possible, UPA basically wanted to do anything but. As *When Magoo Flew* states, UPA had "flattened character designs, streamlined backgrounds and stylized movements."

UPA did a number of one-shot cartoons, but their mainstay stars included The Nearsighted Mr. Magoo and Gerald McBoing-Boing, the sound-speaking boy. Magoo was the creation of Millard Kaufman, and McBoing-Boing by cartoonist and eventual children's book author Ted Geisel a.k.a. Dr. Seuss.

*When Magoo Flew* says, "Robert Cannon was born in Ohio in 1909. Small but strong, he was athletic - a gymnast, a swimmer, and a football player. Cannon grew up in San Bernardino, California, and drew cartoons for the high school annual. Later, he worked as a road surveyor, taught diving, and considered training for the Olympics. After taking classes at Chouinard Art Institute, Cannon found work at Leon Schlesinger Productions, where he assisted animator Chuck Jones. Cannon, who had a round, open face and bushy eyebrows often furrowed in thought, was known in high school as "Bob". Since the animation business enjoyed a panoply of persons named Robert or Bob - McKimson, Clampett, Givens and others - Cannon soon acquired the name "Bobo", which derived from a popular song. He thought that "Bobo" was a bit "too cute and clownish" according to his daughter; so his name was modified to "Bobe", and Bobe Cannon remained."

Cannon worked on "The Dover Boys", a Leon Schlesinger cartoon for Warner Bros. which was an early attempt at a proto-modern cartoon for which UPA was to become famous.

*When Magoo Flew*: "Born in Ohio in 1917, Herb Klynn (family name, Klynitsky) attended East Technical High School in Cleveland. When he was a senior, a former students about his experiences at Walt Disney Productions. "I was just awed by this," Klynn said. "We were fascinated by the stories he told."

"Klynn studied at Ohio State University and Cleveland School of Art. He worked in advertising and later partnered in a firm, Klynn-Walker Studios. World War II diminished the prospects of the Klynn-Walker enterprise, so Herb Klynn joined the Army Signal Corps as a civilian. The Army transferred him from Dayton, Ohio, to the First Motion Picture Unit in Culver City, California, in 1943. There he met and befriended the Hungarian-born artist Jules Engel. "It was really Jules who introduced me to non-objective painting," Klynn remembered.

'Herbert Klynn headed the UPA background department; his assistant was Jules Engel. Klynn and Engel planned each film's continuity in a series of color sketches; these indicate the mood and palette for each section of the cartoon. Furthermore, Klynn and Engel blurred the distinction between foreground and background, as Engel explained: "the character was never in front of the background. The character was always *in* the background."

"In addition to painting backgrounds, Klynn designed the UPA films' opening credits."Titles were my specialty," Klynn recalled, "I enjoyed combining a graphic challenge, a lettering challenge, and the conceptual challenge," As Engel noted, "The title cards on those cartoons for the first time had class."

"Eventually, Klynn was promoted to Production Manager and Engel was promoted to head of the background department. Cannon rose to vice president in charge of production.

"Herb Klynn's secretary, Henrietta "Hank" Jordan was hired as a receptionist at first, and did not wear makeup and was suitably obsequious. However, when Jordan became Klynn's secretary, she asserted herself. She found is ridiculous that UPA charged people five cents for a cup of coffee and altered this policy.

"A more felicitous combination arose when Bobe Cannon joined with the euphoniously named T. Hee. Thornton Hee was born in Oklahoma City, Oklahoma, in 1911. He created caricatures for the Hal Roach Studios, and this skill landed him a job at Walt Disney Productions, where he worked from 1938 to 1946. Hee did not walk the picket line in 1941, as he recalled, "I didn't strike; I was happy as a bird dog in a field of doves." T. Hee was a large man - 6'2", 250 pounds. As one animator observed, "He was built like a giant pear." (Surprisingly, T. Hee ate only vegetables and organic food.)

"In T. Hee, Bobe Cannon found an ideal collaborator. Hee wrote and designed a series of charming cartoons for Cannon to direct. Cannon had difficulty expressing himself in words, whereas Hee was "tremendously articulate", according to Bill Hurtz.

"It was left to assistant animator Alan Zaslove to prepare the cutting. At the age of 23, Zaslove was already an animation veteran. His family had lived across the street from Warner Bros., and as a teenager, Zaslove sold magazines on the studio lot after school. He got a job as an office boy at Leon Schlesinger Productions for 50c an hour and became a protege to animator Bobe Cannon. When Cannon moved to UPA, he said to Zaslove, "I'll get you a raise to 75c an hour,"

"UPA's editorial department, which was then headed by Joe Siracusa. Like Herb Klynn, Siracusa hailed from Cleveland. Siracusa and Klynn put on little marionette shows as children, Siracusa said. After six years on the road as a drummer in Spike Jones' band, Joe Siracusa joined UPA in 1952. Around 1955, he replaced Ted Baker as head of editing. Later that year, Siracusa saw technologies change, as 35mm optical sound tracks were replaced by magnetic tape. During his time at the studio, he was able to hire some of his former bandmates, including Roger Donley.

"By 1959, only the Burbank studio remained. Many of UPA's creative lights were gone. "I could feel studio fading away," Alan Zaslove said. Many explanations for the slow fade were offered. On October 2, 1959, UPA's longest-standing employee, Herbert Klynn, resigned to create a new company, which he said would "carry on in the UPA tradition".

"On June 3, 1960, Herbert Klynn filed a suit against UPA and Stephen Bosustow; Klynn claimed that he was owed vacation pay and a percentage of commissions on advertising sales. Bosustow denied the allegations and pointed out that he was not UPA Pictures. That same month he sold the company to Henry G. Saperstein. Klynn's attorneys amended the suit to name UPA and whatever John Doe Corporations now controlled it. Eventually, Saperstein settled the case to Klynn's benefit.

"Robert Cannon never again found his footing after he left UPA in 1957. Cannon worked for Ade Woolery's Playhouse Pictures. "He was very much at loose ends," Hana Cannon said of her father at the time. Herb Klynn agreed, "Bobe was wandering around, looking for things." After *The Alvin Show*, he resumed work. Cannon tried to persuade William Hanna to make his television product better than it needed to be. Then in 1962, Cannon's luck turned when he landed a job at Walt Disney Productions, but after a little more that five months, Cannon departed Disney's. According to Jules Engel, "Bobe died fairly young, and they say it was from a broken heart." Robert Cannon succumbed to a heart attack on June 9, 1964. He was 54 years old.

"A tremendous wealth of talent was concentrated for a time at UPA, those talents inevitably moved elsewhere or formed companies of their own. The UPA diaspora included Dave Hilberman's Tempo

Productions; Ed Gershman's Academy Pictures; and John Hubley's Storyboard, Inc. Abe Liss formed Elektra Films.

"One of the most fruitful of the UPA epigones was Playhouse Pictures, which was formed by Adrian Woolery in 1952. Playhouse excelled at breezy television commercials with UPA-liked graphics. Bill Melendez formed his own studio, in partnership with Lee Mendelson and in 1965, this new company produced *A Charlie Brown Christmas*, the first of many specials and features.

"Production manager Herb Klynn and background artist Jules Engel formed Format Films. Two years later, Format's *The Alvin Show*, based on The Chipmunks records created by Ross Bagdasarian, premiered on CBS. One of the segments designed to round out the half hours, "The Adventures of Clyde Crashcup," features a Steve Bosustow look-alike who takes credit for others' invention. Many former UPA employees joined Format: T. Hee, Leo Salkin, Alan Zaslove, Rudy Larriva, editor Joe Siracusa and secretary Hank Jordan. However in 1962, Format folded; "It was a really dry year," Zaslove commented. Herbert Klynn revived his company as Format Productions and produced *The Lone Ranger* television series in 1966.

"1959's other major inheritor of the UPA spirit was Jay Ward Productions. The list goes on. Fred Crippen left UPA in 1958 and created Pantomime Pictures, who produced *Roger Ramjet*. Jimmy Murakami partnered with Fred Wolf to form Murakami-Wolf."

Bob Kurtz worked for Format, and discussed his time there, "I never worked for UPA and my first professional job was not at Format. My first job was at Disney doing storyboard and writing and actually directing. The film was never finished and it was called *The Emperor's Nightingale*.

"I started there and my teacher was T. Hee, who later became my partner and mentor, It was Tee who brought me to Disney, and made possible all these great opportunities. Tee also is the one who is responsible for me going to work at Format Films. When I left Disney i already had a job at TV Spots waiting for me. However, Tee still made me go interview with Herb Klynn at Format films.

"At Format, I designed the characters of The Chipmunks and David Seville. That was basically it. Later on, there's probably some incidental ones I designed, but not Clyde Crashcup and Leonardo. I didn't do that. That was Leo Salkin's design.

"For The Chipmunk characters themselves, Leo Salkin did the first rough drawing. He did storyboards with the characters. They don't look anything like what we know them to be now, but they were great drawings. I had been there when Leo had done the network presentation, so when we were starting to design the show, I did my own variation of what Leo had drawn.

"Herb Klynn, again, very knowledgeable, was bringing in outside character designers to design the new Chipmunks. Herb was trying to control Ross and Ross is not controllable. What Herb would say to Ross is, "Well this guy's got 10 years experience and this guy's got 15 years experience," and Ross would say, "I don't care how much experience he has. These drawings suck."

"I was constantly in meetings with Ross and he just would say what was on his mind. As Ross was passing my desk, he saw me doing one of the early storyboards on the Chipmunks. I think Ross had just come from a character design presentation by Herb and he'd gotten really mad at what he was shown, so Ross looked at my drawings and of course, I'm the kid of the group and Ross says, "Why can't they look like this?" There were about six people around including Ross' brother-in-law who was a producer in Ross' company. There were a lot of people standing over me which was uncomfortable.

"Herb said, "OK, Draw Alvin." With all them leaning over me, I started to draw. Needless to say, no artist likes to have people hover over them while they draw. I quickly drew Alvin and his brothers Simon, Theodore and David Seville. They whipped each drawing out of my hands as I finished them.

"Ross said, "That's it! That's what I want!"

"It was a pretty clean sketch, but each character was only in one position. I thought someone will do the turnarounds and make a model sheet, but No! When the director Rudy Larriva got my drawings, all he did was printout the originals and reverse them. There was only two poses for each character, looking left and looking right. A strange way to work.

"Before *The Alvin Show* came to Format Films, I was hired as a writer and I did storyboards. Leo Salkin is the one who did the original Alvin storyboard and was really the overseer and worked real closely with Ross Bagdasarian. The movers of the company were Herb Klynn and Leo who took over that project. I was in a very unique position. I worked on all aspects of the show. I was present when the show was sold to the networks. I was Leo's right-hand man for story editing of freelance writers. I looked up on IMDB and it had freelance credits on equal level with the staff credits. It's all mixed up as to who really worked there full time and who worked only once or twice. I worked very close with Ross Bagdasarian. I was constantly working with him. Because I was one of the young writers and he liked working with me. We would talk a lot. Ross was a strong, opinionated person, but really a pleasure to work with. Always Ross had his own viewpoint of what he wanted.

"Ross was completely involved. In all the story meetings we presented directly to Ross. That's who signed off on the show and he was there all the time. He was a force. He had a lot of energy. He controlled the tracks. When they recorded, we were never around. They recorded off the premises, so the recording aspects I know nothing about other than what Ross would tell me. Voice talents June Foray and Shep Menken would often come into the studio and talk with us.

"Format Films was on 4741 Laurel Canyon Boulevard in Studio City. It was a block north of the 134 freeway in a two-story building. It was a big space actually at that time for an animation studio. We did everything in house except the voices were recorded somewhere else. I know Ross was very secretive on how he recorded "fast". That was his pride. He really was really happy with how he was able to do it. Ross used to tell me that Disney wanted to know how he did it because in his words Disney's Chip and Dale wasn't as good as his Chipmunks, but then that was Ross talking. The real secret was that he had to speak slower and with accents. That's what they did. They sped it up like three times.

"Ross, as you know, wrote the hit song "Come On-a My House", and he was really proud of his Armenian heritage. He and his cousin, the playwright and author, William Saroyan, were very close. Ross even brought William Saroyan into the studio. In fact, very early on, I think it was in the 1940's, while they drove across country together, they made up a character to pass the time. He wasn't named Clyde Crashcup, but it was a character who invented things that were already invented. It was their kind of wordplay as they went across the country and entertained themselves.

"Leo Salkin's drawings were much more in a cartoon world. They were those kind of shapes. I kept their relative proportions. As an aside, Ross came to me to write and illustrate Golden Books. One was titled *Alvin's Lost Voice* and another one was *Clyde Crashcup and Leonardo*. I did the books for him along when he wanted to sell a comic strip. I inked the original strip, but he couldn't sell it. He would come to me for extra work that was outside the studio realm. He said, "Will you do the Golden Books?" I said, "Well, I've never done them before, but sure, why not?" I mean, that's a nice compliment. I didn't work on the Dell comic book.

"I did some of the promotional, stuff occasionally. I think I roughed out stuff for them and they'd have other artists come in and paint.

"Format was artist friendly. Part of it was that Herb was a good background painter before he was a production manager. Then as he became a producer, he had an artistic sense. His partner - a minor partner - was Jules Engel a really good background painter. There was Buddy Getzler - the business guy, so he was always sour. Over all, the studio was filled with many very talented,spirited people. They had some really, really good writers. They had good animators.

"They had Frank Braxton, a close dear friend, who also was the first black animator in American animation. At the time I didn't know that Frank was the first black animator and Frank never talked about it.

"Besides that, Frank was also a wonderful musician. They had a lot of good musicians besides artists working at the studio. At lunchtime, they would play jazz in the screening room. You'd bring your brown bag and listen. Frank would play guitar with them and would play "Samba de Orfeu" from the film *Black Orpheus* for me.

"My memory was that Format was a great place to work and filled with so much talent. There was friction between Ross and the company, because Ross wasn't going to settle for anything less than what he wanted. You had this constant conflict where Herb was trying to appease him or trying to tell him, "We can do this or we can do that," and Ross wanted what he wanted. That's pretty much it. I'm sure Ross was a headache to Herb.

"It was rare to have animation in primetime. I have no idea why the network made the decision to go just one season.

"We did a lot of stuff at Format, but I don't remember doing movie titles because when the show was over, I moved on. I worked on industrial films. I co-authored a industrial film with Leo Salkin. I might have come back once. I was working pretty regularly as a writer, but I wasn't around when they did *Lone Ranger* and the other shows. I was long gone.

"I did do the 60 second Jell-O commercial. I wrote it, did the storyboard and layout. Now if you look at that commercial, it is the closest to my original Chipmunks designs. That was because of Bobe Cannon, who was a marvelous director and animator from UPA. He directed the classic short, *Gerald McBoing-Boing*. Bobe was just a brilliant, brilliant man and one of the legends of animation. Bobe was not working at Format, but he used to come by quite often. We had so many long talks about animation and life. Bobe shared a lot with me.

"Herb Klynn came in and informed me, "You were doing a Jell-O commercial. We're going to have Bobe Cannon animate it."

"I said, "Oh, great!!!" Bobe directed and animated the spot. It was brilliant!!! It's the only time that my characters were drawn the way that I drew them, because I did the layouts, and Bobe was true to the layouts. The studio animators used to square the Chipmunks off with very few curves. I drew straight lines and curves. If you want to know what the original Chipmunks really looked like, you can watch that Jell-O commercial.

"That's the original design and I wish that it would have been followed more closely in the show. Back to the spot, Bobe Cannon could animate beyond gorgeous. When the Jell-O mold is moving, Bobe has got Alvin doing the amazing distortion behind it. So good. It's pure Bobe. I did the drawing, but I never thought it would look like that. I thought, "Oh my God! My work really looks good! Of course, it's done by Bobe Cannon!" You can tell that I'm still excited about that.

"I can tell you one flaw in the Format system and it used to drive the writers crazy. Each writer would go and present his storyboard to Ross, Herb, and a couple other people. There'd be about four or five because there's always a group around Ross. We would do the storyboard presentation. After that, someone would come in and un-pin the board and put it in order and go away. The director was never present in the presentation! Never! The storyboard was taken to the director. I remember thinking it was an awful system that the director's not present in the presentation. The directors would go off and they would plus it.

"They would add or change something without understanding what the essence of the gag or situation or staging or story point. They didn't get it. Cal Howard, one of the great, great comedy gag men and T. Hee and I along with four other writers were all in one big room, but it had gotten so noisy because we had the editorial next door. Joe Siracusa, head of editorial, would remember this, because while they were editing *The Alvin Show*, the editors also were doing sound editing on Popeye. Jack Kinney, who used to work at Disney, shared studio space and he were doing Popeye cartoons. So while we're writing, all this was happening next door, really, really loudly, "Oh, Popeye! Please save me!" This would go on and on, over and over. "Oh, Popeye! Please save me!" All the writers were going fucking crazy!

"T. Hee, Cal Howard, Dick Shaw (who originally wrote the Mr. Magoos and was a wonderful, crazy man) and myself, we were moved out of the writer's room and relocated down the street in a separate building. The other writers were left in the sound tunnel. On Wednesday night, when *The Alvin Show* came on, T. Hee, Cal Howard and I would get together at my house and watch the show. It's probably writer's remorse but oh! we would moan and gripe on the missed opportunities.

"They were in a rush, but it was a stupid rush. Everything was a rush. Cal Howard was the funniest man I had ever seen to deliver a board. Of course, he could make you laugh at anything. Cal was known as one of the best gag man ever. I was trained at Chouinard Art Institute, so I had a fairly contemporary training and drawing and sense of design. Cal drew like Milt Gross, so when Cal's character runs, every joint is all awkward and the thumbs are sticking out. I'm looking at a drawing that's all wrong, but so funny! Everyone else is drawing more contemporary, Cal got these outlandish drawings from the 30s on his storyboard. I gained great respect for funny drawings. Screw how well it's drawn. Is it a funny drawing?

"It was great watching him deliver and then Dick Shaw, he was kind of out there floating. He also was a great character. When Dick would do a storyboard, he did it in layers, so you would have three drawing #44s, one under another under another under another, and they are not even on the same size paper. As he's going through, he's lifting up papers to see what's underneath. It was the craziest presentation. Of course T. Hee's boards were clean, clear and brilliant.

"Leo Salkin was the force and Ross totally believed in Leo and accepted Leo. I don't think Ross believe all that much in Herb. That doesn't mean Herb wasn't right, but Ross accepted Leo. Leo could talk to Ross. If there was a problem or something Ross didn't understand, Leo got through to Ross. If it's anybody's show, it's Leo Salkin's show. He created the show and he followed through. To everyone else, my name is Bob or Bobby but to Leo, my name was Robert. He would smile and say it like he was always correcting me. "Oh! Robert".

"When we were getting close towards the end of the series, Herb came to T. Hee, Cal Howard and me and wanted us to create another show that they could take to the network. Herb set us a room down the street in a motel. We met at night. We were not supposed to let Ross know what we were doing. We started out by doing a special. I don't know why a special, because no network was buying animation specials. We did a thing called "Lock, Stock and Barrel". It was three silly characters: Lock, Stock and Barrel, and it was funny. Herb liked the presentation until we shocked him with the ending. Tee, Cal and I thought it was hysterical because at the end, the villain, not the hero, got the girl. We thought that was really funny. I still do. It was really ahead of its time.

"The show was never made, but we did do the storyboard. When we finished our day job, we would go to the motel to write on the special. It was all in secret. Herb didn't want to have a run-in with Ross. I think Ross was getting more and more feeling he could do it all himself. Herb felt he was losing more control as Ross became more and more confident of his skills as an animation filmmaker.

"It's possible that Ross could have taken the show to another studio. He would not do that in the studio's presence. If it happened, it would have happened behind closed doors. Somebody else might know. Too bad Herb's not around. Herb would have been a very interesting source and a very honest person, so he would have told you everything.

"I can tell you different stories about some of the other artists. There was a great mixture. For instance, there's Alan Zaslove who was Bobe Cannon's protege. He started at UPA and he could draw. Alan was one of the youngest animators to become an accomplished director. He was good. He was a black belt in karate and very athletic. Alan was so fast in animating that he would spend four hours with a big board on his lap doing life drawings during the day and then later in the afternoon he would animate.

"On the opposite side of the desk was Stan Wilkins, who was in the navy until he was 36. Stan went to art school for four years. He was the hardest working guy you ever saw. Stan and Alan had the desks backed up to each other. One guy was hard drawing eight to nine to ten hours a day, and the other one was drawing two to two-and-a-half hours a day. Alan was so good! Alan produced a lot of Disney shows and he also taught life-drawing at the Otis Art Institute because he's an extraordinary draftsman, artist and of course, a marvelous animator.

"Fred Wolf was a good guy. Fred freelanced, so I never saw him there. I haven't seen Fred in maybe 10 years. We saw each other a lot in the 60s. During the 60s, when he came out here, he did a lot of work over at Hanna-Barbera. That was before Murakami-Wolf. But as far as I know, he didn't have a desk at the studio. They had people picking up. That's a different world. You come in, pick up, go home and do the work.

"One of the freelance writers was Chris Jenkyns. Because I was in on all story meetings, I witness how great a storyboard man Chris was. His stuff was so original and just knock-down funny. He was the best freelancer and he was one of the mainstays for Jay Ward. Chris was trained in France and he just was extraordinary.

"There was this one team of writers. I don't want to say their names. One (an ex-Warners Bros. writer) was in the process of probably dying from alcoholism. He was the only writer who came wearing a nice suite and tie. He was in in a lot of pain, bent over and with one hand clutching his side leaning his back against the wall for support. At one time he was a very, very good writer. He's teamed up with this other guy, a big guy (an ex-Disney writer), who starts telling a story. You just can't believe that a pro would deliver a story like this. I remember looking at Leo and Leo looking at me. I watched Ross turn all kinds of mad colors as the second guy is going through the storyboard saying, "Well, first of all (he's referring to Alvin) the little asshole does this. Then, the little asshole runs over here. Then the little son of a bitch will go over here and talks to his brother asshole." He went on and on using these foul words and it was a 10 minute presentation! Alvin was Ross' alter ego, so when the second writer got through, Leo quickly jumped in and said, "Thank you very much. Thank you," and they left.

"Ross leapt up and started screaming saying, "Don't you ever (and he used a derogatory term) ever let him back here with a story!!!!" Ross's explosion was huge! I thought, "That was the dumbest presentation i ever witnessed. Would anyone go into Walt Disney's office and say that about Mickey? 'Now, the little asshole runs around here and does this…" Why would you ever do that? But, they did. It's funny looking back. I'm sure Leo probably told that story many times because I don't think it's ever happened before where you talk about your loveable main character saying, "Then the little son of a bitch runs over here…" It still makes me laugh. Needless to say, their story was not bought.

"A lot of writers came in and couldn't get their stories sold. The majority of the stories were done by the studio's story crew. There was Jan Green, which was rare because they didn't have many women writing in animation at that time. She was really good.

"There was Ed Nofziger, who would to drive up from Laguna Beach to Studio City. That was at least two hours when there were no freeways. He would work and then come back home. He spent most of his time on the road. Ed was a well known *New Yorker* cartoonist and great at drawing animals.

"You had Ed and Jan and then as I said, you had the great Cal Howard and the amazing T. Hee. Tee was so classy, and you had Dick Shaw. Dick was so offbeat funny. Dick drove in in from Newport Beach, near Balboa. He and Virgil Partch (the cartoonist known as VIP) were close buddies. They were two crazy drunks. Dick came in late one day saying that he couldn't find his car because they went drinking last night and they forgot at what bar they left the car.

"They had fun down in Newport Bay in Orange County. It was very upper class, mainly white people, lots of blonde people with tans. They had yachts and small sailboats and they would hold this fancy yacht parade. Dick Shaw and Virgil Partch, co-owned a tugboat, a dirty, dirty unwashed tugboat called "The Michigan". They would take that tugboat out and they would make it a sloppy drinking party with a bunch of drunks and girls in bikinis. They would get in line with all these really elegant boats and just irritate the shit out of them! They blew the tugboat's steam whistle constantly, yell at the other boats and throw beer cans.

"That's the kind of guy that Dick was. Dick would come in late at lunch time. Dick would say "I need to go buy a tie, I'll be right back." We would not see him for four days. Dick was a kind of a guy that things happened to. Joe Siracusa can probably tell the story or confirm it, but Dick came in and he had a polyester coat with a funny weave. He had a small spot on his sleeve. Dick said, "I am going to editorial and clean up this spot." He went into editorial, didn't ask anyone, got a can of acetone, which is a film cleaner, and pour it on a rag. He then gently dabbed it on the spot, and of course, all the fibres just opened up: ping,ping,ping,ping,ping. The editors and Dick just stood watching the hole slowly get bigger and bigger. Dick came back to our writers room wearing that coat. Where there once was a small spot now there was a ragged hole with fibres sticking up in all directions.

"Leo Salkin drove an Austin Healey, an small English sports car. Leo was a very pale person and was the model for cartoon character Mr. Magoo. Strangers would come up to and say, "You know you look like..."

"Leo would reluctantly answer, "I know, I know."

"Leo didn't like the sun. Leo didn't want to see the sun. When he worked in London, he loved it because the sun came out for one day a year he would say. He had this sport car and he never washed it. I think it was either dark brown or who knows what color it was? It was dirty. Why Leo got a convertible, I don't know. He kept the cloth top up all the time. Because we were two doors down from the regular building, he would park his car behind our office. Cal Howard got this idea and said, "Let's polish Leo's car… … with shoe polish!" Dick Shaw, Cal and I, went outside and we polished the car, but only the half the car that faced out in shoe polish. T. Hee was too dignified to join us and he sat there and said, "I'm not doing this." He stayed in the room writing. We spent two hours putting Cordovan brown shoe polish on Leo's car. We knew that someday Leo was going to have to wash it anyway. We polished his car and then we waited. We were like little kids. We waited until 6 o'clock, the time when he usually got his car. We left the door open to our room so we could see him walk by. Leo sees his car and then we come out and he starts laughing. Leo just took it really well considering somebody polished his car with shoe polish. It was good times there.

"There was Vern Jorgensen. He was a fine artist who had come over to animation. He was good friends with Alan Zaslove. He was Scandinavian and was always so proud to be Scandinavian. He was this outgoing, very funny guy so I would address him as one of the finest minds of the 12th Century, and we'd all laugh. He was always shouting, "Vikings rule!".

"There was Ray Aragon, marvelous, marvelous artist.

"There was Sam Weiss, a good layout man and jazz trumpet and piano player.

"There was Rosemary O'Connor, another good layout person in addition to being a background artist. I have a story about Rosemary. *The Alvin Show* was going over budget. Herb decided to have a big meeting with all the writers and he announced, "We're spending too much money. We've got to find a way to write less expensive stories." I remember when the meeting was over, some of the writers were mad. "Oh, what fucking bullshit! Who gives a crap?" They walked away mad saying, "What do you mean, write a cheap story?"

"I thought, "Well, maybe I can do it." I took one of the musical numbers, "Polly Wolly Doodle". Alvin is drawing, laying on the floor and David Seville says something and we go into Alvin's drawings which are kids drawings which then animate and tell the story. I drew with my left hand so I would not be able to control the line. The drawings were very simple kid like. We barely animated them because it of the style. It turned out to be a great short and came in way under budget. Later, it was shown on the Emmy Awards telecasts as part of the opening titles. Animated kids drawings were rare for television at that time.

"A couple years pass and I get the mumps as an adult, which is so uncomfortable. I end up watching a lot of TV and there's a show called *The Funny Company*, which I had never seen before. I'm watching it and it's these kids drawings. I'm looking at it and I'm thinking, "Shit, that looks like my stuff!" but I have nothing to do with that show. It's not like I own the world of kids drawings. I look for the end credits and I see Rosemary O'Connor's name, who was background and layout on *The Alvin Show*. I'm thinking at some point when I see her, I'll ask her about the kid drawings. A few weeks go by and I happen to see her at an animation event and I said, "Rosemary, let me ask you something, I'm feeling kind of like I am going…"

"She says, "Oh Bob! I was afraid that you were going to catch it."

"I said, "Catch what?"

"She tells me that the studio that she was working for saw the kid drawings I had done for *The Alvin Show*. Since Rosemary had done the layout (I had forgotten that she laid out my drawings) they asked her to duplicate my style for one of their shows, and she did it. Rosemary started to apologize.

"It's ok," I said, because I thought I was losing it. I did not want to think that's mine and that's mine from art I had never seen before. It was a funny story, but it started with Herb, when he had a problem. He went to his the crew of artists to ask for help in bringing down the cost of production. Again, it says a lot for Herb.

"I had seen that they did some Road Runners. They were horrendous! All I know is they were cheap. At one time, Rudy Larriva had worked at Warners, so they made him the director of the shorts. I was a good friend with Chuck Jones. I loved the Road Runners and we would talk philosophically, about the Road Runner. The Road Runner shorts were all about timing, timing, timing. The Format Road Runners had NO timing along with being drawn horribly. They were atrocious. Pretty much all the people that had been on the crew of *Alvin* were gone, except Joe Siracusa.

"I will tell you how great Joe Siracusa is. I only had been at Format for a few months. I am this young kid and I look like I am 16 years old. Joe came over to me and asked me out to lunch. Joe just talked to me like an adult. I thought the world of him. He made me feel like I belonged when I was still so young and not belonging. This was before *The Alvin Show*. Joe's always been one of the most caring, open people. He's just a wonderful, wonderful guy and a amazing talent. Many people don't know Joe Siracusa and Herb Klynn grew up as kids next door to each other in Detroit. There's a quite a few people that came out of Spike Jones band who became editors. One of them was Roger Donley, who worked Jay Ward. Roger was my freelance track reader at Kurtz and Friends for about 20 years. Roger was so good and would not charge me. I tried to pay Roger but he would not take any payment. Roger just said that he liked working for me. It was fun!

"There's so many good people. Amby Paliwoda was one of the great animators and certifiably crazy. He would talk to himself out loud passionately while animating.They had to put him in a desk far away in the corner because of these conversations with himself. Again, you can't make this up. Here is this great guy but he was really intense when he talked to you. He would get up from his desk and you almost were afraid to say, "Nice weather today, Amby." You didn't know what Amby would go into. He was a good guy, but he had his own demons. Amby worked in the business forever at many studios. A great, great character.

"When I went to art school and at Kurtz and Friends, we were always damaged souls. We don't fit in to regular society, and I LOVE IT!. I love that you can find a place where you belong. I loved being in art school. I love working with animation people. You don't expect them to be the norm. It's just a great group.

"Jules Engel wasn't that main. He was a minor owner. It was all Herb. What is kind of interesting about Jules is he thought he was a story man. He would be in meetings and he would try and say something about a story point. Nobody listened to him. Later, he became a teacher at Cal Arts and he did experimental films. His experimental films were very interesting. He was a great painter at UPA and a great painter on *Alvin*. Jules was the lead for setting style. However in the studio, Jules was sort of just put up with.

"I remember Jules boasting that he had framed a cleaning rag that he wipe off his brushes and sold it as one of his paintings. Jules thought that was funny. Later on, Jules created the legend of Jules Engel. He wasn't legendary during *The Alvin Show*. I remember once when we were in a story meeting and again no one was listening to Jules, He wanted to explain a story point. He wanted a little character to kick. He walks up to the wall and he wildly swings his foot straight through the wall board. It goes right through up to Jules's ankle. Herb started choking on his dry cigar because the building's rented. They don't own the building! Jules just made a huge hole in the wall. Everybody laughed. I remember Alan Zaslove laughing the most.

"Henrietta "Hank" Jordan was Herb's secretary and she had a sailor's mouth. Her voice was low and rough. She would come on the studio intercom and say, "Herb, get your ass back here in the office!" Every once in a while, she'd say, "Ok Herb, where are you? I'm trying to get you on the fucking phone!" There used to be these crazy announcements coming from Hank over the intercom. It's very funny.

"When I left Disney, I had a week to pack up the film, and I accepted a job with TV Spots. T. Hee informed me, "I made an appointment with you with Herb Klynn."

"I said, "Oh, no! I got a job!"

"Tee said, "No, you've got to see him this afternoon." Now I had seen Herb when I was in school. Don Graham, a master draftsman and a wonderful teacher. He was one of the great ones and a true legend. When I was leaving Chouinard, I told Don that I had been offered two jobs at Disney. Don said, "Now is the time to go see as many studios as you can because when you are working, you will not be able to see other studios." I followed Don's advice and saw as many studios as i could.

"When I went to UPA, Herb came in to interview me. He was smoking at that time. I had one of those cardboard portfolios. Herb opened it about six or eight inches and he kept flicking his cigar ashes on my artwork. He was going, "Uh-huh, uh-huh, uh-huh," and he's flipping really quickly.

"I thought, "He's going to set my portfolio on fire!" There were a lot of glass walls at UPA, and Don Duga whom I knew from Chouinard came walking by holding a rubber cement jar.

"Herb turns to me and says, "You want to be a flunky like that guy?"

"I said, "Uh-huh, yeah." And that was it. The worst interview I ever had.

"So later, Tee says, "You're going to go see him."

"I said, "I don't want to see him."

"Tee says, "No, you're going to go see him."

"So I go there and Hank Jordan is there and I come and I say, "Uh, I have a meeting with Herb Klynn."

"You can't see him!" She yells at me In that raspy voice! "Then I hear from the other room, "Let him in."

"She says, "Ok,but you can't stay long."

"So I open the door and he's laying on the couch. He's had a heart attack since I last saw him. He says softly "Come in, come in." Now Tee warned me not to take any of my Disney work with me. The only thing I had was the same student portfolio he had dumped his ashes into at UPA. That's all I had. I show him my portfolio, While still laying down, Herb takes each piece out separately and holds it up in the air and says, "Ohhh! Ahhh!" He looks at each one like 20-30 seconds. He's doing all this and then he says, "I'll hire you."

"I walk out and I think, "What did I just do? I just said,'yes'." Now I have two jobs to go to on Monday morning. Herb was so sweet to me and everything seem so different.

"I called up TV Spots and I said, "I don't know why I did it. I just accepted a job at Format," and they said, "That's ok. We will wait for you." That was so kind. I called TV Spots a week later, informing them that I was staying at Format. Herb had become a different person. He had softened up. Since Herb couldn't smoke because of the heart attack, he'd have this unlit 10-inch cigar that he'd stick halfway into his mouth. Herb no longer smoked, he chewed. Herb came to work early. So when I came to work, I would find in my trash, this long, wet...it looked like a dog turd or worst yet a horse turd. In the morning, I would come in and without looking, I would take a piece of blank animation paper and cover my trash can. For some reason, Herb liked dropping his wet cigars in my waste paper basket. Herb was this ball of energy. He would scurry from place to place.

"Alan Zaslove, who was a martial arts artist,was working at his desk when Herb, who was so excited to show what he wanted Alan to draw, that Herb took the pencil out of Alan's hand and started drawing on Alan's drawing. Very calmly Alan looked up at Herb and took the pencil from Herb and broke the pencil in half. Then Alan said, "The next time you do that, I'm going to do that to your arm." Herb just did his speedy shuffle right out the door. Herb always meant well. He cared about people. He may crossed the line because he just cared so much. People who knew him, liked him. He was one of us.

"Herb was running the UPA studio a year earlier. He was doing everything. Herb was a dynamo. Herb didn't walk, he shuffled everywhere. His legs were a blur! Just like an animated character! Thinking about it, now...I had a great time. I learned so much, and I learned how to drink there.

"Grim Natwick, who created Betty Boop and whose assistants were Chuck Jones, Walter Lantz, and Marc Davis, taught Cal Howard and also Marc Davis how to drink. So, Cal took it on himself to teach me to drink. We would have these two martini lunches. After one of these wet lunches with Cal, I had to come back and present one of my stories to Ross. I begin to go through my board and I start giggling. I can't stop giggling. Ross is looking at me with kind of a smirk. I know Ross is thinking, "They got the kid drunk," I'm going through the board but I'm thinking, "I'm never going to get through this. I'm going to get fired." When I finally finished my presentation, Ross got up and said, "Love your story," and smiled and walked off. That's the last time I ever drank during the day when working. That was another lesson I learned. You've got to be on your game.

"Ross never got mad at me. He loved Cal, T. Hee and Dick. I have seen Ross get mad at writers. He'd just tear them apart but our little group - our little foursome - he never got mad at. He came in smiling and looking forward to us. He didn't come in like "Show me." He came like "This is going to be fun. What am I going to see next?" It was a very good environment.

"I never did anything for TV Spots. They're still waiting for me! I later did work with Norm Gottfredson and Sam Nickelson, the owners of TV Spots. I was directing on *Roger Ramjet* when they both came in and freelanced layout. It was all switched. Now, I was giving them work.

"People go on. I worked at Disney for a little over a year. I worked probably a year, maybe plus, at Format Films. I wasn't there that long. Everything else I was freelance for a long time until I started Kurtz and Friends. I did work at a place called Filmfair. That was the longest I ever worked anywhere. I worked there three years. They were best known for both live and animated commercials.

"Ross was really a very creative source. He was a very creative man. I don't even know if he could play an instrument. I think he's was musically challenged. He was a hummer, but he was good.

Dale Hale was a writer at Format and discussed his time there, "I wrote some of the shows and I did a lot of the musical breaks. I had kind of a musical background, so that helped. I may have done one or two Clyde Crashcups, but mostly it was *The Alvin Show* and the musical breaks. There was a lot of times where we didn't just do a musical break, but the whole musical part of it. I would visually draw it out and maybe do something as far as a gag goes along with the music.

"We had kind of a big room and went on alone. From time to time, Ross would come in and he'd go to his office and look over something, but he wasn't hanging over us all of the time.

"We had model sheets and we knew what the characters were doing. We'd listen to the music and we had direction. He had a certain way that he wanted them to go. We had to have music in all the things that you do when you were doing cartoons then. As far as if Ross didn't like something, he'd let us know, but he wasn't hovering over us. We would have meetings where he would be involved. Ross was fine to work with. I never had any problems with him. In fact, he inspired me so much, one day he showed up with a big XKE Jaguar and I told him I have to have one. A few months later I bought Hawley Pratt's from him although mine was yellow.

"Before Format, I worked for Charles Schulz and that was doing comic books. I was an assistant on all kinds of stuff, but when I came to LA, my first job was actually on *Clutch Cargo* because I really had no experience at all. I was a writer, basically. I had gone to art school, but it's silly, *Clutch Cargo*, which was totally insane. Some people don't call it animation, but it gave me a rough idea of kind of what was going on. The people that I was working with were all terrific and so it made it pleasant. I had done some freelance stuff for Hanna-Barbera. I think I boarded a show and gagged a show on Hoagy Carmichael. I think it was one of the early ones of *The Flintstones*.

"Then Format called me up and asked me if I wanted to work on *The Alvin Show* and of course, I was delighted to. When I was in high school, I did know two people there, but they didn't know I was even around. When I was in high school, I lived in a little town in Iowa and I had gone about 50 miles or 45 miles with a bunch of friends to go see and hear Spike Jones play. After the show was over, I went back to meet the guys in the band. I was a little pushy and met Joe Siracusa and Roger Donley. It was great fun and I thought I would never see them again. I never knew that 10 years later almost exactly, end up later walking down the hallway at Format Films and seeing Joe Siracusa and Roger Donley. I went in and talked to them. They were editors there and those were the only people there that I knew.

"Tedd Pierce, I think was working with Jack Kinney as writers. I think there were a couple others like Ed Nofziger, John Howard, who was a kick, and Jan Streegen. Then of course, Bobby Kurtz.

"I knew Cullen Blaine Houghtaling and worked with him later on.

"Alan Zaslove was there, and I met him there. Zaslove came over for a visit and soon afterwards he and his wife moved into the neighborhood and bought a house in the area. They lived here for a few years.

"Sam Weiss, the layout man, he was here and he also did the same thing. He came over for a visit one day, liked the neighborhood and he bought a house down the street from me, so we kind of ran into each other.

"I was on staff there. I don't think I did any freelance for them at that time.

"Everything was a surprise then because I was still pretty new in the business. When you get a job in real life compared to animation - which isn't real life - you have it for a long time. The only reason you would not work there is if you screwed up or if the company closed down. It didn't that much, so this was a surprise to us. I worked as a writer and had a hiatus for a few months and come back and work again. Of course, this is on *The Alvin Show*. I never worked on the newer show Ross Jr. had or anything like that. I figured that he probably thought that we were all dead or we were too old-fashioned.

"I did a comic strip called *Figments* for 15 years, plus I ghosted a few others.

"I worked on staff on some of the places. I live down by the beach. It's nice down here. LA is gross to me and I've lived here for 52 years. I would go on staff and then the drive up to the Valley wasn't too awful. I made a deal with the people that I worked with. If you work at home, you have to be fairly disciplined. I get my work done and I didn't get sidetracked. I have a studio separate from the house here and so it was really kind of a paradise. I wanted to be around to help raise my kids. I had three young kids and I wanted to keep my wife sane because I really liked her and I liked being around my kids, so it gave me a chance to do it all. I could take my work in and be in the studio for two or three days of the week or if we're working on a project that they wanted me in there. I would only be on staff for a certain length of time at the beginning to let them know that I would turn in the work when I was supposed to turn it in and then I was there if they needed me on something else. They knew that they could call me. In those days, you could get over to the Valley in about 20 minutes or a half an hour. Nowadays, it's an hour trip. In the Format days, I didn't do that then. I didn't own my house. I was living in a house in Laurel Canyon with my wife. We didn't have any kids then, so I didn't need to then. I was working full time.

"We were working at animation desks, but it really wasn't run like an animation studio. It was more of an office building. In fact, there was a motel next door and they rented some rooms from them. Some of the writers were over there. I'm not sure if they had some rooms with animation tables in them or not.

"I must have done some freelance work for them then after *The Alvin Show* on other stuff. I do recall that the hotel was next door. Going towards the back of the building down a hallway and watching, because I was still learning about the business. When I do something, I go into it whole hog so I understand how it all works. I met the cameraman and I saw him shooting platens and all that stuff. That was fascinating and that's when I ran into Roger Donley and Joe Siracusa. They had their own editing rooms back there. It wasn't set up like Hanna-Barbera because it was smaller. I don't remember anything at all about a sound studio back there. My feeling would be that Ross was doing some pretty technical stuff to make the voices work and he was doing it before they were doing the animation, so he may have had a studio with all the equipment he needed there somewhere. That would be the logic of it.

"I do remember going back and watching camera and watching the guys in editing. As it turned out, I got to be good friends for the rest of the time with Roger and Joe. Joe even calls me now from time to time and he says, "Dale, I'm 92!" or whatever age he is and we'll chat for a while. I haven't talked to him in a while. Roger, it turned out that later on, I bought the tuba he was playing in all those years with Spike Jones. I had it for a long time and carried it with bands. I became a tuba collector. I finally sold it. I was getting into more studio stuff and playing with orchestras that I needed something a little fancier. They needed something more updated, so I purchased a newer one. I've had it for quite a few years.

"I didn't really work with Joe because he was doing the editing and stuff, but we would have lunch together and I went over to his house a few times. He came over a few times, too. In fact, he was here when I bought the house in 1964. A bunch of the guys came out to the house to see it. You'd be surprised about how a house can change in 50-something years.

"I made good friends with Ed Nofziger, which was a kick. In fact, I can look up at my wall and see a couple of originals he gave me. He had a comic strip and Jan Strejan (Green). Jan and I worked on selling a show of our own and Jan was a good writer. She went to doing the layout and she might have done some animation. Last time I talked to her was years ago, maybe at least 10 years ago and she was from Quebec. She had a house there and she had one here, too, and she was also in opera, so she was also in an opera group up there as well. I kept in touch with her until Ed Nofziger passed.

"I used to go down to Laguna and we used to get together with a bunch of cartoonists with VIP and the *Playboy* cartoonists: Ed, Marty Murphy and all those guys. We'd hop in a car and zoom down there. Ed then retired and then he moved up to Ojai with his wife and I went up to visit him a couple times up there. Ed's comic strip was called *Animalogic*. It was more of a panel. That was his thing, and Ed was really good at it. It was crazy, which made it great fun.

"Cal Howard, when he was working over there, he was really brilliant. He was very quiet and kind of to himself. Well, he wasn't that quiet. He worked on the live shows and a very funny gag man. He was very clever and he had funny drawings. You know how guys in the studio draw pictures of each other. I put up the ones I had on Facebook. Cal was very clever. He went on *Truth or Consequences*. Ralph Edwards was hosting that. Ralph said, "Do you want to go on and be surprised out of the past by an old girlfriend?"

"Cal said, "Yeah, I do have an old girlfriend."

"Ralph said, "Do you want to be walking down the street in Hollywood and run into her with your wife? We'll set it up so that you'll run into her and you can stand there and talk to her and totally ignore your wife. We'll have a camera on her and she gets pissed off and you'll probably win a nice prize if you do that."

"Cal said, "Ah, sure."

"We had set it up that Nona and I were eating at The Brown Derby and then we were walking down the street and we ran into this gorgeous redhead which really wasn't my old girlfriend. She was gorgeous, but she wasn't that gorgeous. This was a model. She looked great, but when it came time to talking, she kind of let the ball drop.

"I said, "Oh, my God! I ran into you!" I ran into her and we had to chit-chat for about a minute and a half constantly to get a reaction from my wife. Then they gave us a washer and dryer when it was all over. Then a voice came out from the hidden camera that said, "Do you know that you're on *Truth or Consequences*?"

"Bill Danch worked with the one who worked with Tedd Pierce. They worked as a team and they were freelance.

"Chris Jenkyns. Everybody knew Chris. I knew him. I didn't hang out with him. I knew who he was. As I recall, he was a pleasant guy.

"Leo Salkin was the boss of us all. He was a sweetheart. He was Mr. Magoo. When they were doing Mr. Magoo, he looked just like Mr. Magoo. He was short, bald and had squinty eyes. Mr. Magoo was designed after him. He was smart. He and his wife were truly intellectuals. Really, really smart people. He was a really good boss and he knew how to handle people. I loved working for him.

"Gil Turner worked there. A pleasant guy. They were all kind of in their own place. It wasn't like we were working shoulder to shoulder. I would go in and look over their shoulders from time to time and chat with them. Maybe have lunch with some of them.

"Rudy Larriva was there. I remember Rudy at Format and at other studios. I remember running into him.

"Herb Klynn and I would see socially from time to time. I'd run into him or be invited. He had a nice house out in the Valley and he would invite a few people over to his house from time to time.

"Bob Kurtz worked with T. Hee. Bob was a student of T. Hee's and he and T. Hee worked on some projects together.

"Sam Weiss was the guy that was also my neighbor. He moved in down the path from me. He and his wife lived here for quite a while.

He had a house on the sand, but he got nervous when the high tides were coming up, so he moved over here.

"I knew Frank Andrina. I saw him a few months before he died. He was an armor collector. He had one of the biggest armor collection in the country. He had a whole house full of it. He was movie star good looking. I was always kidding him as I called him the pretty boy of animation, and he was. He just looked like a superhero or a movie star. Even when he was old, I used to kid him. You know, it's not fair. You look that good and you're 78 years old or whatever it was.

"Chuck Downs and John Dunn worked together on stuff. I worked for Chuck over at Hanna-Barbera or somewhere else along the way. He was story editor for a couple of shows that I worked on. We called him Red. He had red hair.

"Ervin Kaplan, I would run into him at some of the other studios. A number of years ago I think I ran into him at a Costco.

Joe Siracusa grew up with Herb Klynn and was a member of Spike Jones Band for a time before getting in to animation editing and timing. For an extended look at Joe Siracusa's years with the Spike Jones Band and with DePatie-Freleng, please consult my other book *Think Pink! The DePatie-Freleng Story* (BearManor Media) (2015).

Siracusa said, "I'm a musician. I came to California to join the Spike Jones Band, but before that I was in Cleveland, going to school in Cleveland, playing in the high school and junior high school band and orchestra all the time. My father was a musician. He was originally from Italy and was a musician and he came to America and played in the Wild West Band and then he came to Cleveland, Ohio, and got into a concert band and I followed in his footsteps. I went to elementary school, junior high and high school playing in the band

and orchestra playing trumpet, clarinet, trombone and French horn and ended up playing the drums as I always wanted to do. I ended up being a drum teacher for the Cleveland Board of Education at 17 years old. I always had been a fan of sound effects. I did sound effects and animal imitations as a young man.

"Then I got into the army. I got in the band in the army after a couple stints in the regular army type of duties. I finally got into the band and definitely started playing Spike Jones like records over the loudspeakers. I ended up in a band in Fort Worth, Texas, near El Paso. It was Ralph Young and his dance band and two concert bands. I played in the El Paso Symphony Orchestra. I played with our army concert band. I started with Spike Jones records over the loudspeakers. I did an imitation of Spike Jones for an army contest and won the contest.

"When I got back and got out of the service, and I got back to Cleveland, I was looking to do that type of thing and couldn't find it, but it was a miracle on how I got to be with Spike Jones. I got back to Cleveland and started playing with the Cleveland youth concert band. They had me be the timpanist and play timpani. I went out and bought a set of two timpani and started in the band and I said that I wanted to be like Spike Jones and everyone said that you should be with Spike Jones, but he was in Hollywood, California making pictures and records and stuff and so I said, Let me take a chance here."

After Siracusa's stint with Spike Jones, a career change was in order. Siracusa continues, "My friend in the cartoon industry, they needed someone to do the arrangements for them and I had been in the army with a couple of different piano players and with a French horns and a tuba. They liked it so much that later on they talked with my friend Herb Klynn and they were already offering me a job if you want to come over to the studio. I said, "Well, let me talk to my wife." I talked to Spike and he understood perfectly. So, that's when I signed up at UPA Pictures. Herb was the production manager at UPA Pictures. I got the job there working as a film editor and I started as an apprentice and in two years, I was head of the department doing music, sound effects, voices and editing film.

"Then, from UPA Pictures, we formed Format Films. We made our own company called Format Films and started producing *The Alvin Show*. We did *The Alvin Show* and that was one of the most fantastic experiences for me working with Ross Bagdasarian. As a film editor, I got to work with him in every area and do the musical things. We got to be such good friends and I've got stories about my playing jokes on him, him playing jokes on me. It became a very personalized thing. In fact, when Ross passed away, I was the only one to do the Alvin voice for NBC. Then from Format, I went to DePatie-Freleng.

"I was film editor and then I became Supervising Film Editor and was working with recording the voices and outlining the dialogue for the animators to do their animation to and I worked with the musicians. I worked with all of them together when I went to the recording sessions and then adapted them to the film and my sound effects and we had to do the sound effects. I became again a film editor on all films done for DePatie-Freleng and worked with David DePatie and Friz Freleng. I had a wonderful experience with David DePatie to England to record music. It was a fantastic experience.

"I just did the film editing and recording with the full orchestra of course, and editorial on each of the cartoons and creating sound effects.

"I worked with the musicians and each musician gave information on various pieces of film. Like certain films when they animated stuff, they did it in a tempo, the drawings were like every eight beats or footsteps like bump, bump, bump, so I gave these films a tempo and then gave the tempo to the musicians. They would record music that would fit the tempo of the animation. That was part of it. Then, I was giving the length of the scene, the tempo and what the director would suggest or recommends. So, I would give the information to the producer and the animators and the musicians, so they all spoke the same language. Then, when they would do the recording, I would make sure that it fit the film properly, or if it had to be edited, I had to edit it to make sure that it was edited to the tempo, and fit the film. It was very natural for me to do, but it also helped me to be a little more creative.

"Of course, I worked with June Foray. She produced a film and I did all the film recording. She wrote it. I did all the technical work for it. She was a dear friend."

The sound effects for *The Alvin Show* were the same as those used for *Rocky and his Friends* and other Jay Ward shows, which also utilized Foray's vocal talents. Keith Scott, author of *The Moose That Roared* said, "Many of them were created by the ex-Spike Jones musicians working at UPA (Joe Siracusa and Roger Donley) and Skip Craig had the reel at Ward Productions for years." In 1998, these same sound effects were sold by a company called Sound Ideas and marketed as *The Rocky & Bullwinkle and Friends Sound Effects Library.*

In the online article "Alvin Might Have Been a Rabbit" by Tralfaz, July 2, 2016, he credits Klynn for getting *The Alvin Show* off the ground, "If it weren't for Herb Klynn, we might only know the Chipmunks today as novelty characters in an old gimmick record heard around Christmas time.

"Klynn was the owner of Format Films and worked out a deal in 1961 to put the Chipmunks in an animated cartoon series. *The Alvin Show* may have lasted only one season in prime time, but it showed the characters were valuable as animated properties and that eventually led to today's Chipmunk empire.

"Not bad for taking someone's voice and speeding it up electronically.

"The voice in question didn't belong to Klynn or anyone on his studio's staff; their involvement ended after producing the original cartoon series (the characters were designed by Bob Kurtz). It belonged to Ross Bagdasarian, who was not only an actor and songwriter but proved to be a pretty canny businessman. He wasn't content with making a quick buck by jumping on the silly record bandwagon. He knew he had something bigger, and he (and after his death, his family) ran with it and built it, step by step.

"Prime time animated shows were the hot thing in 1961, thanks to the success of *The Flintstones*. Networks wanted them. Producers and animation studios sprung into action. Thus, *The Alvin Show* was born. There was some irony in this—the series came after the creation of a syndicated cartoon show starring the Nutty Squirrels. The Squirrels were a sped-up voice novelty record group invented after the first Chipmunks LP. Do you follow all that?"

There was plenty of publicity at the start of the fall 1961 TV season for the various cartoon shows that made it to air. Here's what is supposed to be a publicity piece for *The Alvin Show* in the October 1961 edition of *TV Radio Mirror* magazine. But it reads more like a publicity piece for Ross Bagdasarian himself. Still, he tells the story of the non-simultaneous invention of David Seville and of The Chipmunks:

"Moreover, they've become such hams, they have insisted on squealing and squawking through several new songs and now will be seen over CBS-TV every Wednesday night in *The Alvin Show*.

"Bagdasarian must have realised what a goldmine the cartoon series could be if it took off. Not only did he get paid for voicing the characters, and not only did he get paid for the theme song (which, at the end, spelled out his name musically), but he could use the show to cross-promote other Chipmunks records he was making for Liberty. Things didn't quite work out that way. CBS announced the cancellation of the series by January 31, 1962, less than four months after it debuted. But since the network had rights to rerun the show, it moved *Alvin* to the Sunday ratings wasteland where it wouldn't eat up valuable prime time air.

"Format Films went on to other projects; among other things, it received a contract to make Road Runner cartoons for Warners theatrical release. And, as we know today, the Chipmunks carried on, too."

Klynn shut Format films in 1962, but reopened it in 1965 as Format Productions. At that point, the studio made 11 shorts for Warner Bros.' theatrical Road Runner series which were sublet out from DePatie-Freleng Enterprises. According to animation director and producer Greg Ford, "It was known that Freleng was not only annoyed that he had to work on Looney Tunes again after being fired from them and subsequently opening his own studio, but also he was told to give up on making Pink Panther cartoons in the process."

Freleng refused, but also refused to do new Road Runner cartoons primarily because they were traditionally Chuck Jones' domain and also didn't have the alleged freshness of the other Looney Tunes product of the Daffy Duck/Speedy Gonzales team-ups. In any case, that's why Freleng was willing to farm out the Road Runner cartoons to another studio.

The positive upshot of this was that it helped get Format Films, now Format Productions, back on its feet. Then, when Warner Bros.

reopened their own cartoon studios in 1967 and DePatie-Freleng was no longer in the picture, Format helped with three non-Depatie-Freleng theatrical Daffy Duck and Speedy Gonzales shorts, and produced *The Lone Ranger* series in 1966.

Author and historian Jim Fanning discusses this series on his blog, "There was an animated version of *The Lone Ranger* created for CBS as part of their all-new animated superhero Saturday morning block in 1966. Produced by Herbert Klynn and Jules Engel and their famed Format Films, the show reflected the graphic proficiency of its producers, with stylish designs and distinctive scratchy ink work (actually chinagraph pencil) on the cels. The show was credited as a Jack Wrather Production (Jack for many years held the rights to The Lone Ranger; he may be best known to Disney enthusiasts as the creator/owner of the Disneyland Hotel until 1989, resulting in he and his wife Bonita Granville Wrather being named Disney Legends in 2011).

"The animated *Lone Ranger* ran on CBS from September 10, 1966, to September 6, 1969. The evocative narration ("a man who became a legend...a daring and resourceful man who hated thievery and oppression. His face masked...his true name unknown...with his faithful Indian companion at his side, he thundered across the West on his great white stallion, appearing out of nowhere to strike down injustice and outlawry...and then, vanishing as mysteriously as he came") was spoken by Marvin Miller, who among his many other credits was the narrator for UPA and Walt Disney's *Sleeping Beauty* (1959).

"As opposed to the live-action TV show this animated version had the Lone Ranger and Tonto battling not bandits and desperadoes but rather aliens, monsters and mad scientists—much like CBS's prime-time live-action western / sci-fi / fantasy / steampunk series, *The Wild Wild West*, which had premiered the year before.

Model sheets exist from this utterly unique and unfortunately all-but-forgotten cartoon gem."

Format Productions also created the sequences for several TV series, including *I Spy, Honey West, The Mothers-in-Law*, the animated characters on the television variety show *Hee Haw*, animated various TV commercials, and created film title designs for *The Glory Days* and *Clambake*.

The little animated bits and segments Format designed for *Hee Haw* aired for years and years after their initial debut in 1969 until the show ended in 1992.

Klynn's final contribution to animation was 1984's *The Duck Factory*, a short-lived live-action sitcom with animated bits from MTM whose biggest claim to fame is the first major starring vehicle for a young Jim Carrey, years before *In Living Color* and Carrey's movie career.

Format Films entryway in the early 1960s with Dale Hale.

The location of the former Format Films today.

*TV Guide* article about Format Films from December 30, 1961, featuring Herb Klynn and Jules Engel.

Ever notice how Gerald McBoingboing looks like Alvin if he was a real boy? The UPA influence at Format Films.

Dale Hale then and now (with tuba).

Bob Kurtz today.

Cullen Blaine today.

Joe Siracusa today.

Two books featuring artwork by Bob Kurtz: *Alvin's Lost Voice* and *Clyde Crashcup and Leonardo*.

Article about Format's *The Lone Ranger* TV series from *Jack and Jill*.

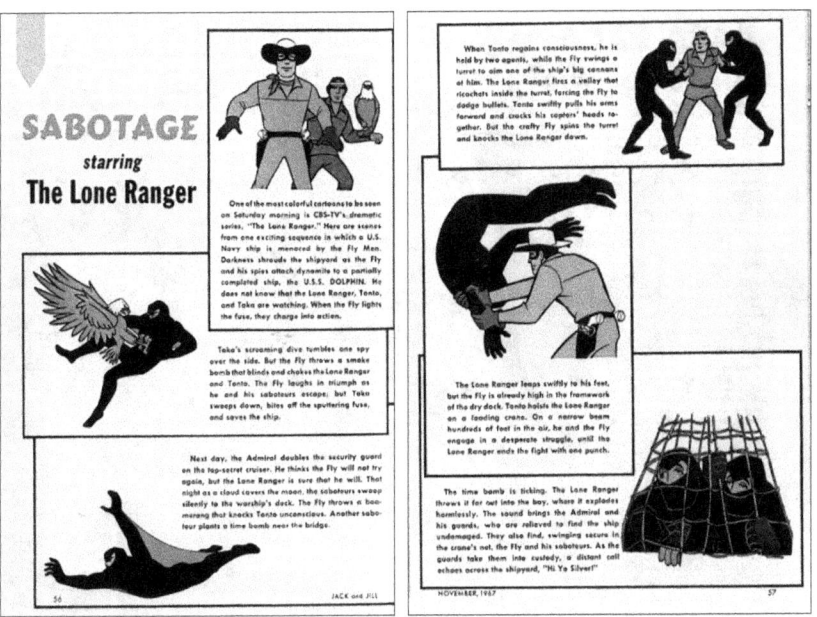

Model sheets from Format's *The Lone Ranger*.

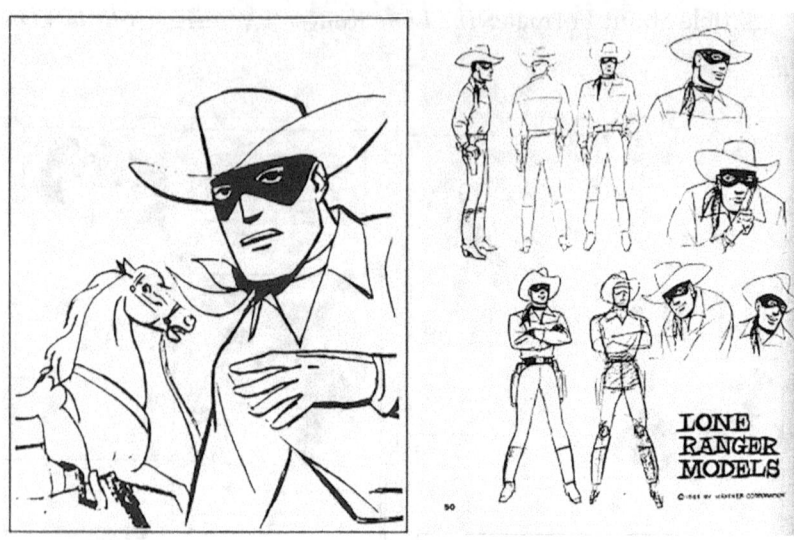

*The Lone Ranger* game:

*The Lone Ranger* button:

*The Lone Ranger Cartoon Kit,* a Colorforms set:

The iconic *Hee Haw* donkey:

# THE ALVIN SHOW

THE ALVIN SHOW WAS the first to feature the singing characters Alvin and the Chipmunks, although a series with a similar concept *The Nutty Squirrels Present* had aired a year earlier. It lasted for one season in prime time (October 4, 1961 – September 12, 1962) on CBS (Wednesdays, 7:30-8pm Eastern), and was originally sponsored by General Foods (Jell-O, Post cereals). It was initially telecast in black and white (color prints of the episodes were not seen until the series entered syndication in the fall of 1965). The Pilot, an early version of "Good Neighbor", was written and produced to sell the show for CBS. The actual show featured a reworked version, which aired as part of the 5th episode.

The voice cast for *The Alvin Show* includes: Ross Bagdasarian, Sr. - Alvin Seville, Simon Seville, Theodore Seville, David Seville, Sam Valiant; Shepard Menken - Clyde Crashcup; June Foray - Daisy Bell, Mrs. Frumpington (partially); Lee Patrick - Mrs. Frumpington; Don Messick - postman and additional voices; Joe Besser - Dragon and additional voices; plus Bill Lee and Johnny Mann - additional voices.

*Cool and Strange Music* #18, August-November 2000 continues, "As The Chipmunks' popularity with children skyrocketed, it seemed logical that Bagdasarian's empire would grow to include a half-hour animated series named for the most popular member of the group,

Alvin. *The Alvin Show* debuted as a primetime series on CBS in 1961, and moved to Saturday mornings in 1962, where it remained for three years, with the episodes surviving as reruns for decades. Bagdasarian continued to perform all the voice of The Chipmunks himself on the TV show while maintaining his alter ego of David Seville.

"It's worth noting here that the look of The Chipmunks changed drastically when the animated series was born. Early Liberty issues depict the trio very much like actual chipmunks, furry little tails and all, but subsequent reissues show The Chipmunks as they appeared on TV. The animated versions have more human features which helped to give them recognizable individual appearances: Simon was the tall one with glasses, Theodore was the chubby one and Alvin wore his trademark baseball cap while sporting a capital "A" on his turtleneck.

"Alvin and The Chipmunks became a lasting influence on American popular culture, spawning dozens of sound-alike children's records featuring everything from cartoon squirrels to cartoon grasshoppers. There was also merchandising a-plenty and toys were made for the toddler to the pre-teen. Chipmunk banks, dolls, puppets, comic books and games found their way into households around the world and Bagdasarian's fame and fortune were secured (even though most of his audience knew him as David Seville)."

Ross Jr. adds from the *Still Squeaky* booklet, "By 1961, pop was growing restless. In a few short years, he had sold 16 million records, launched a successful licensing program, won several Grammys and countless nominations. Nonetheless, he needed something new.

"Something new came in the form of a primetime animated television series. *The Alvin Show* debuted in October 1961 on CBS. He provided ideas for the stories, created new characters and composed all the songs and background music, including the show's hit theme song:

"This is *The Alvin Show*
*The Alvin Show*
You're positively going to love
*The Alvin Show*
There's Dave Seville
And what is more
Here's the boy who giggles
Known as Theodore
And now you see
On camera three
The brother known as Simon
On the family tree
And here's the star of the show
Alvin... Alvin... Ready, here we go, it's *The Alvin Show*!

"As if this weren't enough, pop also supplied the voices of Dave, Alvin, Simon, Theodore and several ancillary characters. I got into lots of fights with kids at school when I told them that my dad, Ross Bagdasarian, created The Chipmunks. "No, he didn't," they'd say, "David Seville did!"

"That's my dad," I'd say, "David Seville is his stage name," but they usually didn't believe me until I took them home to meet him. Since my brother and sister both had the same problem with their friends, pop's office was soon overrun with kids.

"One of the reasons for *The Alvin Show*'s success was The Chipmunks' dramatic makeover. Gone was the realistic look - the bushy tails, pointy noses and sharp teeth that looked like they could give you rabies. It was replaced by a stylized, more anthropomorphic look. This made the characters appear much friendlier.

"Although Alvin, Simon and Theodore were clearly the stars of the show, pop created new characters for them to interact with: - like Sam Valiant - Private Nose; the fast talking shylock who wasn't above petty larceny; Stanley the Eagle, an eagle who was afraid of heights; Mrs. Frumpington, a blueblood socialite who felt rock and roll was society's undoing; The Ostrich, who sits on a small sports car and tries to hatch it with The Cruise Director, an overbearingly perky man who drove Alvin nuts.

"Perhaps the most memorable of these new characters was Clyde Crashcup, a mixed-up inventor, and his capable, but exasperated assistant, Leonardo. Clyde was an eternal optimist. He was positive that he had invented everything from happiness to the baby. Clyde had a very distinctive way of introducing his inventions; he'd say, "That's ba for ba and -aby for -aby, baby." There was always something fundamentally wrong with Clyde's inventions, whether it was the five-legged horse or the airplane made of bricks. Nonetheless, in the face of disaster, Clyde always held his head up high and proclaimed to the world, "So far, perfect!"

"Clyde's loyal assistant and best friend, Leonardo, was as shy as Clyde was immodest. Leonardo didn't talk, he whispered, but he was much smarter than Clyde and tried, generally unsuccessfully, to get Clyde to see the error of his ways.

"Pop's humor permeated the entire show and made is absolutely original. What I didn't know until much later was how important it was to him to create a show that was non-violent. This was an era when a host of animated characters routinely slammed, exploded and otherwise destroyed one another, if only for a cartoon moment. Pop was intent on steering away from this successful cartoon formula and creating instead a kind of musical variety show.

"Pop also decided to veer from tradition and not use a laugh track. In face, *The Alvin Show* was the only animated show of its era and one of the few comedy shows that did not use a laugh track. Pop felt if the show was funny, people would know when to laugh without being prompted."

The classic animation fanzine *Mindrot* featured an article about *The Alvin Show* in its 12th issue, November 1, 1978. The article was by Lucinda Ann Sanderson and Michael J. Tawney, "The 1961-62 television season was something of an animated cartoon lover's paradise. Four fully animated shows could be seen on primetime television (not counting Walt Disney, which was sometimes animated). These four were Hanna-Barbera's *The Flintstones* and *Top Cat*; *Calvin and the Colonel* and last, but not least, there was Format Films' *The Alvin Show*.

"The Chipmunk records sold so well that Alvin, Simon and Theodore soon had several gold records to their credit. It seemed as though the most famous Disney characters and the early Hanna-Barbera characters had some formidable rivals in the three Chipmunks. The mention of Disney and Hanna-Barbera is apt, for Bagdasarian soon decided to produce an animated series himself.

"The cartoons for *The Alvin Show* were made by Format Films, an animation studio in Tarzana, California, which still exists today [1978]. Bagdasarian did not own Format Films in the sense that Disney, Hanna-Barbera and Jay Ward owned their studios. There was really no need for Bagdasarian to establish an animation studio of his own.

"When *The Alvin Show* was in the planning stages, the physical appearances of The Chipmunks were changed and they acquired distinct personalities.

"Alvin was mischievous and clever and these two qualities often went hand in hand. He was egotistical and proud of his success as a recording star and performer, but he had a right to be proud. Girls couldn't help loving him and he new this. He was more interested in girls than were Simon or Theodore.

"Theodore, however, was more interested in good things to eat. He was the fattest of the three and giggled much more often than the brothers did. He was not nearly as clever as Alvin; in fact, he could be called simple-minded. He was almost as much of a mischief-maker as Alvin, though.

"Simon was particularly intelligent, hence his glasses. He would never had gotten into mischief on his own, but was often dragged into it by his brothers. When Simon was not singing or playing with his brothers, he was usually a bookworm.

"David Seville was a caricature of Bagdasarian himself. He is presented as a bachelor, likeable and easygoing. He is patient with the Chipmunks' antics. He and The Chipmunks live in an average home in an average neighborhood.

"When the cartoons were in production, the cels were thrown away as they were completed. A few were rescued by collectors, but the vast majority are lost. This is especially tragic today in view of the extent to which Bagdasarian and The Chipmunks have been forgotten by the general public.

"*The Alvin Show* premiered on CBS Television on October 4, 1961. Each show consisted of four cartoons with The Chipmunks and David Seville also appearing in some of the commercials. The first cartoon on the show was always about David Seville and The Chipmunks, presenting them in a conflict situation of some kind. The conflict was often resolved by Alvin's cleverness. The second and fourth cartoons on the show were built around songs sung by

The Chipmunks, while the third was about a wacky inventor named Clyde Crashcup.

"The Chipmunks' singing was occasionally heard in the first cartoon on the show as well as in the song cartoons. For example, in one such cartoon, the operator of a radio station refuses broadcast Chipmunk music, so Alvin climbs into the broadcasting room of his station through a window and puts on of his records on the turntable. The station owner is dismayed when he hears the music and promptly puts a stop to it, but soon his phones are ringing with calls for more Chipmunk music. The radio station owner is thus the villain in this cartoon.

"There was no regular villain on *The Alvin Show* to compare with *Beany and Cecil*'s Dishonest John or Rocky and Bullwinkle's Boris Badenov. Many of these cartoons had no villain at all. The conflict sometimes arose between some well-meaning individual and our heroes. In one cartoon, for example, David Seville feels the need for the services of a private eye for some trivial reason, but at Alvin's suggestion, hires a private nose instead. The nose turns out to be a long-nosed fellow with poor eyesight who pokes his nose into everything. "The Nose knows" is his favorite remark. He means well, but ends up making a nuisance (or rather, a nose-sance) of himself, at least in David Seville's judgment.

"In another cartoon, Dave and The Chipmunks visit a jungle to record some exotic sounds and are confronted by a native who apparently keeps trying to shoot darts at them from a blowgun. It turns out that his blowgun is really a musical instrument - a wooden flute of some kind - which the native was trying to play for them because he wants to take part in their recordings and musical shows. So the native is clearly not a villain.

"*The Alvin Show* was in fact a good example of a non-violent cartoon show. The uproar over cartoon violence had not broken out when the show was made, yet Bagdasarian and the storyboard personnel at Format saw to it that the cartoons were as non-violent as any congressional committee or PTA might have wished. All the conflict in these cartoons was built around simple domestic situations. There was a cartoon where Alvin becomes angry about something and decides to run away from home. There was another in which The Chipmunks encounter a friendly eagle who cannot fly and they meet him in the yard of their own home, not on a trip to the mountains. They teach him to fly by attaching cymbals to his wings and instructing him to clash them together.

"Another cartoon with a villain of sorts was one in which The Chipmunks' neighbor complains about their rehearsing during the day because he works nights. The Chipmunks peek into the window of his dwelling and discover that he is a devout admirer of anything connected with the word mother (mother of pearl, Whistler's Mother, etc.). The Chipmunks win him over by singing a song in praise of mothers in general, but while he is off his guard Alvin ties a skyrocket to him and lights it. He (their neighbor) ends up orbiting the Earth still attached to the skyrocket and sending back signals by saying the word mother at regular intervals. The first showing of this cartoon almost coincided with Colonel John Glenn's orbital flight! In spite of the comic ending, this cartoon may well have been made to compensate for the fact that there is no mother in the home where David Seville and The Chipmunks live. This brings up a very interesting part of The Chipmunks' story - their relationships with the fair sex.

"The Chipmunks were a favorite with girls from the days of the earliest recordings - little girls, teenage girls and a few more mature ladies. There was Daisy Bell, a little girl who lived in the same neighborhood as Dave Seville and The Chipmunks and visited them from time to time. Daisy was a human, not a girl chipmunk. The well-known voice artist June Foray provided the voice for Daisy. Daisy liked Dave and The Chipmunks, but she seemed to have a crush on Alvin. Alvin treated Daisy as a good friend, though he had no crush on her. He seemed to prefer teenage girls.

"The most important cartoon about Daisy Bell is one in which she and Alvin play together. They make believe that he is a knight and that she is a princess whom he rescues from a dragon. The dragon is really the Davenport and the castle with barred windows in which the princess is held captive are really the bars on the back of a chair. The cartoon alternates back and forth between the everyday world and the fantasy that Alvin's and Daisy's imaginations make of it. It is remarkable for its portrayal of the workings of children's imaginations.

"The Chipmunks did not care for middle-aged ladies. In one cartoon, Dave arranges for such a lady to babysit The Chipmunks, but she babies them to an extent which they find most displeasing. Alvin's cleverness prevails again, however. He tricks her into drinking something alcoholic which Dave happens to have on hand, and by the end of the cartoon he has her sitting in a tree acting as though she is a bird. Then he calls the men in the white coats to come for her.

"The Chipmunks, and especially Alvin, enjoyed having female admirers, but the notion of having a mother made them feel uneasy. There is a delightful cartoon in which The Chipmunks mistakenly believe that Dave is going to get married. Actually, he is going to put in a swimming pool, but it is being installed by the Sweetheart Pool Company, operated by Mr. Sweetheart. When Dave talks to him on the phone, he addresses him as Sweetheart and The Chipmunks overhear him and of course they misunderstand the situation. They are more frightened than happy at the prospect of Dave's supposed marriage. Theodore wonders out loud, 'Do you think we'll have to call her mother?'

"There is an interesting cartoon in which Alvin falls for a pretty girl he sees at the beach. He tries to get their attention, but she wants nothing to do with him. Then he sees her play one of his records (this is still on the beach). She is one of his fans, but apparently had not recognized him before. When he finally does get to recognize him, she immediately wants to give him a big kiss. He is frightened at this and runs away with her in pursuit.

"The song cartoons were an important part of *The Alvin Show*. Bagdasarian had, after all, started as a songwriter. Many Chipmunk songs existed on records before *The Alvin Show* was on television; some of the song cartoons were built around these and others were built around songs composed specifically for the cartoons. Not all of the songs recorded by The Chipmunks were composed by Bagdasarian. Some were old favorites like "Home on the Range" or "On Top of Old Smokey" or "The Band Played On" or the spiritual "Swing Low, Sweet Chariot" which Bagdasarian arranged for The Chipmunks.

"Many of the song cartoons do not have much of a story. They depend on the effect of the song. In some of these cartoons, the song begins almost as soon as the cartoon does. We might see Dave and The Chipmunks riding in their car as the cartoon opens, and after a few bars of music, The Chipmunks begin to sing.

"Many of the song cartoons are built around trips made by Dave and The Chipmunks to some foreign country. These were the most educational of *The Alvin Show* cartoons, since interesting information about the country they were visiting were often provided. This information was usually provided by David Seville and sometimes by Simon. It was built into the script; on a trip to Scotland, for instance, Dave tells Alvin that the ancient Romans called Scotland Caledonia. Theodore, of course, was most interested in sampling the cuisine of the country they were visiting, while Alvin would usually get into mischief of some kind.

"Sometimes Alvin's antics were very innocent and endearing as in "I Wish I Could Speak French". It was a different story on their visit to Japan. Alvin decides that he wants a banana to eat. When Dave informs him that none are available in Japan, The Chipmunks burst into a song about the "Japanese Banana" - or rather, about the absence of Japanese bananas. Dave is perturbed by their song and Alvin further exasperates him by referring to a samisen player as "the worst banjo player I ever heard." The shamisen is a Japanese stringed instrument which vaguely resembles a banjo. That is another example of the educational "facts" in the cartoons of this type. The melody of "Japanese Banana" is pseudo-Oriental, just as the melody of "I Wish I Could Speak French" is more or less pseudo-French. When Bagdasarian composed a song for a cartoon in which The Chipmunks visit another country, he naturally composed the music to sound like the kind of music associated with that country.

"Speaking of foreign countries, The Chipmunks were popular in foreign lands practically from the days of their earliest recordings. Chipmunk albums turned up in Germany and Mexico, sung completely in the language of those countries. This probably means that The Chipmunks' voices for these albums were provided by persons other than Bagdasarian. Presumably, The Chipmunks were popular in many other countries, too. June Foray turned on the television in a hotel room somewhere in Africa years ago and there was *The Alvin Show*.

"As mentioned previously, there was also one cartoon per show about a wacky inventor named Clyde Crashcup. His voice was provided by an artist named Shep Menken. Clyde had a small, bald-headed laboratory assistant named Leonardo. Leonardo never spoke out loud; he communicated by whispering into Clyde's ear. Clyde's next lines would then make clear what Leonardo had said. Clyde did not invent non-existent things such as time machines, anti-gravity devices or machines that turned lead into gold; instead, he invented such items as the stove, the telephone or the bathtub. Apparently, Clyde and Leonardo live in a world which nothing exists except what Clyde invents. He "invents" things not by putting pieces of machinery together with tools, but merely by drawing pictures of them with a pencil.

"A typical cartoon begins with Clyde deciding that he needs some particular item in his home and then attempting to invent it. The results are always laughable. For example, when he decides to invent the bathtub, he first comes up with a long, narrow affair like a giant test tube and then jumps into it head first with his feet sticking out the top. "Leonardo," he complains, "I'm not comfortable in here."

"In another cartoon, Clyde tries to invent jokes. He causes Leonardo to slip on a banana peel and then cannot understand why Leonardo does not think the joke is funny. On another occasion, he invents himself a wife - whom he names Pictorial - but what he draws is an ugly hag with a personality to match. She henpecks him, and when he invents a vacuum cleaner and other accessories with which to do housework, she makes him use them. Thus, Clyde's inventions always get him into trouble of some kind, but all his cartoons have happy endings.

"Besides June Foray and Shep Menken and Bagdasarian himself, the only other voice artist on *The Alvin Show* was Bill Lee. He provided the voices for characters such as the man who complains about

The Chipmunks rehearsing because he works nights and sleeps during the day.

"*The Alvin Show* was moved to Saturday mornings after its first season, but it was still a success, remaining on television through the end of the summer of 1966. Only one season of Alvin cartoons was made.

"Bagdasarian himself would seem to have become disillusioned with producing *The Alvin Show*. The amount of time and effort involved in making animated cartoons is great and can be very disillusioning to a person like Bagdasarian, who became involved with animation comparatively late in life with little knowledge of the industry. If a 30-minute cartoon show is not ready to meet the air date, the studio or producer can be fined. Obviously, this did not lessen the pressure on Bagdasarian. Therefore, he stopped producing cartoons after the first season. He entertained no thoughts about an hour-long television special or a feature-length cartoon about The Chipmunks. Such a cartoon would have been a magnificent climax to the success story of Alvin, Simon, Theodore and David Seville. Instead, Bagdasarian was content to let *The Alvin Show* remain on television as a rerun and to continue overseeing the production of his records and toys from the offices of Bagdasarian Enterprises."

Since *Alvin and The Chipmunks* got their start in music, it was inevitable that a soundtrack album featuring songs as well as stories from the TV show would appear as *The Alvin Show* Soundtrack LP. A review online states, "This album, the soundtrack to the TV show, features audio versions of comedy bits and songs that appeared on the very funny program.

"After opening with the bouncy theme song ("This is the *Alvin Show*, the *Alvin Show*"), we hear the story of the Margaret Dumontesque Mrs. Frumpington, an anti-Rock crusader from the pre-PMRC activist group, The Society for Quiet and Universal Appreciation of Refined Enterprises. Upon introduction, Alvin comments, "And you are the head of the SQUARE's, I take it?" She then (oblivious of The Chipmunks' identities) demonstrates what she sees as the most heinous of all music by playing snippets of the Chips rockin' tunes "Coming 'Round the Mountain", "Old MacDonald Cha Cha Cha" and "Witch Doctor". Alvin begins to brutally curse her out, but David stops him.

"So Alvin goes to plan B: "I decided Mrs. Frumpington was going to sing my kind of music whether she likes it or not!" He goes to her house, gives her a flower, then starts discussing nature while his brothers hide outside and play instruments. He has her consider her love of the wind through the branches (guitar plucking), the sound of the bullfrog (bass fiddle) and the birds (a fake woodpecker playing percussion).

"As she gets more and more swept up into the rhythmic groove, he asks, "Do you like families? Don't you just love a baby, a baby?" She responds, "A baby? Baby, baby baby!" Now that he has her worked up, he asks, "And how about a daddy, a daddy?" She now has lost control to the demon rhythms of Rock and Roll and starts screaming, "DADDY, DADDY, DADDY, BABY, BABY, BABY!" A full horn section kicks in as she works herself into an erotic climax, "BABY, BABY, BABY, DADDY, DADDY, DADDY, BABY, BABY, BABY! Ohhhhhh!"

"She can't get out of the groove and howls her orgasmic Rock 'n' Roll vocals until men in white coats take her away. Thus, the most sexually charged kiddie record ever proves that everything this woman feared was true - Rock music is Satan.

"The album side ends by attempting to desexualize Alvin a little by reprising "I Wish I Could Speak French", but ending it by having Alvin's sexy encounter with the French girl turn out to be nothing but a (wet) dream.

"Side two opens with a TV interview. The boys sing a song (a new version of "Chipmunk Fun") to the reporter about what they like to do (play baseball, go swimming, watch *Gunsmoke*). The song and interview end with David pleased at their good behavior, but as the TV dude signs off, Alvin reprises the tune with new, naughty lyrics. "I like to break dishes and fight with the squirrels. I like to pull pigtails when they're on girls. We like to eat candy and talk in school. But we don't like to study math. Arithmetic makes me sick." "I knew it!" laments David. Perhaps the squirrel line was a jab at their animated rivals, The Nutty Squirrels.

"We then meet Clyde Crashcup, a scientist character introduced for the cartoon. His humor is very Ernie Kovacs-esque, but it doesn't really fit in with the rest of the stuff. Dave then starts "Witch Doctor" solo, but the boys stop him and they sing it together. The album ends with a reprise of the TV theme, some goodbyes and a few more Crashcup jokes. All in all, perhaps the wildest Alvin album ever."

The album was engineered by David Hassinger and orchestrated by James Getzoff. Once again, Pate/Francis & Associates did the cover design. The Frumpington segment plays about the same, but there is added Alvin narration to explain the more visual gags and the Clyde Crashcup segment is severely truncated on the album.

CBS reran the series on Saturday mornings for a few years after the show's prime time run ended, and segments from the show were syndicated in the mid and late 1960s under the package title *Alvin and the Chipmunks*. The series later was revived on NBC-TV, again promoted under the title *Alvin and the Chipmunks* (with the introductory *Alvin Show* title card cut off the beginning of the show opening) Saturday mornings between March 10, 1979 and September 1, 1979. TBS also reran the show sometime in the 1980s as well.

Ross Jr., launched a new animated series in fall 1983 on NBC. It was called *Alvin and the Chipmunks* and featured redesigned versions of The Chipmunks. To coincide with the new series, Viacom Enterprises distributed reruns of *The Alvin Show* to local stations.

Later incarnations have phased out the Crashcup characters, but in 1981, Crashcup did make a cameo appearance in *A Chipmunk Christmas*. More recent network airings of the special have cut this sequence out, due to network time constraints for advertising.

In 1990, *The Alvin Show* versions of the Chipmunks and Clyde Crashcup reappeared in an episode of *The Chipmunks Go To the Movies* entitled "Back to Our Future" (a spoof of the 1985 movie, *Back to the Future*).

Cable station Nickelodeon picked up the rights to *The Alvin Show* sometime in 1994 and ran the episodes daily until late 1995. During this time and shortly after, individual cartoons and musical segments were inserted into episodes of *Weinerville*. In 1996, Nickelodeon stopped showing *The Alvin Show* segments altogether, and no television station has aired them since.

There were two VHS releases from Buena Vista Home Video, both of which featured 11 songs from *The Alvin Show*. On September 8, 2009, Paramount Home Entertainment released the first episode of the series, and in 2015, three complete episodes (#01, #04, and #10) were released together on DVD and Blu-ray.

Early newspaper announcements for *The Alvin Show* in *Daily Capital News*, April 15, 1961; *Variety*, May 4, 1961; and *The Times*, June 18, 1961.

## CBS Plans New Cartoon Series

"Alvin and the Chipmunks," a new animated cartoon series starring Alvin, the mischievous singing chipmunk, and his brothers Simon and Theodore, will make its debut as a weekly feature over the CBS Television Network next fall.

The program will be scheduled on Wednesday at 6:30 p.m. The starting date will be announced.

In addition to Alvin and his brothers, songwriter David Seville also will appear on the series in cartoon form. David Seville is the professional name used by Ross Bagdasarian, the composer who wrote and recorded "The Chipmunk Song," the Christmas novelty which sold a record 4,000,000 copies in seven weeks following its introduction in 1958.

Bagdasarian has since recorded three full albums of the singing chipmunks and total record sales have hit the 12,000,000 mark.

### Cartoon Production Peak

## CARTOON PROD'N AT ALLTIME PEAK

STARK, HYMAN PAY 500G TO FILM NEW TENNESSEE WILLIAMS PLAY

Animation Bonanza In TV Booms Outlay To $14 Mil This Year, Survey Shows

Poaching Sponsor Blasted On Air By Clete Roberts

44 WB Writers At Work On 44 Vidpix; Eye More

## TEEN ETIQUETTE
# Songwriter Offers Success Cues
**By KITTE TURMELL**

Want to succeed? Break the "rules" for success! Want a career that will bring you around a million dollars? Then be willing to drop the career you trained for, should a better one come along. Does the effort have to be pretty grim? Not at all—it can even be a little crazy, and a lot of fun!

That's what you conclude after you talk with one of today's most successful songwriters, Ross Bagdasarian. Usually you teen graduates get your formulas for job success from bank presidents or industrial tycoons.

I called on this former grape grower from Fresno who now, as David Seville, rides herd on three singing chipmunks. He provided these boyhood memories.

"In my teens I drove a tractor in my father's vineyard—at two miles an hour—and the studio passing me drove me crazy," fans recalled with his flash-grin. "So I used to sing at the top of my voice—which kept jackrabbits away, too—and at it. I composed my first song there, 'Nuts to You.'"

• • •

"THEN WILLIAM SAROYAN, my cousin, gave me the part of the Pinball Maniac, in his play, 'The Time of Your Life'. That was great for me but a disappointment to my family. After four years' service in the war, I thought maybe my father was right, so I got married and went back to grape farming. That year the bottom fell out of the market. My wife and I ate a lot of grapes!"

Eventually, he took wife, two children, $200 and an unpublished song called "Come on-a My House" to Los Angeles. There things began to happen. Rosemary Clooney recorded the song and the movies took both him and his music.

• • •

SINCE THEN Ross has been too busy to develop success formulas, but he says you can pretty well sum things up in these five thoughts:

DO YOUR BEST—"A girl just-turned-teens told me she got a B in spelling. I reminded her she usually got A's. But B was good, she felt, because everyone else got D. I didn't agree. I asked her is she judged herself by what she did or by what others didn't do. As my favorite chipmunk, Alvin, would put it: 'You're wrong, kiddo. Do the very best you can and to heck with everybody else.'"

BE YOURSELF—"This doesn't mean you have to be a non-conformist. Some people are only happy if they go along with the crowd. But I don't think that any teen should have to like a thing simply because family or friends insist.

"That goes when you pick out records, too. Let your own good taste tell you what to get. Develop that taste, otherwise, you won't know how to choose."

FORGET YOUR YESTERDAYS—"Don't fall in love with what you did in the past, so that people say, 'Sure, we know what you did then. But what are you doing now?' I can't remember half the lyrics I've written for songs, Kitte. I use my time to do my work and look ahead. The great adventure that interests me is in the week that I must do next."

• • •

DON'T FEEL SORRY FOR YOURSELF — That can be as bad as any disease. Many of us waste time — and taste it so important — feeling sorry for ourselves because our parents don't live in a big house or don't drive a new, impressive car. Neither your parents or the world owe you a living. If you don't have much to start with, be thankful you've got the chance a clinch so much further."

AND EXPERIMENT — What worked for Edison works for Bagdasarian, too. His best-seller records follow many, many hours of singing into his tape recorder and tinkering with the result. "All I can say," observes Ross, "it that I love Witch Doctors, chipmunks, and—most of all—tape recorders!"

"How can you find the right career—and be the success every Dad wants his teen-ager to be? For a list of helpful career-guide pamphlets, send a self-addressed, stamped envelope to Kitte Turmell, care of The Hammond Times, for Kitte's leaflet, 'M Career Booklets and Job Leaflets.'"

SUCCESS ISN'T necessarily stuffy, says Songwriter Ross Bagdasarian, shown with his daughter, Carol (seated), 12, and secretary, Carol Macciotra. Career can even be found in offbeat tinkering with tape recorder according to former grape grower known as David Seville.

## DEAR KITTE TURMELL:
# He's All 'Broken Up' After Break Up With Girl Friend

"DEAR KITTE TURMELL: My girl friend and I broke up after going together for over a year. She is going out with a friend of mine, and says she wants to go with both of us. I am M. I have not slept since we broke up, and it has got to the point where I can't take it any longer. What can I do? Jan W."

DEAR JIM: Go out with her, and...

## An *Alvin Show* script.

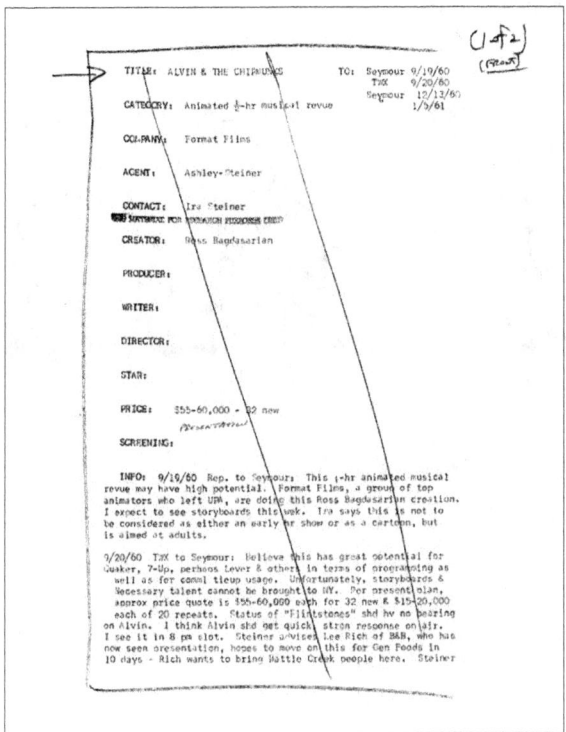

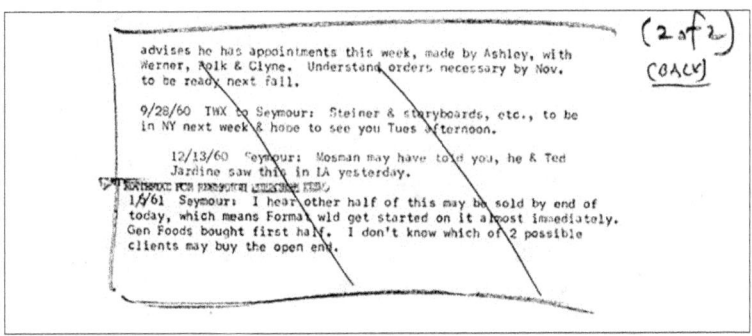

*Alvin Show* prototype design drawings for Alvin and The Chipmunks and David Seville.

Complete *Alvin Show* storyboard.

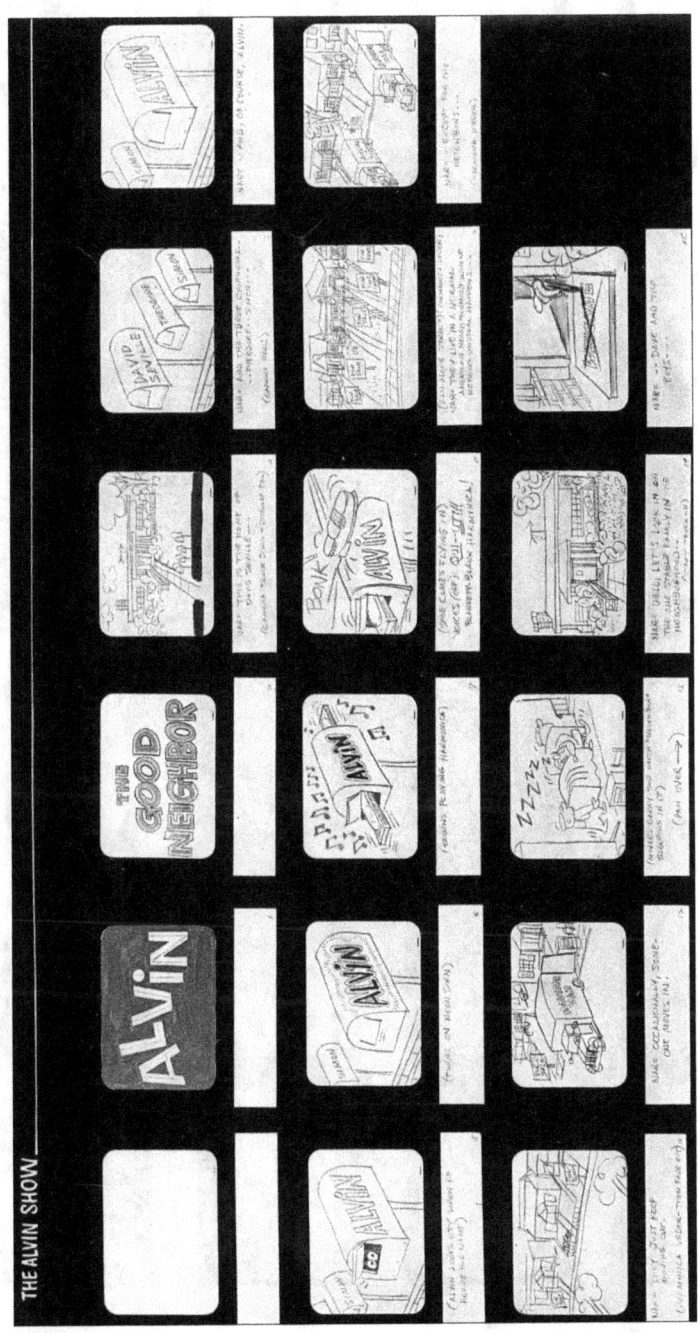

# *AAAAALLLVIIINNN!*: The Story of Ross Bagdasarian, Sr., ...

# Liberty Records, Format Films and *The Alvin Show*

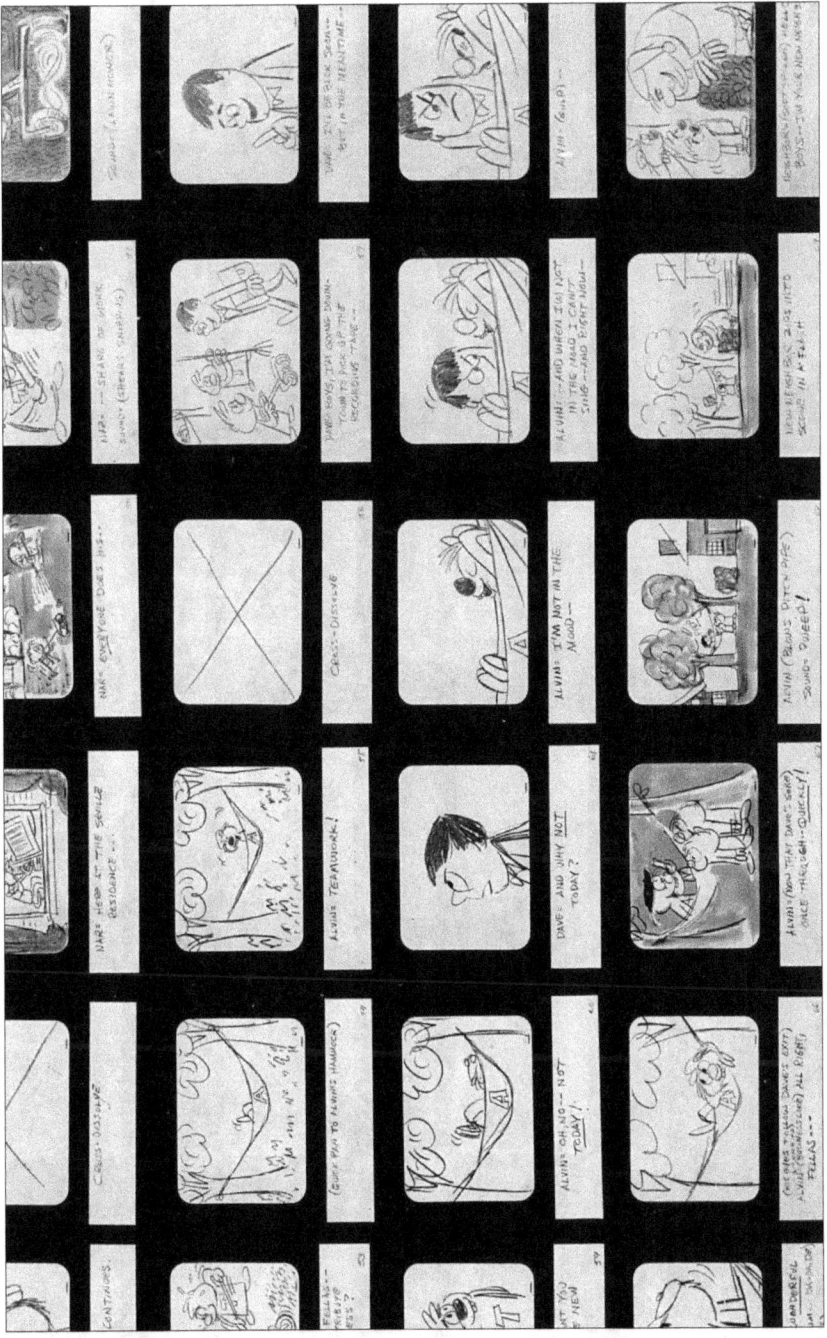

# AAAAALLLLVIIINNN!: The Story of Ross Bagdasarian, Sr., ...

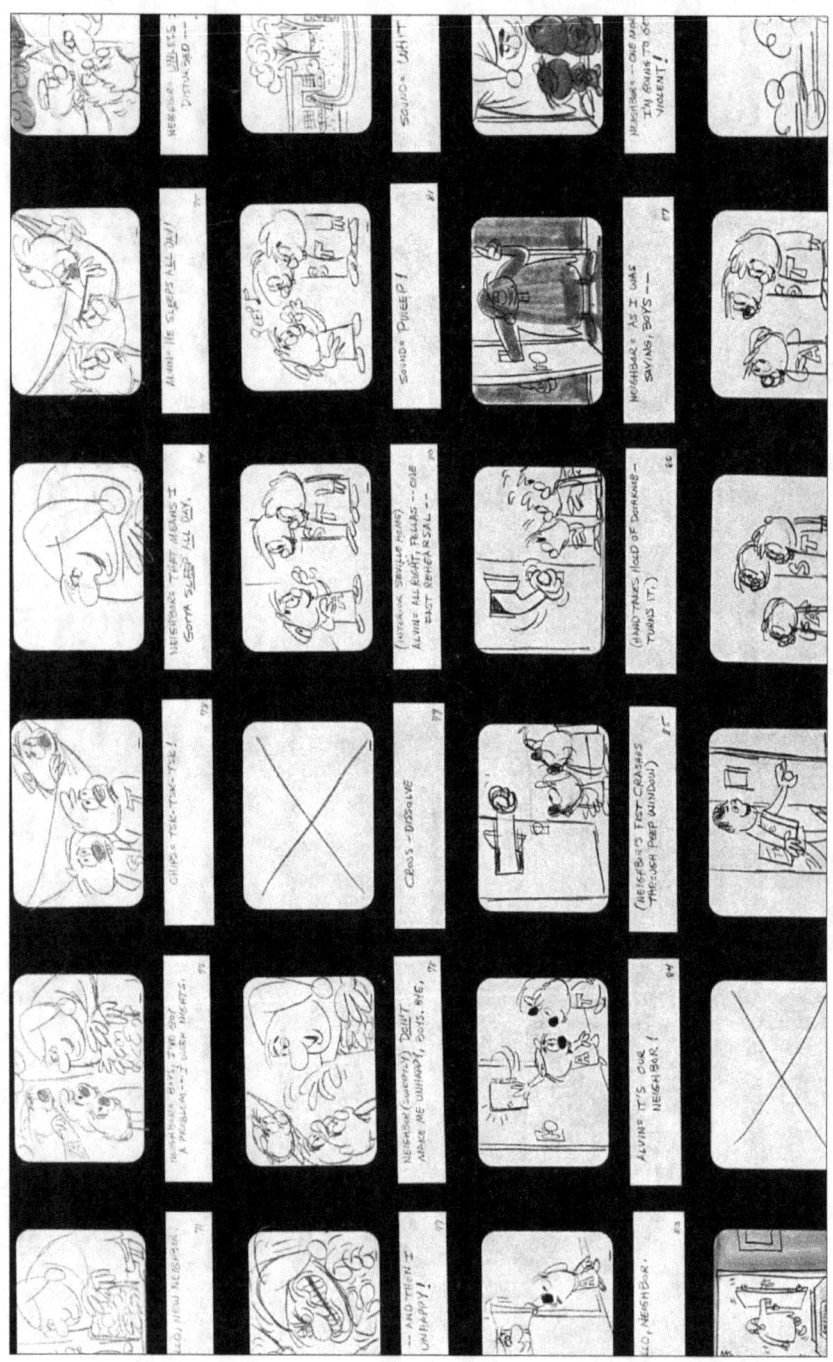

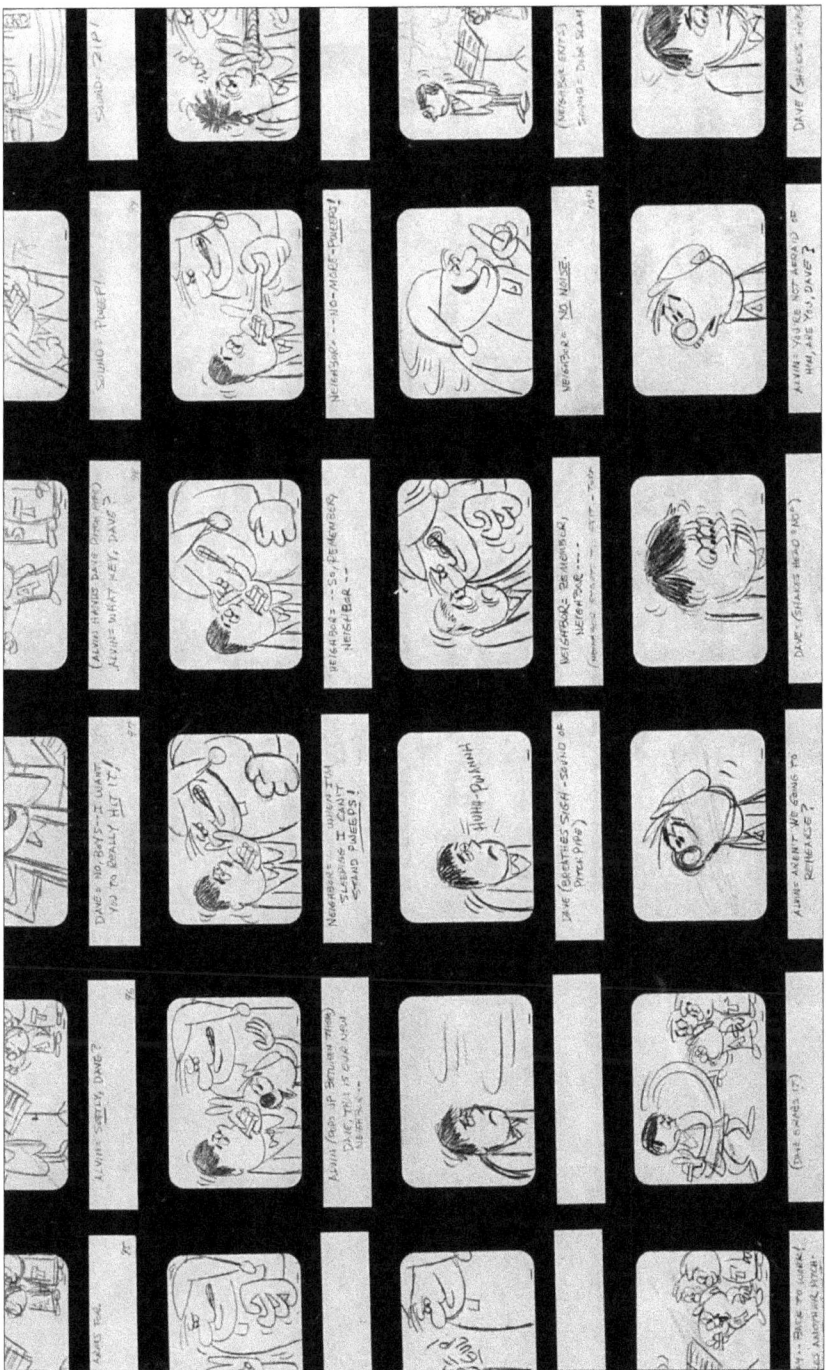

# AAAAALLLVIIINNN!: The Story of Ross Bagdasarian, Sr., ...

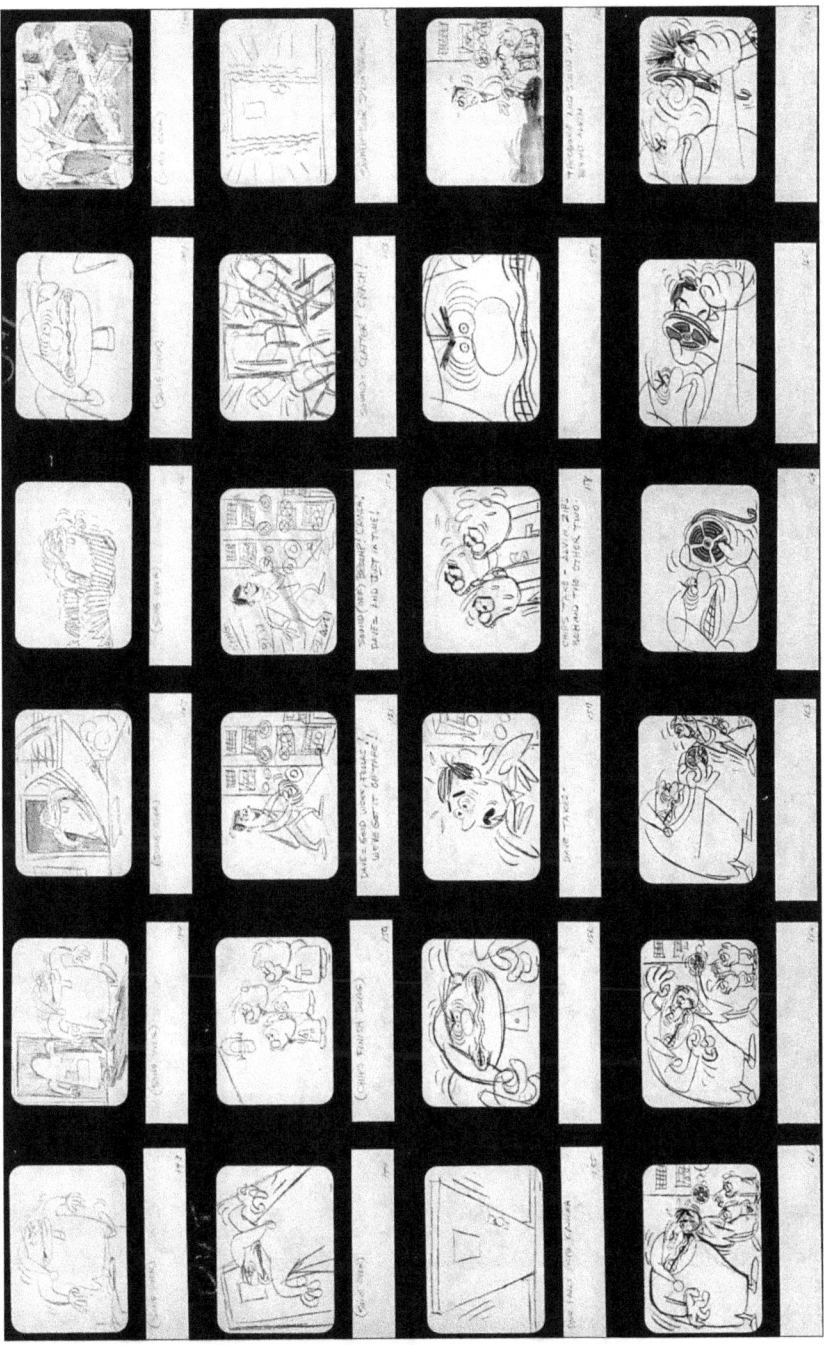

# *AAAAALLLVIIINNN!*: The Story of Ross Bagdasarian, Sr., ...

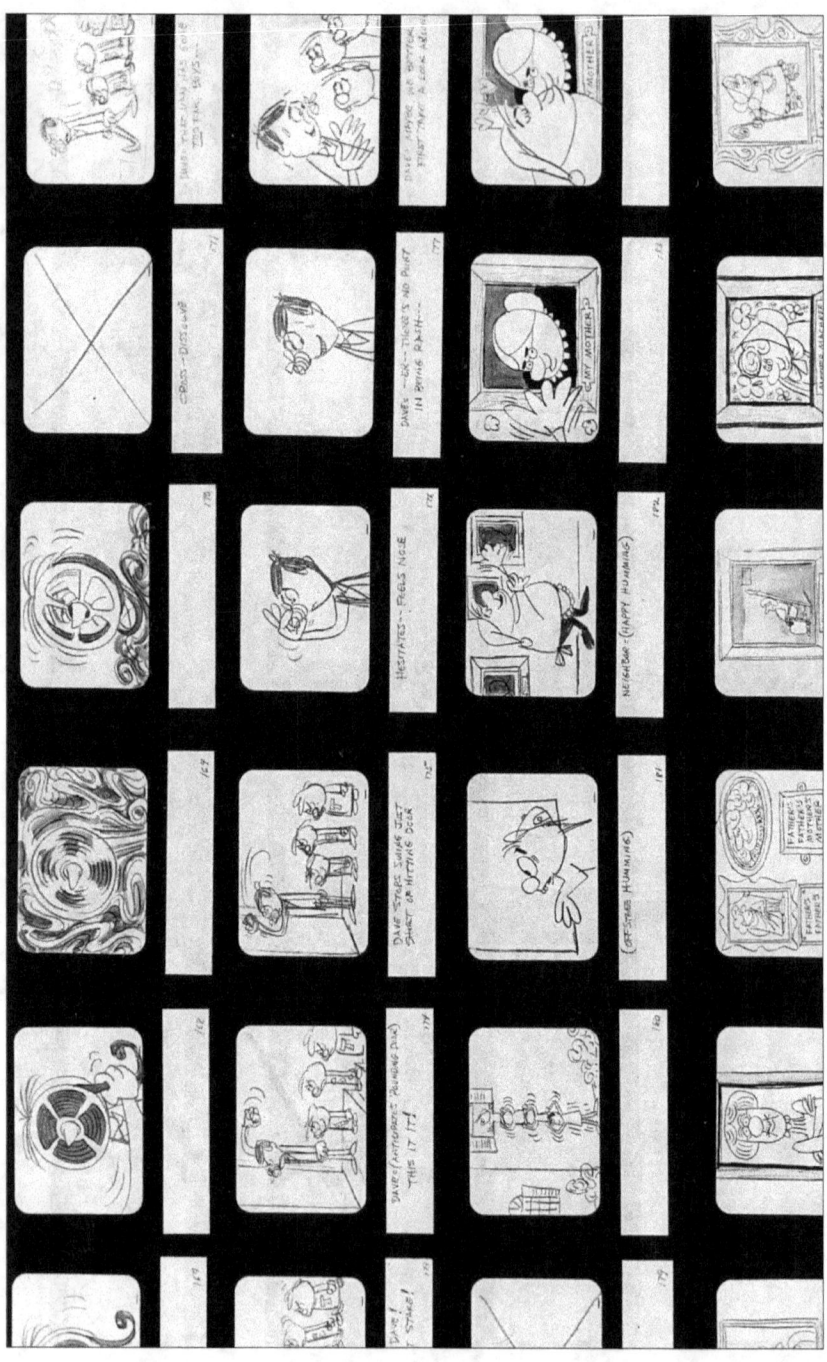

# Liberty Records, Format Films and *The Alvin Show*

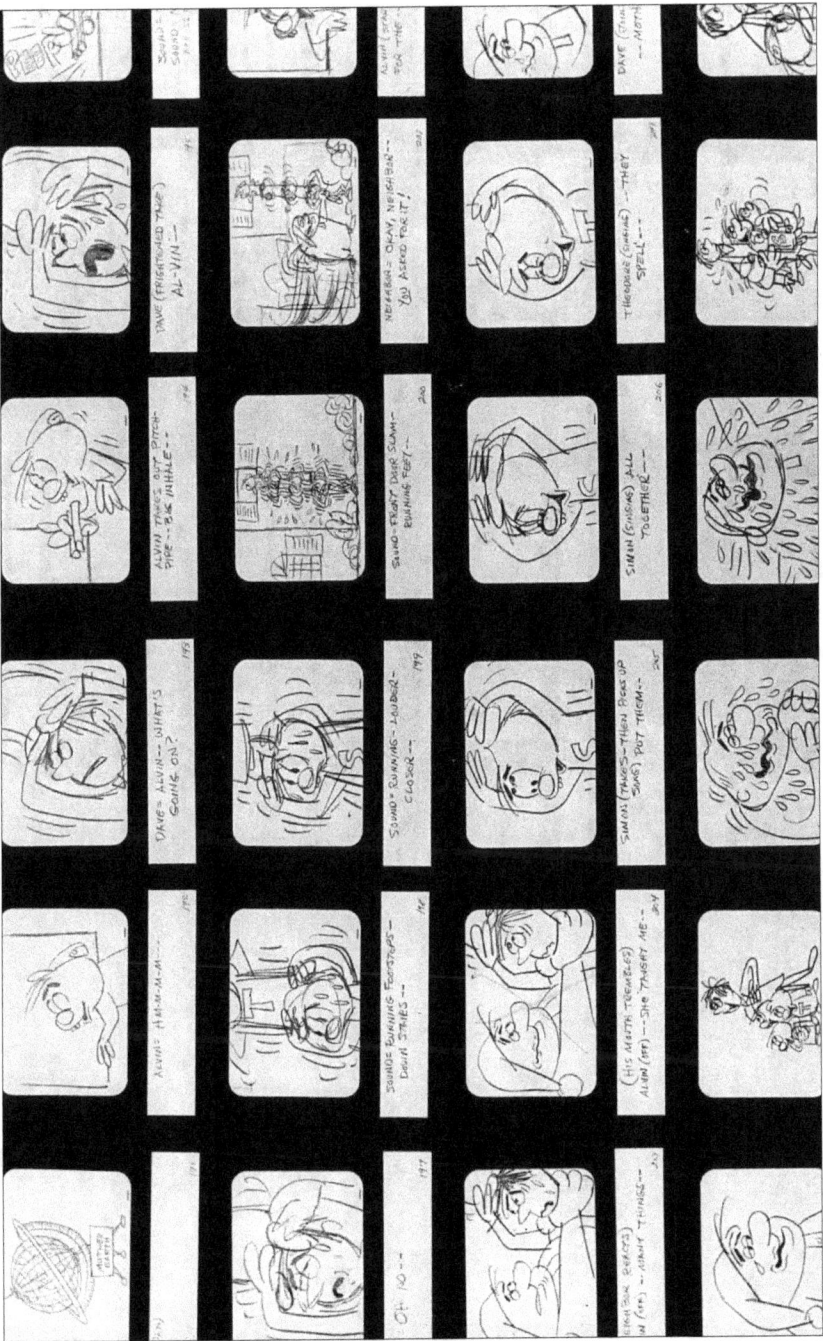

## AAAAALLLVIIINNN!: The Story of Ross Bagdasarian, Sr., ...

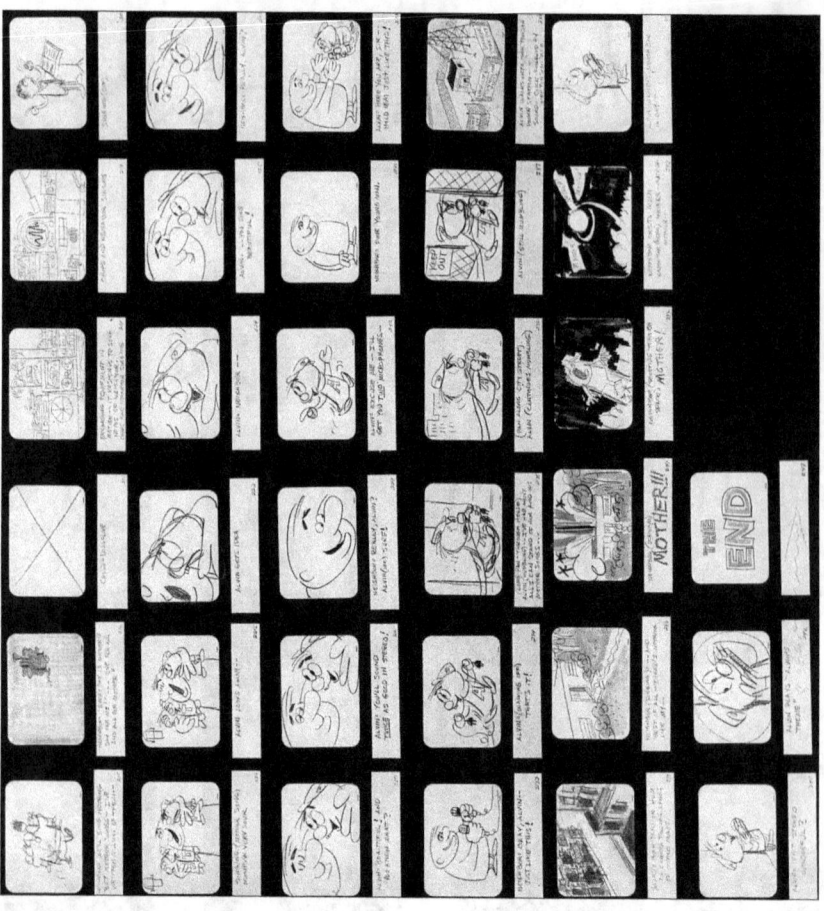

Promotion for *The Alvin Show*, September 23, 1961, and *TV Guide* Fall Preview issue.

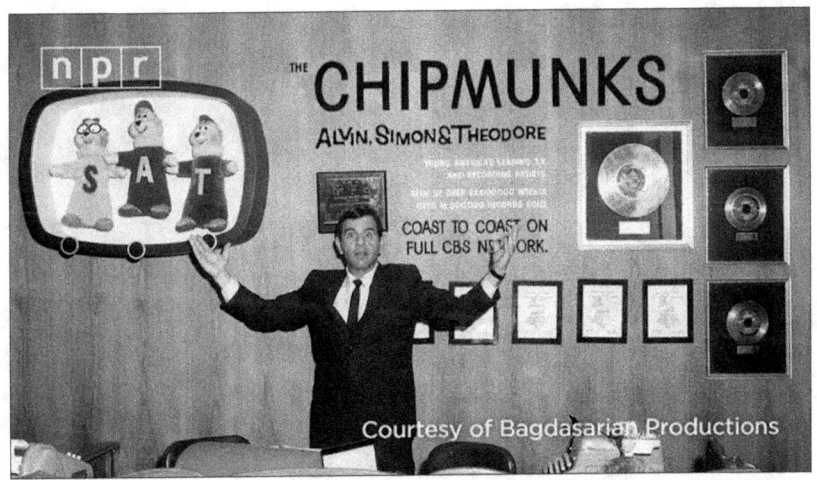

*Alvin Show* photo shoot with Ross Bagdasarian.

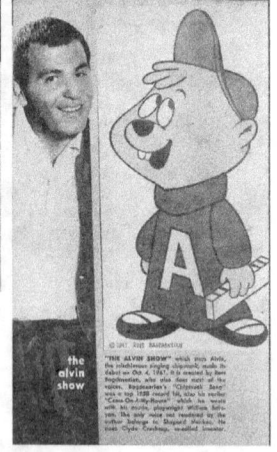

Complete *Alvin Show* press kit.

I'M THEODORE. EVERY TEAM NEEDS A BIG EATER. (REMEMBER BABE RUTH?) P. S. I ALSO HAVE THE HOT DOG, PEANUT, POPCORN, ICE CREAM AND SODA POP CONCESSIONS.

*Alvin Show* press photos.

*Alvin Show* slides featuring the show logo, the Bagdasarian Film Productions logo, Jell-O and Alpha-Bits.

Various *Alvin Show* animation drawings and cels courtesy of Heritage Auctions.

*AAAAALLLVIIINNN!*: The Story of Ross Bagdasarian, Sr., ...

## Liberty Records, Format Films and *The Alvin Show*

## *AAAAALLLVIIINNN!:* The Story of Ross Bagdasarian, Sr., ...

# Liberty Records, Format Films and *The Alvin Show*

*AAAAALLLVIIINNN!*: The Story of Ross Bagdasarian, Sr., …

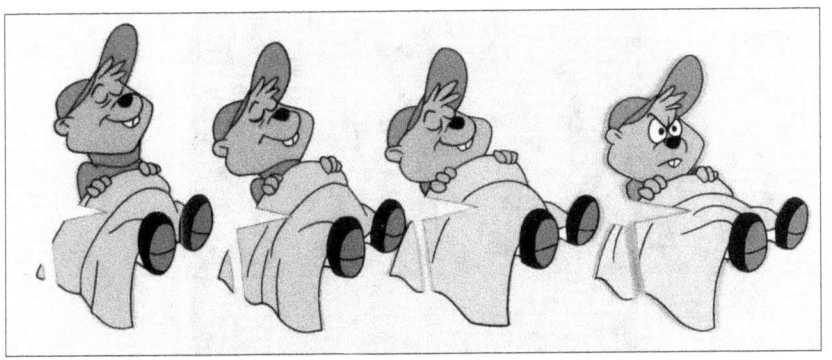

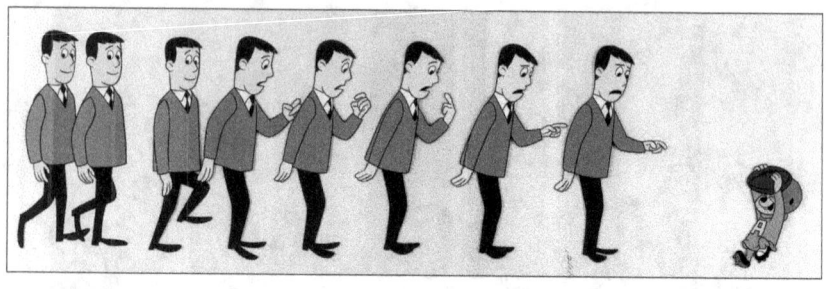

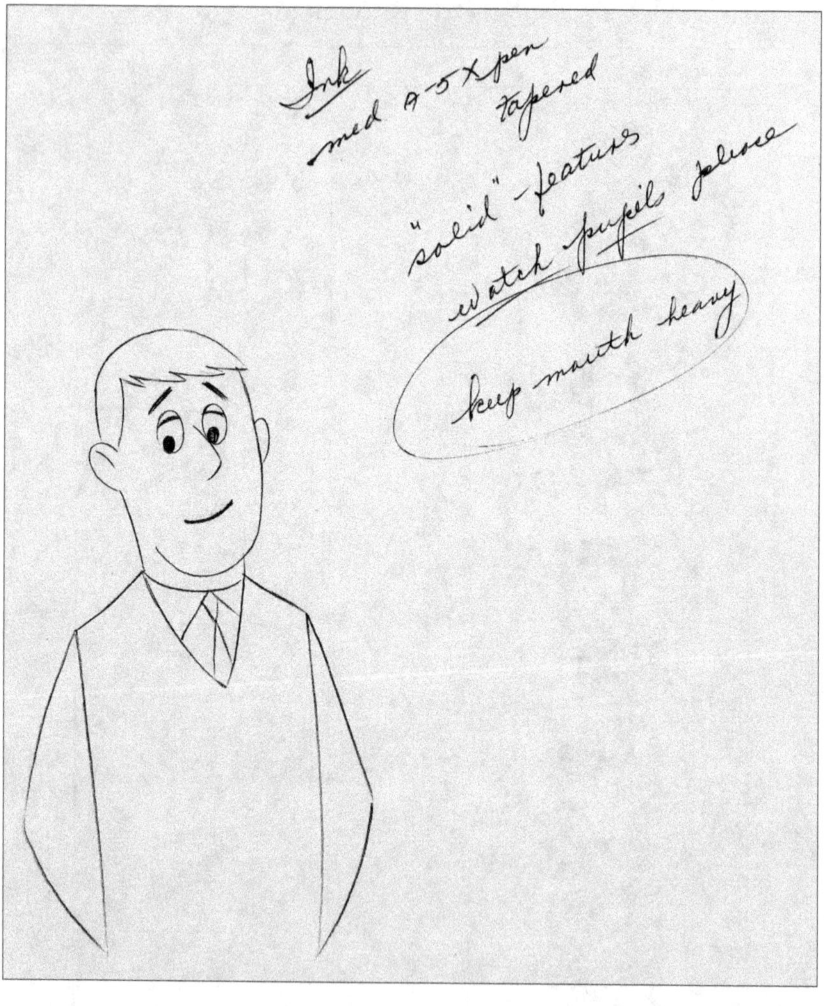
Ink
med A-5 X pen
tapered
"solid" - features
watch pupils place
keep mouth heavy

The fourth Chipmunks album, the soundtrack to *The Alvin Show*, front and back covers.

# THE MIXED-UP WORLD OF BAGDASARIAN

AFTER THE CANCELLATION OF *The Alvin Show*, the 26 episodes produced continued to appear on Saturday mornings starting in the fall of 1962, airing initially at 10am on CBS. From this point forward, The Chipmunks were essentially regarded as only children's entertainment; the appeal towards adults was severely limited. Bagdasarian would only release songs and albums targeted towards adults under his own name leaving the David Seville for only Chipmunks releases and his cartoon image. There were a few more experimental releases, which will be detailed in this chapter.

There was a new slew of merchandising, now featuring the re-designed characters as they appeared on *The Alvin Show*. Even The Chipmunks first three albums and some of their singles were reissued with redesigned sleeves reflecting this changes.

As *The Alvin Show* entered into reruns on Saturday mornings, two comic book series debuted from Dell Comics, *Alvin* which lasted for 28 issues from October-December 1962 through October 1973, with writing attributed to Don Segall and *Clyde Crashcup* with lasted five issues from August-October 1963 through September-November 1964, with writing attributed to John Stanley.

There were also two one-shot comic books *Alvin For President*,

August-October 1964 and *Alvin and his Pals in Merry Christmas with Clyde Crashcup and Leonardo,* December 1963-February 1964 and reissued in abridged form in April 1966, with writing attributed to Don Segall and John Stanley and pencils by John Stanley.

The earliest Chipmunk-related comic book predates *The Alvin Show* and was called *The Three Chipmunks* and was part of Dell's *Four Color* series #1042, October-December 1959, with writing attributed to Paul S. Newman.

John Stanley, a writer and artist best-known for his work on *Marge's Little Lulu,* also for Dell Comics is mentioned in Bill Schelly's biography *John Stanley: Giving Life to Little Lulu,* "After all the comic books he created except *Thirteen "Going on Eighteen"* were canceled, John Stanley needed more work. He filled in by writing five issues of *Clyde Crashcup* in 1963. Stanley's stories of the crackpot scientist from the 1960s animated television series *The Alvin Show* were drawn by Irving Tripp (Stanley's art partner on *Marge's Little Lulu*). Stanley also wrote much of the exhaustively titled *Alvin and his Pals in Merry Christmas with Clyde Crashcup and Leonardo* #1, February 1964."

Singer Chubby Checker had a #1 hit with the same record TWICE! It was the popular dance single called "The Twist". The song originally hit #1 on September 19, 1960 where it was a hit with teenagers. Then strangely, in late 1961, the craze caught on again with adults, and hit #1 again on January 13, 1962.

Never to miss an opportunity at this point in his career, Bagdasarian quickly recorded and released "The Alvin Twist" in February 1962, and it charted at a respectable #40. A review of the single states: "The Alvin Twist" / "I Wish I Could Speak French": "The 1962 Top 40 hit "The Alvin Twist" showed the hard-core commercial side of The Chipmunks. Not a "novelty" or children's record, it was a serious stab at mainstream pop radio success. No side stories, no yelling David Seville, just layers of piercing vocal harmonies on top of rocking Twist music provided by LA's best studio session men."

The A-side appeared on the upcoming *The Chipmunk Songbook* while the B-side appeared on both *Around the World With The Chipmunks* and *The Alvin Show* soundtrack album.

*The Chipmunk Songbook* was the next Chipmunks LP, released in April 1962, along with an EP with the same title. The album occupies an interesting spot as being the first follow-up project after *The Alvin Show*, although all of its songs were featured on the show, so it was a no-brainer release. For some reason, The Chipmunks' versions of "Clementine" and "Jeanie With the Light Brown Hair" from *The Alvin Show* have eluded inclusion on this or any Chipmunks album or single.

An online review of this album states, "The Chipmunks from the start were perceived as perfect for kids, but also so clever and amusing that adults would groove on the jokes as well. Must of this is attributable to the sophistication of Ross Bagdasarian's humorous instrumentation and songwriting. As evidenced by the nearly instrumental B-sides of the early Chips singles, all the whimsy and humor of the group can be also matched just by the originality of Bagdasarian's personalities, their was a bit of a wake up call about the Chips' audience.

"Originally aired in primetime, a la *The Flintstones* or *The Simpsons*, *The Alvin Show* was a commercial flop despite its super high quality. It then moved to Saturday morning where the kiddie audience grooved to it for several successful seasons. This may have been a blow to Ross' ego because all the LPs released post-*Alvin Show*'s time-slot relocation seem more squarely aimed at the kids, and they now rely less and less on original songs and more on children's standards and covers of pop songs. The pop covers would prove to be the least inspired, but that was several years off.

"For this album, after the charming (though not particularly comics) original "The Alvin Twist", we get a dozen or so kids songs / Vaudeville numbers, with plenty of funny Alvin / Dave-isms. "On Top of Old Smokey", "Twinkle, Twinkle, Little Star" and "Bicycle Built For Two" are all particularly pleasant. At this point (and on the Christmas LPs to follow), Bagdasarian may not be composing as much magic, and his work may be less sophisticated than on his recordings with a broader audience in mind. However, his respect for the craftsmanship of the songwriters of yore seems to lead to inspired arrangements and a genuinely joyous execution. By 1964, inspiration would become rarer, as most Chipmunks records would be just rote covers of current hits."

This was followed in May 1962 by the second single from the album, "America the Beautiful" / "My Wild Irish Rose" where a review says, "The boys sing a patriotic hymn and a drinking song! The former could drive you to drink and the latter could make you want to leave the country." Both sides were taken from *The Chipmunk Songbook*.

*The Chipmunk Songbook* was nominated for a Grammy for Best Recording for Children. The cover design is credited to Francis and Manahan, Inc.

Also in May 1962, was a puzzling reissue of "Armen's Theme" / "Russian Roulette (Dark Eyes)", although this time it was released under the name Ross Bagdasarian. Both songs end up on Bagdasarian's 1966 LP.

By the end of 1962, *Christmas With The Chipmunks* as an LP and EP were released, which seemed to be a natural considering how The Chipmunks got their start. An online review states, "The four-year-old "Chipmunk Song" is repeated here from their first album. This LP has a humorous cover drawing featuring the lads opening their presents four days too early (according to a wall calendar). Seville's still getting as much mileage out of The Chipmunks' biggest hit as he can. Four years later, Alvin is still asking for a damn hula hoop. As for the rest, when Seville is not yelling at Alvin and company to keep in line, he gets a couple of solo turns, as do The Chipmunks themselves. There's even a guest vocalist, Rudolph, the Red-Nosed Reindeer, on the song of the same name. Highlights include: "Here Comes Santa Claus", in which Alvin starts orating the lyrics like John Barrymore, forcing David to scold his overacting, and a straight version of "Up On the Housetop", a great tune for The Chipmunks style. Yuletide music at its kitschy best. The original LP has the fancy foil and the non-foil covers. The 1980 reissue is the same as the original, but omits "Over the River and Through the Woods" and "We Wish You a Merry Christmas".

In addition, "Rudolph" also is a repeat, originally appearing on *Around the World With The Chipmunks.*" The Christmas album hit #84 and has become a Christmas perennial and also spawned a sequel album at the end of 1963. Studio Five did the cover design.

As 1963 began, Bagdasarian released one of his most ambitious Chipmunks singles, "Alvin's All-Star Chipmunk Band" / "Old MacDonald Cha Cha Cha". An Internet review states, "The A-side is remarkable because we learn that Alvin and his brothers aren't the only mutant human-esque Chipmunks. He brings in a bevy of them to jam with.

"The flip is one of the most charming Chiptunes (and a four year old album cut) where the Chips (over a pleasant pseudo Mambo rhythm) sing "Old MacDonald", adding "cha cha cha" after every line (it doesn't replace e-i-e-i-o). The best part is the interactive portion where David tells the kids at home to do the "cha-cha-chas" and the Chips keep quiet. Try to not sing it!"

To add to this review, the A-side is a really impressive experiment long before Bobby McFerrin did it with "Don't Worry, Be Happy". That is, vocalizing all of the instruments along with the actual vocals themselves. So, Bagdasarian performs all the trumpets, bass, trombones, violins, etc. with his voice and overdubs it so that it sounds like a full orchestra, plus the tune ain't bad, either. The song never appeared on any of the original albums and only occasionally appears on greatest hits collections. Bagdasarian is presumed to have performed a version of it on the March 6, 1963 edition of *The Tonight Show Starring Johnny Carson*.

As stated, the B-side originally appeared on *Let's All Sing With The Chipmunks*.

Bagdasarian still was trying to gain traction on the charts with a February 1963 reissue of "Gotta Get To Your House" / "Cecilia" and a new single in September 1963, "Lucy, Lucy" / "Scalawags and Sinners", both released under his real name. Both flopped. It is assumed that the Lucy of the song was named for Lucy Saroyan (1946-2003), William's daughter and Bagdasarian's niece. "Lucy, Lucy" features a straight female chorus while "Scalawags and Sinners" is a fast sax song that sounds like "The Bird on my Head". Both are on Bagdasarian's 1966 LP.

In Fall 1963, *The Alvin Show* continued on Saturday mornings on CBS, now airing at 9am, the spot it will remain in until Fall 1965, when the show will enter syndication.

In October 1963, Bagdasarian released one of the bizarrest Chipmunks singles: "Eefin' Alvin" / "Flip Side". An online review states,

"This is either a record that makes no reasonably sane sense whatsoever, or it's the single greatest example of a novelty record Natural Law inevitability. "Little Eefin' Annie" by Al Perkins popularized an awkward, unnatural, pseudo hillbilly vocal gimmick where you kinda do a rural asthmatic scant, sorta playing invisible harmonica by wheezing and puffing, gulping and swallowing and expelling air, hitting two half notes on the exhale. It's hard to describe and not easy to do, though I think Southerners can do it at birth. Mac Davis used to do it on his show, and one of the highlights of "eefing" has to be Jimmie Riddle's self-explanatory "Yakety Eef". I don't know if it is ever supposed to have historically been done for non-comical effect, but basically if you put eefing on "Amazing Grace", it becomes a novelty song. So imagine how much more absurd this becomes when this is sped up Alvin style! The record is either Grammy material or a sign of the Apocalypse."

To add to this, "Eefin' Alvin" has to be one of the most difficult Chipmunk songs to obtain that originally appeared on Liberty Records. The song has never appeared on a legitimate compilation and when uploaded onto YouTube, it is usually taken down, quickly. A complete Chipmunks and Seville/Bagdasarian Sr. compilation is greatly needed and wanted. The producer of this strange single was Thomas "Snuff" Garrett (1938-2015), who was a staff producer at Liberty Records starting in 1959 and became the label's head of A&R, before leaving in 1966. His path would cross with Bagdasarian again after leaving Liberty.

As stated, it is a very strange record, but considering the direction that The Chipmunk records were going from this point forward, not as strange as they would soon become. The B-side is the same B-side from "Ragtime Cowboy Joe".

1962's *Christmas With The Chipmunks* inevitably begat *Christmas*

*With The Chipmunks, Volume 2* as both and LP and EP in October 1963. The new album proved to be even more popular than its predecessor, peaking at #9. It has also become a Christmas perennial with tracks from both albums mixed and matched and re-released annually. Studio Five one again did the cover design.

The tremendous success of The Chipmunks' Christmas albums have led to countless reissues and reconfiguration over the years including a white vinyl version released for Christmas 2018.

A review of this sequel album says, "This is Seville showing his sentimental side. Though he tries to act like a tough on wax, you can tell his heart is bigger than the post-transformed Grinch's by just how sweet and straightforward this album is. Apparently, the spirit of Christmas isn't something to be irreverent about, as there's hardly any shenanigans here. Sure, Dave tries to get mad at Alvin when he starts improvising during "Twelve Days of Christmas", but you can tell his heart isn't in it. Conflict like that is rare here, and most of these carols are sung with reverence. Dave even sings lead twice, on a sappy but earnest "Have Yourself a Merry Little Christmas" and on a Beatnik version of "Night Before Christmas". Overall a pleasant album, but definitely more of a real kiddie record than most Chips stuff Russ Sr. did."

A single was also released of "The Night Before Christmas" / "Wonderful Day" which was reviewed as, "David Seville delivers a Be-Boppin "Night Before" that sounds kind of like your math teacher trying to do a rap about integers to "really connect with the kids".

"Wonderful Day" is the follow up/sound alike to "The Chipmunk Song", and at the end Alvin starts harmonica jamming to his dad's dismay. (Dave: "YOU'RE PLAYING THE WRONG SONG IN THE WRONG KEY!") We learn a secret of The Chipmunks: Alvin only has moderately adequate chops. Maybe Dave should have let him play more." Both sides were taken from *Christmas With The Chipmunks, Volume 2*.

At the end of 1963, President John F. Kennedy was assassinated and the US went into a general funk until four lads that shook the world landed on our shores. Then, in 1964, The Beatles had such an impact on our country's youth and pop culture that it seemed inevitable that Bagdasarian would have teamed The Chipmunks up with them in some way.

But before the release that you think will be discussed here is a single that was rush released on February 29, 1964 with yet another Bagdasarian pseudonym, The Begbugs. The single was "Yeah, Yeah" / "Lucy, Lucy". "Yeah, Yeah" is an upbeat rocker with Bagdasarian singing and talking to himself and adapting a British accent that's almost as bad as Dick Van Dyke's in *Mary Poppins* released the same year. It's amusing with the sound of cash registers ringing to the beat at the end. The song itself is reminiscent of "The Alvin Twist" and was a total Beatles cash-in. "Lucy, Lucy" was the same Ross Bagdasarian song released as an A-side in 1963, but on this remake, it is slower and notable for the "Shut up, Henry, and go on home!" ending. These two songs appear on Bagdasarian's 1966 LP.

During 1964, Bagdasarian signed a special deal with Columbia Records Productions to record five different cardboard record greeting card songs, plus a promotional cardboard record sing about Soaky the Fun Bath, all as by The Chipmunks with David Seville. The five greeting card records are "Well, Happy Birthday Anyway", "Happy Birthday" (one with an image of them playing Pin the Tail on the Donkey and another with a drawing of them singing), a Valentine's card called "Because I Love You" and a get well card called "It Sure is Rough Being Sick". These cards were available in gift shops and dime stores sold along with the other greeting cards. The three Happy

Birthday records have the same "Happy Birthday" song, but with different humorous spoken word comments on each. The love card and get well card both have unique songs and dialogue.

"Soaky the Fun Bath Sends Greetings from The Chipmunks" reworks their "Wonderful Day" song to include lyrics about this special record and Soaky the Fun Bath. The mail away record was available from Colgate-Palmolive, the makers of Soaky. This song on this record is completely different from the "Soaky Soaks You Clean" song used in the TV commercial to promote the Soaky bottles shaped like Alvin, Simon and Theodore.

Another rare Chipmunks promotional record released during 1964 was "Cooperative Forest Fire Prevention Campaign" by The US Department of Agriculture. The 10 second, 20 second and 60 second tracks were also used as the soundtrack to an animated public service announcement airing on television at the time called "Smokey's A-B-C's". It is unknown as to whether Format was the animation studio responsible for the animation on the PSAs because Format Films was in limbo until 1966. It is possible that Era Productions, Inc. animated these spots as they also animated other Smokey Bear PSAs of this same vintage for the Ad Council.

As stated earlier, 1964 was the year that The Beatles hit America. Bagdasarian was so enamored by their success that he actually sought out and met with The Beatles and their manager Brian Epstein to get their approval to do a Chipmunks Beatles album. The Beatles agreed, but only if The Chipmunks did it straight, so there is very little humor and banter on the subsequent LP and EP release of *The Chipmunks Sing The Beatles Hits* in September. It must have worked as the album was the highest charting Chipmunks release in quite some time and the last charting record for the group, reaching #14.

Ross Jr. said in the *Still Squeaky* booklet, "In 1964, The Beatles eclipsed "The Chipmunk Song" for the fastest-selling song of all time. Figuring if you can't beat them, join them, pop visited The Beatles in London. With their blessing, he released *The Chipmunks Sing The Beatles Hits*. The album, like many Chipmunk albums that came before, sold millions of copies."

Bagdasarian said of the project in *The Daily Tribune* on September 9, 1964, "The one who suggested it was Nick Draklich, who runs Bagdasarian Enterprises for me. I told him he was nuts and to forget it, but he kept pressing me, and then the Liberty Record heads started in on me. No, no and no, I declared, the whole idea is ridiculous."

Bagdasarian then gave in and said, "Two things I insisted on, I wasn't going to poke fun at The Beatles - they are sacred to too many kids - and I wouldn't do the album without The Beatles permission. They gave it happily."

An online review said, "There are a number of old time Rock and Roll fans who think The Beatles ruined everything (usually citing *Sgt. Pepper* and the art-ification of rock). Well, I'm not going to take a position on that, but I will say that they kind of screwed up The Chipmunks. For the first time ever, the creativity and verve of Ross Bagdasarian is totally stifled. Of course, it's funny that The Chipmunks appear in Beatles wigs on the cover with Alvin holding a Beatles bass. For the most part, this is very much like the 80s Chipmunk revival where they just did straight covers of Michael Jackson and Cyndi Lauper songs with slick studio musicians, sped up vocals and no real jokes or banter. They don't even respect The Chipmunks continuity. On "Love Me Do", the harmonica solo is replaced with a melodica! Not surprising, considering Alvin is playing his harp backwards, with the wrong end in his mouth on the cover. The most spirited track may be "Twist and Shout", where David Seville makes a brief appearance (mixed low) to tell Alvin his wig is falling off, and where they actually improvise some vocal arrangements getting a little more soulful than The Beatles. The best part of that is the scaling up vocals at the end which climax with atonal shrill Chip-shrieks. Seville is actually becoming less involved, which I guess is a good metaphor for Baby Boomer generation gap development. Overall, the cover art is the whole joke, and this is the first uninspired Chipmunks LP."

For this album, Engineer Dave Hassinger won a 1964 Grammy for Best Engineered Recording - Special or Novel Effects. Studio Five again did the cover design.

One single was also released, "All My Loving" / "Do You Want to Know a Secret?" and reviewed online, "Harmless rote covers of The Beatles tunes with no Dave and no edge. Cute, but there is no Chipmunk flavor here. This might as well be The Chippers or Woody the Chipmunk."

On later pressings on the Sunset label and all reissues on vinyl, cassette and compact disc since, the opening guitar chord on the song "Do You Want to Know a Secret?" is partially cut off. This has led to speculation that damage may have occurred to the master tape on this song, but this has not been officially verified.

Overall, The Chipmunks perform the proceedings fairly straight. During the instrumental of "Twist and Shout", David Seville does tell Alvin that his wig is falling off, but other than that, it's faithful interpretations of early Beatles hits.

Starting with this album, there was far less direct Ross Bagdasarian involvement. In Stephen Cox's article "The Chipmunk Song" Turns 60: Secrets of a Holiday Novelty Smash", he reveals the secret singers behind this and the remaining Chipmunks album of the 1960s,

In every interview he ever gave, singer-songwriter Ross Bagdasarian took sole credit not only for his 1958 holiday hit "The Chipmunk Song (Christmas Don't Be Late)," but also for all the musical performances by the rodent trio - Alvin, Simon and Theodore - that came before his death in 1972. But as the high-pitched phenom exploded, spawning dozens of albums, a TV series and multiple films, the songwriter called in ringers - who've been silent until now about this quirky chapter in their careers.

"When albums like 1964's *The Chipmunks Sing the Beatles Hits* appeared, it became too much for Bagdasarian. He engaged session singers, though he never copped to the hired help.

"Speaking about the work for the first time, Ron Hicklin, 80 - a member of guy-group The Eligibles that took over the harmonizing on five albums, "With Ross and The Chipmunks, it would be maddening work," says Hicklin. "It was a long, involved process. We'd sing in slow motion for everything. It was one of the hardest things we had to do. What was a four-bar phrase for The Beatles became an eight-bar phrase. You'd run out of breath. The sheer work of doing it was remarkable." Stan Farber, 81, remembers fighting to restrict the vibrato that's intrinsic in a trained singer but wouldn't sound right the sped-up final track. "Vibrato would ruin the sound of it and if you did it, the words would come out like machine gun fire. You had to sing a very straight tone," Farber explains, adding "Ross was there and would supervise, but he had done his stuff alone. We didn't sing with him."

"The session singers were not assigned any particular character, he says, "because when it was completed, all the voices sounded about the same. It didn't matter. Basically, we came in and did our job because Ross got tired and he got old - and rich."

"These Eligibles harbor no regrets. "I didn't seek any celebrity," says Hicklin, now retired in Palm Springs. "I just wanted to do the best job I could in all of my work. I have fantastic memories from that period. I mean, one day I was working at Capitol Records and Frank Sinatra walked into the studio and approached me. He came up to me with some sheet music and said, 'Kid, how does this go?' Sinatra didn't read music. I had to sing it for him. He thanked me and left. How do you top that? I walked among kings."

This hits the nail on the head for many longtime Chipmunks fans as to why the post-Bagdasarian Chipmunks leaves everyone a little bit cold as they seldom have the bite or the humor of the original records or TV shows. These Beatles covers from Bagdasarian are the beginning of the end, as rote covers seem to be more the rule than the exception. The upshot of the *Beatles Hits* album is that it was the only Chipmunks album apart from the Christmas releases to remain perpetually in print and the first to be released onto CD in the 1980s.

Moving into 1965, The Chipmunks ditch The Beatles and release *The Chipmunks Sing With Children* and its accompanying single "Supercalifragilisticexpialidocious" / "Do-Re-Mi" in March. An online review states, "Here's my theory: Some people can't stand The Chipmunks high-pitched shtick, and some people can't stand to hear children singing. On top of that, show tunes like "Hello Dolly", hippy kiddie songs like "Puff (The Magic Dragon)" and songs that have had their definitive recording done and are in no need of Chipmunkization ("Que Sera Sera", "Tea For Two") and going to rub some people wrong. That's three strikes against you and that's likely why this record never seems to pop up used, meaning it's likely that hardly anyone bought it. While The Jimmy Joyce Singers are clearly not the all-time most annoying kids choir, and while Bagdasarian's liner notes indicate he was genuinely challenged and excited by this project, Alvin really doesn't need the competition and this isn't the soundest concept. Still, it's one of the weirder Chips LPs, and if you think of the kids as the equivalent of the theremin on "Good Vibrations", you can consider this The Chipmunks' *Smile*, a doomed masterpiece that's years ahead of its time (so many years it hasn't arrived yet, 'cause I still don't dig it.)

"Though sales figures are not available to me, I suspect the album (and this single) where The Chipmunks sang along with a real-live children's choir might have been their worst-selling, because I certainly almost never see used copies. Alvin, Simon, Theodore and the label must have loved these songs, though, because they appear again three years later on their movie tribute album. Of course, that was the album that buried their careers for over a decade."

The Jimmy Joyce Children's Chorus featured arrangements by Pete King. Their version of "Supercalifragilisticexpialidocious" was nominated for a Grammy for Best Recording for Children. The above review is a bit harsh as apart from the dubious choice of having The Chipmunks sing with a children's chorus, it is the temporary return of the loudmouth David Seville character, yelling at Alvin in many cases to keep him in line and not be overbearing. Even the chorus has to chime in sometimes to set Alvin straight.

The producer was Dan Blocker instead of Bagdasarian, the engineer was Bob Doherty, photography was by Robert Marchutz and the design by Studio Five.

As the cover notes state, Bagdasarian stated this about the project, "The making of this album has been a delightful experience for me. Unlike previous Chipmunks albums, a new dimension was added - that of children's voices - and I must say I was apprehensive. Where could a group of children be found that could sing like children and behave like adults during the complicated recording sessions? The answer turned out to be the wonderful group of kids on the cover with The Chipmunks - Jimmy Joyce Singers. My sincere thanks to Jimmy and and to all of his talented kids - to Pete King for the imaginative orchestrations - to Bob Doherty for his fine engineering work and to Dan Blocker for the great help he gave me in putting all of the elements together. To one and all I am grateful."

Author Stephen Cox adds, "On the photo on the back of *The Chipmunks Sing with Children* album, Ron Hicklin of The Eligibles is the younger guy next to Bagdasarian. The other two are technicians." These are the same singers who ghost sang on *The Beatles Hits* album, and would continue to do so for the remaining 1960s albums, and come back again for *Chipmunk Punk* and *Urban Chipmunk* in the 1980s.

In June 1965, Bagdasarian tried to release another stillborn effort under his own name with "Navel Maneuver" / "La Noche", plus a reissue of "Come On-a My House" / "Gotta Get To Your House" in October. All but "La Noche" appear on Bagdasarian's 1966 LP. "Navel" is an instrumental featuring middle eastern finger cymbals, guitar, sax and trumpet.

Also in 1965 was the debut of car designer George Barris' Alvin's Acorn car. Barris also designed the Munstermobile and went on to design perhaps his most famous creation, his version of the Batmobile for the 1966-1968 *Batman* TV series. According to an article in the *Pantagraph Sun* from October 15, 1967, the car was designed at the request of Bagdasarian with enough legroom to go hunting with his close friend, comedian Jonathan Winters.

The George Barris website describes the Alvin car: "Alvin Acorn's Safety Car (Alvin the Chipmunk). Styled for Ross Bagdasarian's famous cartoon character, Alvin the Chipmunk and his friends. This is the first vehicle to be adapted to a cartoon character. The primary purpose was to impress the importance of safety to the young, potential drivers.

"From the many design renderings and engineered drawings, this car has been created with many different innovations such as: four inch hand built chassis of oval frame construction, unitized on each end with U-bends and heliarc welds. A 289 cu. in. LED (Lowest Exposure to Danger) Ford engine which will tilt and absorb impact shock by hinging on he center transmission mount, was installed with multiple carburetors covered by a unique spun aluminum flared intake air cleaner, while the fuel supply is generated by Dual Dupree Electric Chrome Dome fuel pumps; the engine is coupled to a dash control lever automatic transmission, which carries the power to the rear wheels through the Ford Mustang rear end. The rear end is complete with fore and aft spring mountings, safety stabilizer bars and functional road coil-air shock levelers. For added handling safety the front undercarriage is equipped with air frame coils and adjustable torsion bars. The radiator is installed horizontally with dual electric fans to assist cooling at slow speed driving. Looped roll bars are mounted directly to the frame with fore and aft adapter bars, fully chrome plated, and acting as the frame for the front and rear dome. The single rear rumble seat, which is used by David Seville, who is the human companion of the Chipmunks and Alvin's back seat driver, is also housed by a complete chrome roll bar. The passenger-driver compartment is covered with fore and aft bubble windshield and rear glass, while the doors slide on ball bearing rollers between the center roll bars, moving up in gull wing fashion to provide easy entry and exit. Mounted directly between the upper roll bars is a closed circuit wide angle TV camera that is used as a rear view projector, viewed through the monitor installed on the dash panel. This eliminates the need of a rear view mirror, and provides for better observation to the rear and less distraction from driving. The wheels are of lightweight one piece alloy incorporating Airheart disc brakes with dual master cylinders front and rear. In addition the "Acorn" has been outfitted with a Dietz parachute for assistance in braking at high speeds, conserving dangerous radical wear to the brakes. Unique hydraulic bumpers are telescopic upon impact, absorbing the shock and eliminating a portion of the danger in the event of a slow speed accident. Upon impact force they cushion in then release hydraulically. The steering wheel is collapsible and the steering column energy absorbing upon impact, reducing the chance of chest or facial injury should a collision occur. The entire undercarriage is triple chrome (blue/white) plated as are the array of roll bars.

"Quad individual tire-form fenders made of aluminum house unique lighting systems. General Electric sequential directional lights are located on the ends of each fender. A complete attached road-warning system is mounted on each side of the body panels. This system is completely in association with the driver's intention, ie: the red is for tail-light, blue for deceleration, green for acceleration, yellow for slight braking and changing to bright red for full stop.

"For the exterior finish, the exposed frame is painted Acorn Amber metalflake in 40 coats of acrylic; while the Acorn center section is done in the matching Acorn Amber. The front and rear of the body has been finished in Chipmunk Yellow pure pearl of essence imported from Sweden. The center section is trimmed at the belt line with Acorn Gold fringe foam Masland Duran, coordinating the interior with same. Rock scatter shields are mounted on the ends of each fender and covered with matching vinyl, and the major portion of each is finished in Snowflake metal-flake pearl, which includes multicolors of white pastel blues and yellows.

"The overall value of Alvin's Acorn was $30,000 back in the late 60s when it was built. But there was a toy model available for all the fans."

In September 1965, the *Chipmunks à Go-Go* LP appeared. A special note about this and other Bagdasarian recordings: The instrumentation of many if not all of The Chipmunks and Seville recordings were done by Los Angeles' famous Wrecking Crew, who handled many of the musical backgrounds on such groups as The Beach Boys, The Monkees and Sonny and Cher among many, many others. The producer was Dave Pell, the engineer was Dave Hassinger and the cover design was by Edwin Francis. The briefest mention was alluded to at the beginning of the excellent 2015 documentary called *The Wrecking Crew!* which features a small snatch of "The Chipmunk Song". Interviews are included with Dick Clark and Snuff Garrett among others.

It has been mentioned before that Bagdasarian did not perform the vocals on this record, and a slowed-down listen courtesy of Chipmunks on 16 Speed on "Mr. Tambourine Man" and "This Diamond Ring" reveals that if Bagdasarian did sing on this album, it was with help as there are singers that are distinctly not Bagdasarian. It is possible that Bagdasarian's smoking habit prevented him from belting out lyrics like "What's New, Pussycat?" at this point in his career, or maybe he disliked these tunes.

In any case, it turns out that Bagdasarian recruited The Eligibles again for this album as revealed in Stephen Cox's "The Chipmunk Song Turns 60: Secrets of a Holiday Novelty Smash".

"Ron Hicklin remembers one nerve-racking day in August 1965. "One of my strongest memories was when we were recording at RCA on Ivar and Sunset in Hollywood," Hicklin says, "and we were inside doing The Chipmunks when the Watts riots were breaking out at the time. We'd heard there were snipers on top of the Knickerbocker Hotel shooting at people. When we finished the session, I was with Ross and he was walking nervously with his back to the wall on the outside of the building, looking everywhere to get to our cars, and Ross had a .45 handgun with a shoulder holster that he was licensed to carry. I remember laughing later how here we were inside recording Chipmunks and then going outside with Ross, who's packing a pistol."

"Hicklin likes to describe his unique professional niche as "a ghost singer." He and additional experienced singers who worked on the Chipmunks albums (including Stan Farber, Al Capps, Bob Zwirn, Buzz Cason and Gene Morford in different configurations) hopped from gig to gig supplying background vocals for albums, TV show themes, films and commercials at a breakneck pace. Their voices brought themes for classic TV shows from *Happy Days* and *The Monkees* to *The Jetsons* and *Batman*." The Eligibles even sang the revised *Gilligan's Island* theme for the series second and third seasons. Incidentally, Buzz Cason was also Snuff Garrett's assistant in 1962.

Perhaps because they didn't date as well as the other 10 tunes on this album, "Sunshine, Lollipops and Rainbows" and "The Race is On" were removed when this album was reissued to cash in on The Chipmunks resurgence in 1982. Early pressings of the original release called the song "Sunshine, Lollipops and Roses".

One online review said, "Remember the episode of *The Alvin Show* where The Chipmunks and David Seville appear on some *Bandstand*-type TV program to perform "The Yellow Rose of Texas", with Alvin wiggling his hips Elvis-style to the delight of the girls present? And square Seville totally trying too chill Alvin's shit ("Come on, you know we don't do that kind of music!") Well, by '65 the Chips were older and wiser and rocked while Seville wisely stayed in the background on his drum kit (see cover). Here, they play catch-up with their second all-rock album in a year (after The Beatles tribute, natch), with an album cover depicting the Chips and Seville rocking with go-go girls in the background. So, are they doing any abrasive garage-punk or wyld soul? No, the song selection is straight down the middle of the road: "What's New, Pussycat?", "Mrs. Brown, You've Got a Lovely Daughter", "This Diamond Ring", etc. There's a surprising cover of George Jones' "The Race is On", but that's probably because lounge singer Jack Jones had a version around this time. Dobie Gray's poppish "The In Crowd" is the closest the Chips come to soul music (could you see them doing "My Girl" or "Respect"? Maybe "Baby Love"...), while the nearest to rowdy rock we get is Dino, Desi & Billy's "I'm a Fool". "I'm Henry VIII, I Am" even has a better guitar solo than the original by Herman's Hermits. No "Louie Louie" or "Wipe Out". Even when they're trying to, they never really could master that kind of music."

"I'm Henry VIII, I Am" / "What's New, Pussycat?" was the single released from the album to no chart action. When the album reappeared during The Chipmunks resurgence in the early 1980s, it did so minus two tracks (as did *Christmas With The Chipmunks* and *The Chipmunks Sing The Beatles Hits*.)

Also in fall 1965, *The Alvin Show* ended its Saturday morning run on CBS and first entered syndication. It was also the first time the series aired in color. As a result, a new slew of *Alvin Show* and Chipmunks merchandise entered the marketplace during 1965 and 1966.

*Mindrot* said, "With the demise of *The Alvin Show* in 1966, the popularity of The Chipmunks began to decline. The heyday of

Chipmunk music was over and Chipmunk albums became ever more scarce in record stores, finally disappearing around 1969."

Carrying on into 1966, Bagdasarian made one more attempt to cash in on his own name with his final solo LP release *The Mixed-Up World of Ross Bagdasarian*, which collected some of the random single tracks that had been quietly released over the past three years, some dating back even further. Like the single tracks, they didn't chart, but all make for quite interesting listening. The album is long out of print and somewhat difficult to find. "Judy" became "The Prom" for this release and the version of "Come On-a My House" is a remake featuring a background chorus and a rock arrangement with brass.

Meanwhile, on March 6, 1966, older brother Richard Bagdasarian passed away at the age of 56.

The only 1966 Chipmunks release is probably their most bizarrest, but then you could say that about "Eefin' Alvin" or their 1968 team-up with Canned Heat as well. Apparently, Ike and Tina Turner were huge Chipmunks fans and in the days of audial and chemical experimentation, the idea of having The Chipmunks provide the backing vocals to one of their records proved irresistible. The resulting single was "Betcha Can't Kiss Me (Just One Time Baby)" / "Don't Lie To Me (You Know I Know)" on Innes Records. The Chipmunks only appear on the A-side. Later releases of the song mix The Chipmunks out and is probably for the best as The Chipmunks voices was a noble experiment, but adds nothing to the proceedings and in fact, kind of detract from the record. The track is also available on Ike and Tina's *So Fine* album from 1968, released on Phoenix Records through Atco/Atlantic.

*Cool and Strange Music* adds, "He longed to move on, though, and in 1967 decided to retire the famous animated trio and return to songwriting full time. Liberty had released a sort of "best of" LP in 1966, *The Mixed-Up World of Bagdasarian,* and a few singles would follow."

Mary Campbell in her entertainment news article, "Cosby Relives His Funny Childhood" from *The Kansas City Times* on August 20, 1966 said this about the album, "You might expect *The Mixed-Up World of Bagdasarian* to be comedy, but it's not. It's also not capable of being categorized at all - it's so diverse - but it's enjoyable."

By February 1967, Liberty Records was having financial difficulties again. Producer "Snuff" Garrett who had produced "Eefin' Alvin" asked Bagdasarian if he would be interested in being produced again at his new digs, thus becoming the one and only Chipmunks release on Paramount's Dot Records. It was an amusing send-up of Herb Alpert and the Tijuana Brass music with "Sorry About That, Herb" / "Apple Picker", but it too, failed to chart, despite large ads in *Billboard*. Promo copies are slightly easier to find than stock copies, but essentially this is probably the rarest Chipmunks release, even rarer than the cardboard greeting records or the Ike and Tina Turner record. Maybe on a par with the US Department of Agriculture record as far as rarity. "Apple Picker" sounds like a standard Bagdasarian solo tune of this time, perhaps a little more psychedelic than usual, until The Chipmunks chime in on the chorus.

Later on in October 1967, Bagdasarian again released a single under his own name and back on Liberty Records: "Red Wine" / "The Walking Birds of Carnaby". Both songs have never appeared on an album.

Meanwhile on December 16, 1967, Bagdasarian's daughter Carol made her professional acting debut and the first of five guest appearances on *Mannix* starring fellow Armenian actor and Bagdasarian friend, Mike Connors (1925-2017), whose real name is Krekor Ohanian, and was also born in Fresno, California. Carol's cousin and daughter of

William Saroyan, Lucy Saroyan also made an appearance on a 1971 episode. Connors was one of Bagdasarian's oldest friends being friends for over 25 years at this point and was crucial in getting Carol the part. Bagdasarian also has a small cameo on this episode and it turned out to be his final acting role portraying an Armenian merchant.

On December 19, 1967, 20th Century Fox released their highly-anticipated musical version of *Doctor Dolittle* starring Rex Harrison. The expectations were so high that many tie-in albums and toys and other memorabilia were licensed including *The Chipmunks See Doctor Dolittle*, released in January 1968. Unfortunately, the film was a colossal dud that almost bankrupted Fox and this tie-in album sank without a trace. One single with a picture sleeve ("My Friend the Doctor" / "Talk to the Animals") was released and also sank without a trace. This album was the first released on Liberty Records' new budget line, Sunset Records. Previous Chipmunks albums were re-released with a Sunset Records sticker affixed over the Liberty Records logo and sold at a lower price.

Here's an Internet review, "Note the title isn't *The Chipmunks SING Doctor Dolittle*, but rather *SEE Doctor Dolittle*. The narrative here is great, the Chips have just seen the movie and they are stoked! Understand that at the time, the pre-release hype on *Doctor Dolittle* had everyone ready for this big budget flick to have the impact *Star Wars* would a decade later. It didn't happen. But everyone committed to tie-ins before the film flopped. Thus, a lot of big names invested: The Chips, Sammy Davis Jr. and Bobby Darin rushed out LPs covering the songs from the film, and Dr. Seuss' imprint published a series of books. The movie ended up being a legendary financial disaster, but that doesn't mean quality stuff didn't come out of it.

"This LP likely tanked commercially, but it's a ton of fun! Dave takes the boys to the movie, but they beg to see it again. He then challenges them to take a *Doctor Dolittle* test, and if they pass, they can go again. Thus, they spend the LP joyously recounting the story and the cool parts of the movie, and of course, singing all the songs with David.

"As opposed to the pop cover LPs where Seville is a non-entity, this is all about the warm, loving relationship David and his kids have. Some of the lyrics are altered to be specific to Seville talking with The Chipmunks. There's not much bratty acting up here (though Alvin delights in squealing like a pig on the last note of Dr. D's theme). As a reward for their good behavior, and good singing, at the end Dave takes them back to the theater for another Pushmi-Pullyu fix. Note that the Chips are now on Liberty's budget imprint, Sunset, and indicator of their fading commercial appeal."

"Talk to the Animals" opens with Dave singing, and he's no Sammy. Then the Chips join in, curiously wishing they could talk to animals... yet they are animals! Perhaps the paradox is why Dave sings a bit more on this than he normally would.

"My Friend the Doctor" has Seville doing an Irish turn (he kept away from ethnic humor more than most novelty tunesmiths, but he'll dive into it occasionally), and he changes some lyrics to address talking to chipmunks specifically rather than animals in general."

Both sides are from *The Chipmunks See Doctor Dolittle*, the only original LP never to be officially released to CD. There are only eight tracks, but there is more dialogue between tracks on this album than on others. Bagdasarian returned as producer, the arranger was Pete King, the engineer was Bob Doherty and the cover illustration was by Phil DeLara (1914-1973) with art direction by Woody Woodward.

The Chipmunks kept soldiering on as Bagdasarian and The

Chipmunks made personal appearances throughout 1968 and 1969, but he also spent more and more time at his Fresno grape plantation and less time devoted to music. He bought a winery, Sierra Wine Corporation, that supplied product to Gallo and other brands.

In June 1968, he did release a few more singles released under his real name with "The Winds of Time" / "When I Look in Your Eyes" and unreleased "Yallah" / "Navel Maneuver". All slipped out with nary a trace. Little is known about the song "Yallah". "The Winds of Time" has some nice guitar and vocals and appears on Bagdasarian's final LP *A Summer Day's Delight*. "When I Look in Your Eyes" is a solo version sans Chipmunks from *Doctor Dolittle*.

*Cool and Strange Music* continues, "He also released a novelty single in June 1968 on Liberty using yet another two-person pseudonym: Bruce & Dutch. "The Song of Bruce & Dutch" / "I Remember Dillinger" featured Bagdasarian playing both parts of a screwball dialogue, with one character speaking in a lispy, stereotypical gay male voice and the other in a thick, cartoonish Chinese accent. The B-side was an instrumental. The heyday of novelty records was long past, and Bagdasarian's brand of so-called "serious" music was, by the late 1960s, beginning to sound a bit old-fashioned. Rock groups like The Beatles and The Doors had caught the ear of the young listeners, and great soul artists like Otis Redding, Aretha Franklin and Marvin Gaye were winning fans the world over. Bagdasarian's time had passed."

Apparently, Bagdasarian also thought so and on June 1, 1968 entered into an agreement that would have lasting repercussions into 2010. According to the agreement, "On July 1, 1968, Bagdasarian, in both his personal capacity and as the president of Monarch, entered into a written agreement to sell to Liberty master recordings encompassing 112 musical selections in exchange for a lump sum payment of $200,000. This 1968 agreement is at the center of the instant dispute.

"Monarch and Artist [Bagdasarian] hereby assign and grant to Liberty all rights of every kind, and the complete, exclusive, perpetual, unencumbered, unconditional and worldwide right, title and interest in and to said Monarch-Artist master recordings and all records and reproductions made therefrom together with such rights to use and control the same and the performances embodied thereon for the purposes of manufacture and distribution by Liberty and its licensees of reproductions or records which for the purposes of this agreement include discs, tapes or any other article or device now or subsequently known or developed, and for such other purposes as are set forth herein. Without limitation of the foregoing, Liberty and/or its subsidiaries, affiliates and licensees shall have the exclusive, perpetual, unlimited and complete right to make, manufacture, sell, license, distribute, advertise, exploit or otherwise use or control the use of or dispose of or deal in said master recordings, the matrices, mothers, stampers, duplicates, records or other copies or derivatives produced from said master recordings and the performances embodied thereon, and all or any part or parts thereof, edited, excerpted, altered or changed in any manner or by any means whatsoever—in connection with the manufacture and distribution of said reproductions or records throughout the world or any part thereof, under any label, trademark, trade name, or other identification, and by any means or method, upon such terms as it may desire, but Liberty at its option, may refrain from doing any of the aforementioned."

In short, Bagdasarian seemed to have apparently sold the complete rights to his music publishing company, Monarch Music, and the master recordings of his work to Liberty Records. Problem is,

Liberty Records and Bagdasarian are both no longer around and Capitol Records and Ross Jr. both became their respective successors. Ross Jr. had originally understood that he had no rights to the materials until 2007 when he realized his views were mistaken and the lawsuits began. The court ruled in favor of Capitol in 2009 and this may help to explain why virtually all of The Chipmunks albums done by Bagdasarian were released to CD in remastered form in 2008. It is assumed to help Capitol defray court costs.

Ross Jr. filed an appeal as disagreements still arose as to what Capitol actually has the rights to in regards to both the songs and their recordings. One thing is for sure, the master recording and song publishing for the song "Alvin For President" was and is still maintained by Ross Jr. for Bagdasarian Productions.

In the end, the judgment was reversed and some rights reverted back to Ross Jr. and Bagdasarian Productions on August 18, 2010.

Here are some edited highlights of the revised ruling, "While Capitol may have the right under the 1968 agreement to license the master recordings in connection with the manufacture and distribution of movie soundtracks, the right to license the recordings for use in the film itself belongs not to Capitol, but to Bagdasarian Productions.

"The 1967 recording agreement, in which Bagdasarian granted Liberty, Capitol's predecessor, possession of the physical master recordings and all copies of the master recordings for the duration of the recording contract, contains a similar reservation allowing Bagdasarian access to recordings in Liberty's possession.

"Monarch-Artist have not heretofore granted any right or license inconsistent with or which may impair and/or curtail any of the rights or licenses granted hereby, and Monarch-Artist will not grant, lease, license, sell or assign to any other person rights in or to said master recordings, nor will it itself suffer or suffer to be done any act, or acts, in derogation of the rights of Liberty hereunder.

"According to Capitol, the recitals of the 1993 agreement conclusively demonstrate that Capitol owns all the rights to the master recordings. As discussed, however, those recitals pertain only to the ownership of the master recordings and their use in connection with the manufacture and distribution of records, rights that are not disputed by Bagdasarian Productions."

Back to 1968, more time at the winery when Bagdasarian got a call to add vocals for a re-recording of "The Chipmunk Song". The new version was released in November 1968 just in time to stiff for the Christmas holidays. Many didn't realize it was actually Bagdasarian. providing the Chipmunk vocals, but he apparently agreed that 10 years later, The Chipmunks were ripe for parody.

Here's an online review: "The Chipmunk Song" / "Christmas Blues": "No one twisted Canned Heat's collective arms into doing this. It was actually their idea! During the 60s blues revival, LA's Canned Heat were one of the prominent names in the genre, right along with The Blues Project (from New York) and the Paul Butterfield Blues Band (Chicago). Unlike those other two bands, the Heat actually charted a few singles in the Top 40 ("Going Up the Country" is the best remembered). The band also had a broader sense of humor than the usual young blues unit. Singer Bob "The Bear" Hite had a diverse record collection as massive as he was. Seeing as how the Heat recorded for the same label as The Chipmunks (who hadn't had a new release for a while), Hite thought it would be a gas and a giggle to team up. This is one record where trying to describe it is like dancing about architecture, but I'll make an attempt: somehow The Chipmunks and Canned Heat find themselves booked in the same studio at the same time, arguing furiously. Hite interrupts The Chipmunks' original 1958 "Chipmunk Song" with his own band's patented boogies, and after some resistance form Alvin, the Chips finally cave into the beat. I never thought I'd hear the word "psychedelic" coming from a Chipmunk's mouth (the cartoon characters, not the actual forest creatures), but here it is. Hite made doubly sure that a copy worked its way to LA oldies DJ Art Laboe (owner of Original Sound, the label that virtually invented the oldies compilation), but airplay was not forthcoming. With all the soldiers not coming home from Vietnam, I guess there was precious little to laugh about that Christmas."

After being disassociated with official Chipmunks releases for years, this song finally made it onto one of the umpteenth *Christmas With The Chipmunks* CD in 2007, the ONLY Chipmunks Christmas CD that has all 25 original Chipmunks Christmas songs (including this one) on one disc.

On April 6, 1969, Dickran Bagdasarian, Bagdasarian's father, passed away at the age of 84, and as a result, Bagdasarian spent even more time at his winery and new record releases became even more sporadic. Despite the fact that Bagdasarian was only 50 years old, he and The Chipmunks were essentially retired, there was to be one more album and a few more singles and a few more public appearances, but everything was really winding down. *The Alvin Show* was still running and Liberty Records was still struggling.

A couple more solo singles saw release: "Jone - Cone - Phone" / "Spanish Pizza" in May and "You've Got Me on a Merry-Go-Round" / "You Better Open Your Eyes" in October. Both singles came out on Liberty's subsidiary label, Imperial. Only "You've Got Me on a Merry-Go-Round" made it onto an album; in this case *A Summer*

*Day's Delight*. The song is sung with chorus and calliope. "You Better Open Your Eyes" is an upbeat sax and piano song with vocals.

In September 1969, the final original Chipmunks album and single was released. *Chitty Chitty Bang Bang* was a children's musical comedy feature film released on December 18, 1968. The film was a flop, although not as big of flop as *Doctor Dolittle*, but Bagdasarian and Liberty Records were not going to hedge their bets on a complete album devoted entirely to the film, so the resulting album was called *The Chipmunks Go to the Movies* with a single release of "Chitty Chitty Bang Bang" / "Hushabye Mountain".

Here's the online review of both the single and the album: "Two playful, funny numbers from the Chips movie album. These aren't nearly as great as David Seville original songs (in which Bagdasarian's enthusiasm for the tune seemed to translate into funnier comedy and better Chipmunk singing, if you'd believe it), but you could tell that Ross appreciated kiddie showtunes more than Rock and Roll, so he is somewhat invested.

Both songs are from *The Chipmunks go to the Movies*, the final original Chipmunks album: "I really like this record because it makes me feel like David Seville really has fun with his kids, taking them to the movies and being a good friend. Mostly, it's the cover art that does this for me. They look the happiest they've ever been crossing the street to go to a big movie theater with searchlights and palm trees and the whole shebang. As they cross the street, Dave is holding their hands like a responsible parent (of course, Alvin is running wild. Dave only has two hands!). The songs are great, from *Oliver!*, *The Wizard of Oz*, *Chitty Chitty Bang Bang* and other family friendly flicks. Highlights include "Consider Yourself", "Supercalifragilisticexpialidocious" and "The Bear Necessities"."

The album featured two repeats: "Supercalifragilisticexpialidocious" and "Que Sera Sera" from *The Chipmunks Sing With Children* to help save on the budget. There is also only 10 tracks total in comparison to the typical 12 of most other Chipmunks albums. Bagdasarian was producer, the arranger was Pete King, the engineer was Dave Hassinger and the cover illustration was by Phil DeLara with art direction by Gabor Halmos.

1970 was a major turning point for both music and children's entertainment. The Beatles, The Monkees, and The Turtles all broke up, and Jerry Lewis, Don Knotts, and Warner Bros. Looney Tunes and Merrie Melodies stopped producing films. For a time, birth rates were declining and the dumping ground for animation was on Saturday morning TV, and Disney became the only place that long-time family-friendly character actors could seemingly get work.

Ross Jr. said in the *Still Squeaky* booklet, "After years of producing The Chipmunks, pop was ready for a change. The Chipmunks had sung with everyone from Canned Heat to Tina Turner. They had sold everything from Jell-O to Soaky dolls, hula hoops to musical plush. Their television show was currently playing in 80 countries around the world. Pop had done more with The Chipmunks than he had ever dreamed. Besides, he was impatient by nature. He gave 100% to whatever he did and then, having done it, moved on."

In May 1970, Liberty Records slipped out one final US Ross Bagdasarian release which as usual by this time, went nowhere: "I Treasure Thee" / "Lie-Lie". "I Treasure Thee" is much more modern sounding and upbeat than most Bagdasarian tunes. It has a late 60s funky sound with brass and violin and is strongly reminiscent of 1967's "Can't Take My Eyes Off You" by Frankie Valli of The Four

Seasons. "Lie-Lie" meanwhile, is upbeat as well, but has more of a Middle Eastern flavor as typical of other Bagdasarian tunes.

In frustration, Bagdasarian self-released his final album on his own Monarch Music label called *A Summer Day's Delight* in 1970; a very difficult album to find. The other new songs are unique to this album: "House of Romona", "Be a Star", "Holding You Now", "The Vineyard" and "The Girl in the Ocean" and seem to be Bagdasarian's final recordings.

The LP also features a new version of "Armen's Theme", now with vocals. "Holding You Now" sounds like the "Third Man Theme" with added vocals. "Holding You Now" / "Armen's Theme" became Bagdasarian's final single release in his lifetime, being released in March 1971 in the UK only on Philips Records.

Bagdasarian also made a rare, brief Broadway appearance in 1970 and daughter Carol continued her acting career on TV with appearances on *Ironside* and *Mannix* and in films like *The Strawberry Statement*.

Essentially retired to harvest his grapes in 1970 and 1971, Bagdasarian, a lifelong smoker, was found dead of a heart attack in Beverly Hills, California on Super Bowl Sunday on January 16, 1972, 11 days before his 53rd birthday. It was the Cowboys vs. Dolphins in Super Bowl VI. The Cowboys won 24-3. Bagadsarian's body was cremated at Chapel of the Pines Crematory in Los Angeles.

An *Alvin Show* vinyl lunchbox and Thermos.

Alvin's Christmas Cards promotion available through Nestle's Quik.

*Alvin Show* slide puzzle with images decidedly off model.

Alvin bubble gum and tattoos.

An *Alvin Show* marionette.

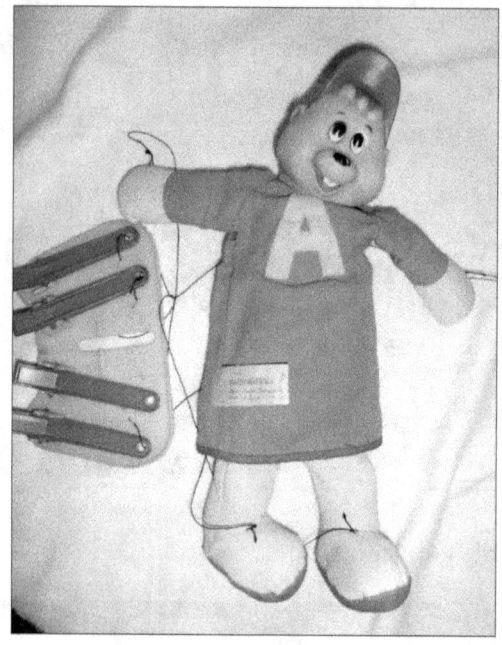

Chipmunks chalk.

Chipmunks balloons.

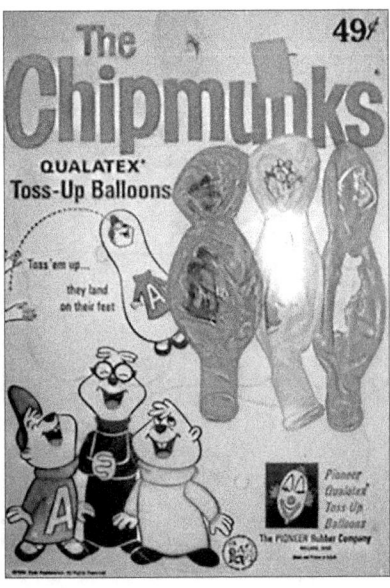

A Chipmunks card game with card samples.

*Cartoon Carnival* View-Master set featuring slide reels for *King Leonardo* and *Supercar*.

Two Chipmunks frame-tray puzzles.

Various Chipmunks-related coloring books.

Chipmunks blow-up dolls.

A Chipmunks Christmas stocking.

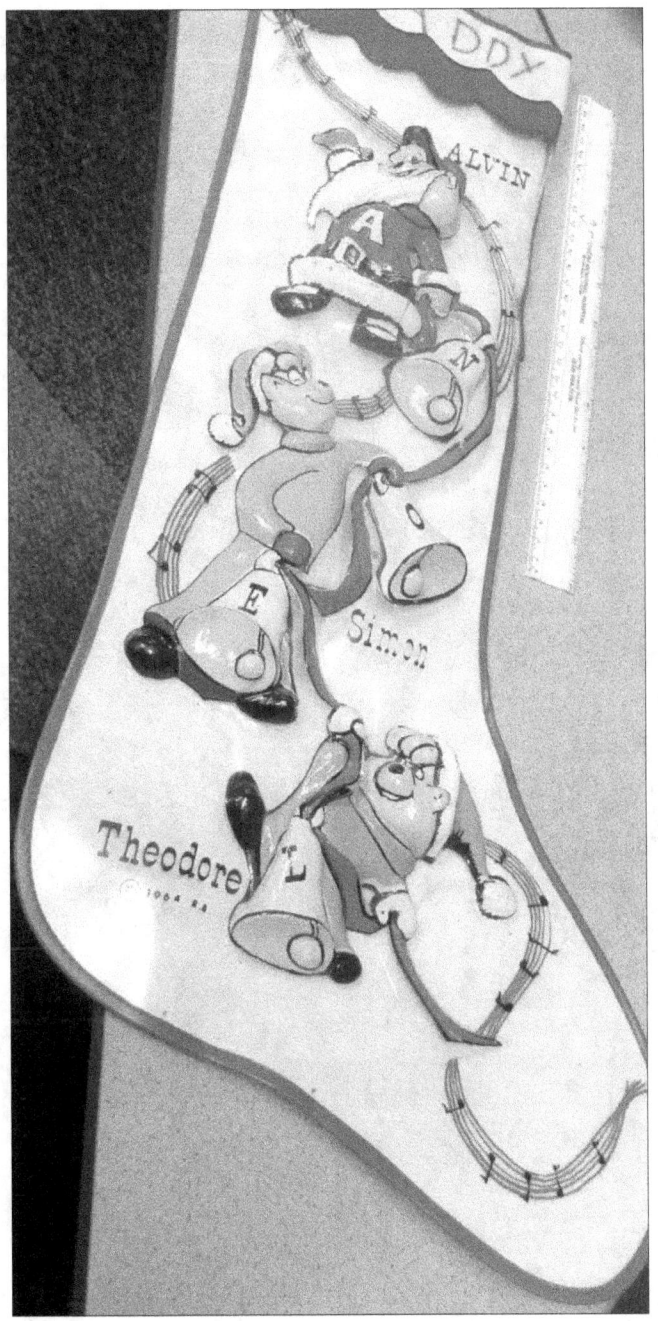

A Give-a-Show projector with Chipmunks slides.

The Chipmunks comic book photo gallery:

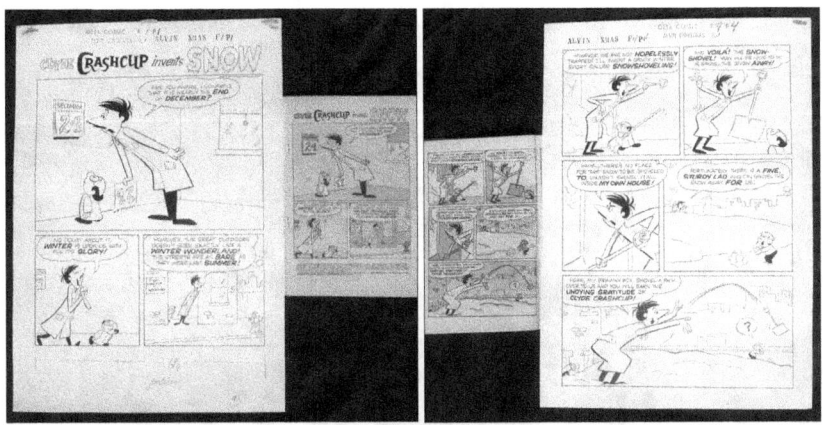

"The Alvin Twist" sheet music and buttons.

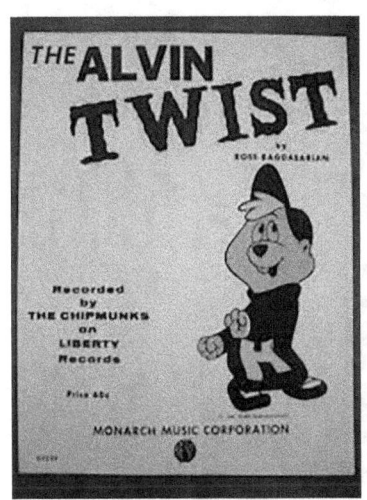

The fifth Chipmunks album, *The Chipmunks Songbook* (1962).

The sixth Chipmunks album, *Christmas With The Chipmunks* (1962).

Liberty Records, Format Films and *The Alvin Show*

"The All-Star Chipmunk Band" picture sleeve and print ad.

The seventh Chipmunks album, *Christmas With The Chipmunks, Volume 2* (1963), front and back covers, and promotional ad.

"Wonderful Day" picture sleeve.

The Chipmunks cardboard birthday, love and get well records.

The Chipmunks Soaky record and bottle toys.

The 1964 Smokey Bear PSA record label and a still from the PSA. This was not animated at Format Films and could possibly be Era Productions, Inc. as they did other animation for other Smokey Bear PSA's of this vintage.

The eighth Chipmunks album, *The Chipmunks Sing The Beatles Hits* (1964).

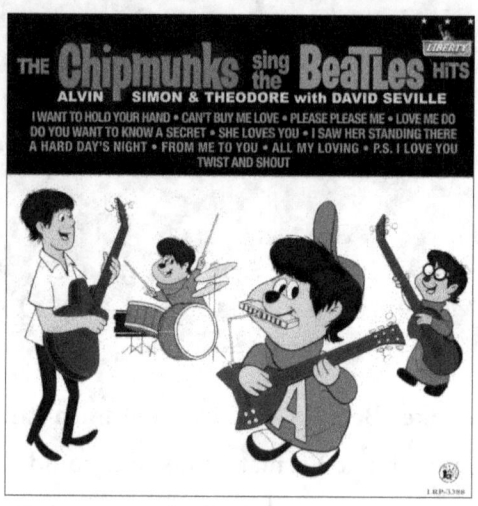

"Do You Want to Know a Secret" picture sleeve.

An article about *The Chipmunks Sing The Beatles Hits* from *The Daily Tribune*, September 9, 1964. The ghost singers who appeared on *The Chipmunks Sing The Beatles Hits* and later Chipmunks albums, better known as The Eligibles.

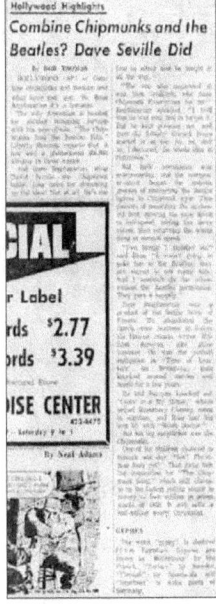
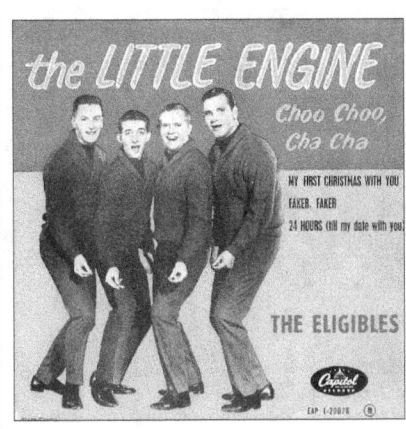

The Chipmunks appear at The Rose Parade, January 1, 1965.

The ninth Chipmunks album, *The Chipmunks Sing With Children* (1965), along with an ad from Billboard, February 27, 1965.

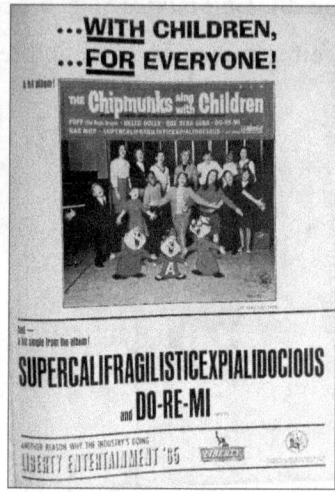

Alvin's Acorn, a 1965 car designed by George Barris, best known for his version of the Batmobile from TV's *Batman* (1966-1968), plus article from *The Pantagraph Su*n, October 15, 1967, about the car.

One of my favorite star cars wasn't a car after all—but rather a Jeep which Ross Bagdasarian (he's "daddy" of "The Chipmunks") asked me to redesign into a California-ranch hunting wagon with leg room enough, Ross joked, so that one of his hunting pals, comedian Jonathan Winters, could stretch out in comfort.

I suppose Ross could have asked Jonathan to tuck in his legs, but it seemed easier simply to stretch the Jeep, which I did, adding three feet to its length. Then I outfitted Ross' "BagBunny" for he-man hunting with a high-powered engine, four plush aircraft bucket seats, guns racks, bullet trays by each seat, and bright-as-day road lights for night hunting.

The tenth Chipmunks album, *Chipmunks à Go-Go* (1965).

A 1965 Chipmunks ad and an updated article about Bagdasarian from the *St. Louis Post Dispatch*, October 19, 1965. Strangely the article makes no reference that Bagdasarian does or does not perform on *Chipmunks à Go-Go*; instead it is just a standard history piece.

The *Ocean Blues* book and related merchandise from 1966. Phil DeLara did the artwork on these and on the upcoming *Doctor Dolittle* and *Go to the Movies* albums.

Bagdasarian in 1962 surrounded by the merchandise of his Chipmunks empire.

An article promoting Bagdasarian's second solo LP, *The Mixed-Up World of Bagdasarian* (1966) from the *Kansas City Times*, August 20, 1966, and the album cover.

The very rare "Sorry About That, Herb" Chipmunks 45 on Dot Records, with an ad claiming it is a best seller, and a brief article mentioning it from *The Chicago Tribune*, February 10, 1967.

An article promoting Bagdasarian's appearance on *Mannix, San Antonio Express,* October 8, 1967.

EXPRESS and NEWS Sunday, Oct. 8, 1967 PAGE 13

**No Chipmunk Role This Time**

NEW YORK — Ross Bagdasarian, famous for his "Chipmunks" songs, neither looks nor sounds like a chipmunk (or their friend David Seville, for that matter) when he plays a small role in an episode of "Mannix" this season.

Bagdasarian, a long-time friend of series star Mike Connors, plays an Armenian merchant.

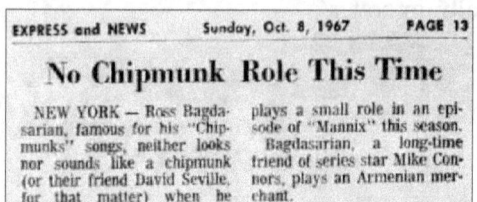

A Chipmunks album sale ad from *The Morning Call,* December 19, 1967.

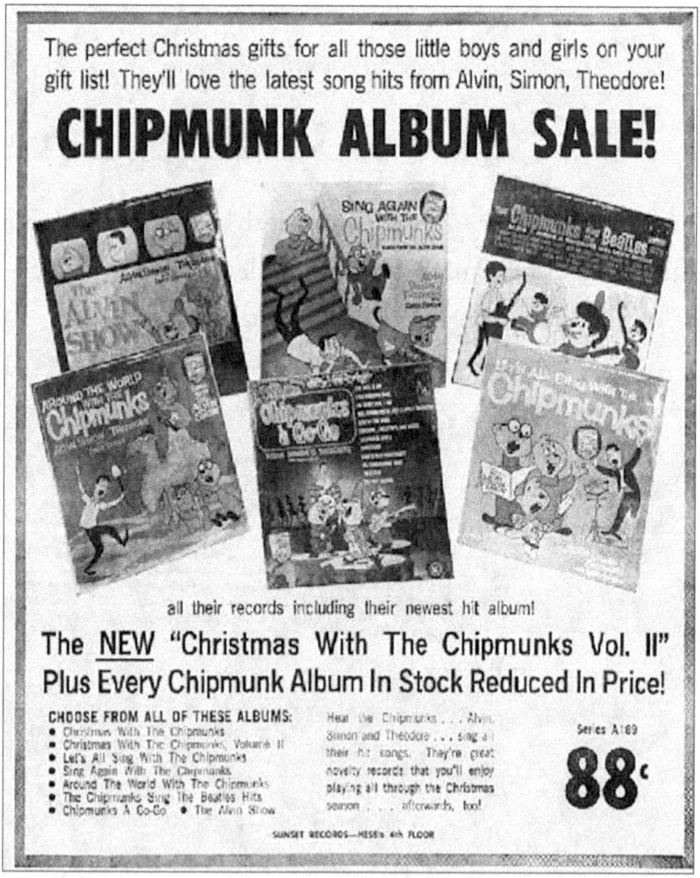

The eleventh Chipmunks album, *The Chipmunks See Doctor Dolittle* (1968), front and back covers.

"My Friend, the Doctor" picture sleeve.

A Chipmunks Christmas ad from *The Lebanon Daily News*, December 9, 1968.

French "Christmas Blues" picture sleeve.

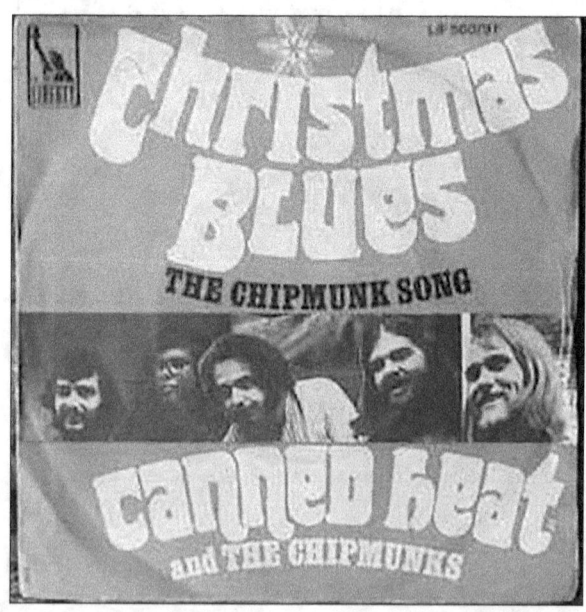

Liberty Records, Format Films and *The Alvin Show*

Obituary for Dick Bagdasarian, Ross' dad, from *The Fresno Bee Republican*, April 7, 1969.

The twelfth and final original Chipmunks album, *The Chipmunks Go to the Movies* (1969).

"Chitty Chitty Bang Bang" picture sleeve and ads.

Various ads promoting The Chipmunks in Person: *The El Paso Herald Post* from April 15, 1964 and March 2, 1966, *The Evening Review* from July 10, 1968, and *The Dominion News* from April 22, 1969 (same ad).

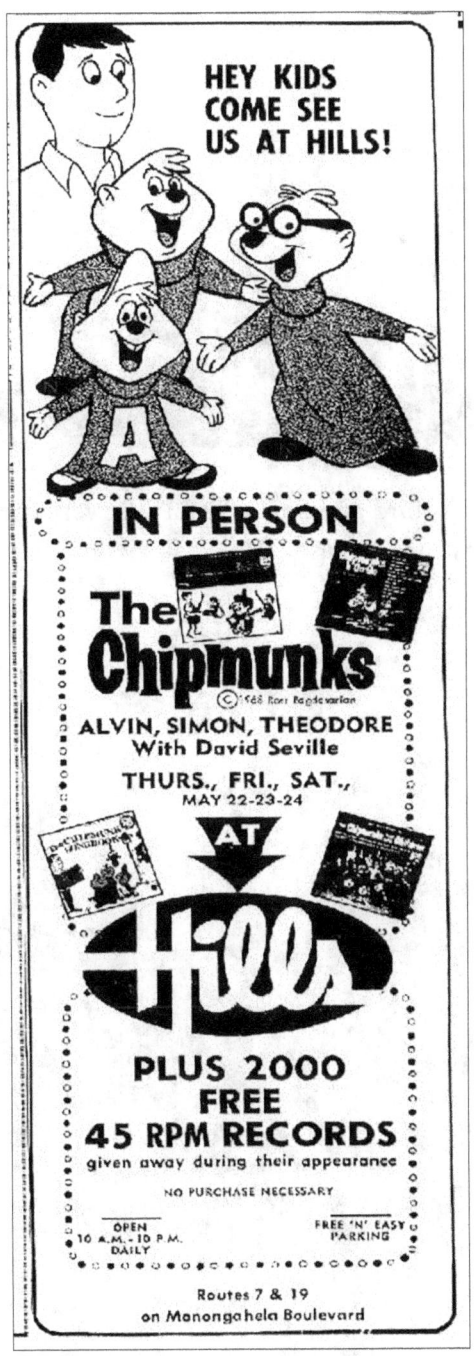

Bagdasarian promotional shots from the late 1960s and early 1970s.

Bagdasarian's third and final solo LP, the very difficult to find *A Summer Day's Delight* (1970).

Liberty Records, Format Films and *The Alvin Show*

The *Time of Your Life* revival from *The Colorado Springs Gazette Telegraph*, November 18, 1970 and an article promoting the acting careers of Carol Bagdasarian and Lucy Saroyan from *The Honolulu Star Bulletin*, January 24, 1971.

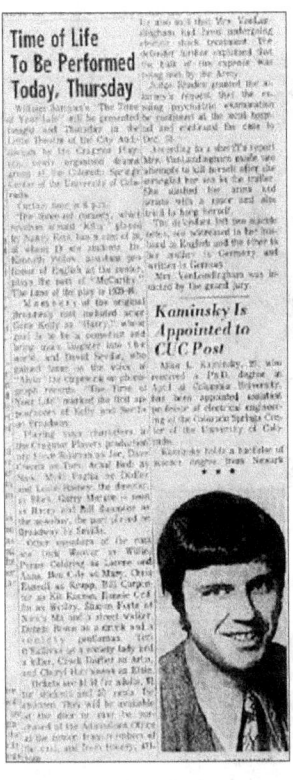

Various Bagdasarian obituaries from January 18, 1972: *The Indiana Gazette*, *The Los Angeles Times*, *The Odessa American*, *The Akron Beacon Journal*, *The Troy Record*, *The Wilmington News Journal*, and *The Courier Journal*, plus *The Evening Independent* from January 19, 1972.

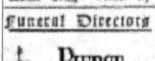

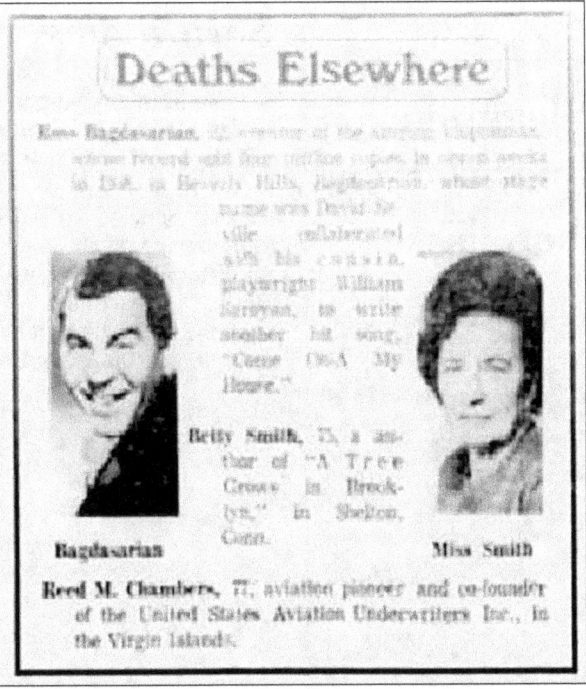

**Chipmunk Creator Dies**

BEVERLY HILLS, Calif. (AP) — Ross Bagdasarian, 52, creator of the singing chipmunks, whose record sold four million copies in seven weeks in 1958, died Sunday. Bagdasarian, whose stage name was David Seville, collaborated with his cousin, playwright William Saroyan, to write another hit song, "Come On-A My House."

*Other deaths*

## Bagdasarian, Chipmunk Song author, dies

© L.A. Times-Washington Post Service

BEVERLY HILLS, Calif. — Songwriter Ross S. Bagdasarian, 52, an Armenian who rocketed himself to fame and fortune when his 1958 recording of "The Chipmunk Song" sold four million copies in seven weeks, is dead.

Bagdasarian, who used the stage name David Seville, died Sunday at his home here. An autopsy will be performed to determine the cause of death.

At the time of death Bagdasarian was a composer and executive with Monarch Music Co.

At one time he was a poor raisin farmer and bit-part actor but became an overnight millionaire with the success of his creation of the three chipmunks — Alvin, Theodore and Simon — for whom he was also the voice.

The Chipmunks were used in "The Witch Doctor" and "Alvin's Harmonica," but their greatest success was in "The Chipmunk Song" that by 1961 had sold more than 12 million copies.

Bagdasarian was a first cousin to playwright William Saroyan, and they wrote "Come On-a-My House," which was made famous by singer Rosemary Clooney. It sold more than one million copies.

Yet for all his success Bagdasarian never learned to write songs, preferring instead to put his compositions on tape and then hiring somebody else to do the actual writing.

He is survived by his wife, Armen; sons, Adam and Ross Jr., and daughter, Carol.

*Other deaths:*

## Seville dies

BEVERLY HILL, Cal. (AP) — Ross Bagdasarian, 52, creator of the singing chipmunks, whose record sold four million copies in seven weeks in 1958, died Sunday. Bagdasarian, whose stage name was David Seville, collaborated with his cousin, playwright William Saroyan, to write another hit song, "Come On-A My House."

# CHIPMUNK PUNK AND BEYOND

After Bagdasarian's death, Ross Jr. took it upon himself to resurrect The Chipmunks. What was supposed to be a quick turnaround took eight years to come to fruition.

Ross Jr. said, "It really wasn't until he passed away in 1972 when I went up to his office and started listening to the albums and looking at the shows that I really became excited about The Chipmunks.

"I started in right away to revive The Chipmunks, but nobody else did. I went around to the record companies and networks and said, "Gee, The Chipmunks should be back out again. It's a wonderful idea," and they said, "No, that's ancient history. No one cares about it."

"We simply wanted to get the record company to re-release the albums he had made or get the network to play his old episodes. But unfortunately, we couldn't interest anyone because The Chipmunks had become passé at that point."

Ross Jr. also attended law school upon recommendation from his dad before he passed. It wasn't until after he passed that Ross Jr. realized that he needed to know the laws about creation, ownership and music publishing since he was handed this Chipmunks legacy. He passed the bar in 1975, but never officially practiced law. It has been stated that he put his energies into reviving The Chipmunks full time starting in 1977.

Ross Jr. said that first they went to CBS to talk to them about a revival since they had run *The Alvin Show*. They liked what his dad did, but again were greeted with a pass and that The Chipmunks were old news and that history had moved on. They had similar results with the music side of things.

Meanwhile, United Artists Records had acquired the Liberty Records catalog in 1972 and released a couple Chipmunks singles reissues in 1973: "The Chipmunk Song" / "Ragtime Cowboy Joe" and "Alvin's Harmonica" / "Rudolph the Red-Nosed Reindeer" and "The Chipmunk Song" / "Rudolph the Red-Nosed Reindeer" in 1974. "Witch Doctor" / "The Bird On My Head" by David Seville was also reissued in 1973.

Also in 1973, Dell Comics ceased publication on the long-running *Alvin* comic book series with issue #28, October 1973. The title had actually been in reprints since issue #20, October 1969.

In 1974, United Artists Records reissued *Christmas With The Chipmunks* as a two LP repackage of *Christmas With The Chipmunks* (1962) and *Christmas With The Chipmunks Vol. 2* (1963), the first album reissue since Bagdasarian's death in 1972.

Next in 1974, The Chipmunks resurfaced to perform on a 60-second Chipmunks radio commercial for Smokey Bear as they did 10 years earlier for the Ad Council. Since Bagdasarian was gone, voice actor John Erwin (1936-   ) (He-Man; Morris the Cat; Reggie Mantle on *The Archie Show*) stepped in to play the David Seville role. A slowed-down listen reveals that he also performed The Chipmunks as well, and he does and admirable job. The spot also appeared on an April 1975 promo record called "Thanks - 1975 Smokey Bear Radio" FP 475.

Also in 1975, *Christmas With The Chipmunks* was successfully reissued again as two separate albums on Mistletoe Records from Springboard Records, a budget line label.

In December 1976, just in time for the holidays, United Artists issued the first Chipmunks compilation called *The Very Best of The Chipmunks* which used three of the four Chipmunks tracks reissued on singles in 1973-74 and sporting the same cover image from *The Chipmunk Songbook*. It was later issued on CD in 1995 by Capitol Records.

*The Alvin Show* continued to air in syndication during the 1970s and actually made it back onto the NBC Saturday morning schedule (with Ross Jr.'s help) from March 10, 1979 to September 1, 1979. This same year Ross Jr. married Janice Karman.

All this activity was build up for The Chipmunks pending return with *Chipmunk Punk*, which was released to great fanfare on June 15, 1980, resurrecting the act that has continued in some form or another for almost 40 years.

The inspiration for *Chipmunk Punk* came when KMET DJ Chuck Taylor played the 12" version of the Blondie song "Call Me" at double speed and jokingly announced that it was the Chipmunks' latest single. So many requests came for this "new" Chipmunks release, that Ross Bagdasarian, Jr. and his collaborator Steve Vining rushed to record an album, issued on Excelsior Records.

*Chipmunk Punk* turned out to be the final project released as by Bagdasarian Enterprises, for in 1981, Ross Jr. officially changed the name and the logo from Bagdasarian Enterprises to Bagdasarian Productions.

Ross Jr. comments on *Dr. Demento* and other places about this lengthy return to the top for The Chipmunks, "It took Janice and me many years before we were able to interest anyone. Finally, in 1980 we made a new album that went platinum. We followed that up with The Chipmunks first Christmas special, which Janice and I wrote, produced, voiced and funded. Janice also redesigned the characters for that special. My dad's look was very stylized, which was the norm in the early 60s. But Janice didn't stop there, she further redesigned them for the TV series (1983-1991) when she also created, designed and voiced The Chipettes, then further redesigned them for the films and again, for our new series.

"But she also did much more. She expanded the personality of Theodore and Simon in major ways. My dad's show was a wonderful series that highlighted the relationship of Alvin and Dave. Theodore was basically someone who giggled and ate. Simon was mostly smart. Janice made both characters much more dimensional. Theodore became the baby of the family, innocent, honest, naive and sweet. Simon grew from just being smart, to having a quick wit and a person who stands up for his principals. She made these changes in our TV series in the 80s and in the movies, as well as our newest series.

"The fact is that no one has done more for Alvin and The Chipmunks over the past 37 years than Janice. She spends seven days a week working to make these shows as special as they can be. She not only designed the characters and the look of the new series, but calls out every color of every background, prop, costume, etc. She voices Theodore, Brittany, Jeanette, Kevin, Miss Smith, Miss Croner and others, and directs the rest of the voices as well as the show itself. She listens to every pre-mix and makes sure that every cue not only captures the emotion of the scene, but enhances it."

Animator Mark Kausler adds, "Janice should give a bit of credit to the late Toby Bluth and Corny Cole for re-designing the Chipmunks. Toby did a lot of work on the Chipettes."

After The Chipmunks resurrection on records with *Chipmunk Punk* (June 15, 1980) (*Billboard* #34) and *Urban Chipmunk* (1981) (*Billboard* #56), the Chipmunk characters returned to animation in a one-off special by Chuck Jones called *A Chipmunk Christmas* (1981) with a companion soundtrack album (*Billboard* #72). June Foray, who did voices for *The Alvin Show*, returned for this special to voice Mrs. Claus and Mrs. Waterford.

Meanwhile, Bagdasarian's cousin and co-writer of "Come On-a My House", William Saroyan (born August 31, 1908) passed away on May 18, 1981 at age 72.

This was followed by a new animated TV series called *Alvin and the Chipmunks* (later called *The Chipmunks* and *The Chipmunks Go to the Movies*) which ran from 1983-1991, originally by Ruby-Spears and later by DiC. The albums continued with *Chipmunk Rock* (1982) (*Billboard* #109), *The Chipmunks Go Hollywood* (1982) and *Songs From Our TV Shows* (1984).

The difference between the original Chipmunks and this updated incarnation is that David Seville (now voiced by Ross Jr.) became a much more soft-spoken and sympathetic character than Bagdasarian's version, which sometimes border-lined on psychotic and abusive towards Alvin. Bagdasarian also used to voice all of the three Chipmunks, while Ross Jr.'s wife and collaborator Janice Karman took on the voice of Theodore as well as The Chipettes, a new creation of Karman's that has appeared in every new Chipmunks project since.

Many follow-up animated TV specials followed including *I Love the Chipmunks Valentine Special* (1984), *A Chipmunk Reunion* (1985), *Rockin' Through the Decades* (1990), *Cartoon All-Stars to the Rescue* (1990; guest appearance), *Trick or Treason* (1994), *A Chipmunk Celebration* (1994) and *The Easter Chipmunk* (1995).

1987 saw the fully-animated Chipmunks feature film release, *A Chipmunk Adventure*, again with accompanying soundtrack album. More albums followed with *Solid Gold Chipmunks: 30th Anniversary*

*Collection* and *The Chipmunks and The Chipettes: Born to Rock* (both 1988), *Rockin' Through the Decades* (October 16, 1990) (based on the TV special) and *The Chipmunks Rock the House* (1991) as well as some direct-to-video animated films including *Alvin and the Chipmunks Meet Frankenstein* (1999), *Alvin and the Chipmunks Meet the Wolfman* (2000) and *Little Alvin and the Mini-Munks* (2003).

The namesake for Alvin, Al Bennett, passed away on March 15, 1989, at the age of 82.

Bagdasarian's widow, Armenouhi Kulhanjian (born November 13, 1927), and the mother of Ross Jr., Carol and Adam Bagdasarian, passed away on November 11, 1991, passing along the rights to The Chipmunks to the children.

1992 saw a return to form, chartwise, for The Chipmunks with the *Billboard* #21 placing *Chipmunks in Low Places* featuring The Chipmunks cover of "Achy Breaky Heart", a duet with Billy Ray Cyrus which charted on the *Billboard* country singles chart at #72.

In 1993, Ross Jr. and Janice bought out the rights to The Chipmunks from siblings Carol and Adam Bagdasarian. Adam Bagdasarian went on to become a published writer with books *Forgotten Fire* (2002) and *First French Kiss: And Other Traumas* (2005). Carol, meanwhile, had a few more acting roles, but has essentially retired from the profession.

From 1993-2007, Alvin and The Chipmunks continued on with many more new song albums including *The Chipmunks' 35th Birthday Party* (1993); *Here's Looking at Me!* (February 1, 1994); *School's Out for Summer* (cassette only) and *A Very Merry Chipmunk* (*Billboard* #147) (both 1994); *When You Wish Upon a Chipmunk* (October 31, 1995); *Club Chipmunk: The Dance Mixes* (October 8, 1996); *The A-Files: Alien Songs* (May 26, 1998); *Little Alvin and the Mini-Munks*

(2003). There were also repackages of the Ross, Sr. years during this period, which are detailed in the discographies in the back.

The namesake for Simon, Si Waronker, passed away on June 7, 2005, at the age of 90.

In 2007, Alvin returned in a big-screen adventure - this time in live-action. David Seville was portrayed by character actor Jason Lee (*My Name is Earl*). The film and the accompany soundtrack called *Alvin and the Chipmunks: Original Motion Picture Soundtrack* (November 20, 2007) restored The Chipmunks ongoing popularity in the movie theaters and on the album charts peaking at #5 on the *Billboard* charts.

The newfound chart success caused The Chipmunks to quickly release a non-soundtrack follow-up called *Undeniable* (November 4, 2008) which hit *Billboard* #78. The first film also begat an equally successful live-action sequel called *Alvin and the Chipmunks: The Squeakquel* in 2009. It's accompanying album *Alvin and the Chipmunks: The Squeakquel: Original Motion Picture Soundtrack* (December 1, 2009) charted at *Billboard* #6.

The success of the second live-action film paved the way for a third in 2011, with an accompanying album called *Alvin and the Chipmunks: Chipwrecked: Music from the Motion Picture* (November 15, 2011). This album peaked at *Billboard* #36.

A Christmas album called *Chipmunks Christmas* (October 9, 2012) charted at *Billboard* #111 featuring two newer and 16 older Christmas songs.

*We're the Chipmunks (Music From the TV Show)* (September 25, 2015) It was the soundtrack for the new CGI animated Chipmunks series called *ALVINNN!!! And the Chipmunks*, which debuted in the US on August 3, 2015 after an international debut on March 30,

2015. It is still in production as of this writing. The soundtrack CD from Target stores featured four extra tracks.

In 2015, the fourth live-action feature film came out with its accompanying soundtrack called *Alvin and the Chipmunks: The Road Chip: Original Motion Picture Soundtrack* (December 11, 2015) It charted on *Billboard* Soundtracks #9.

As fortune shines on the current live-action and CGI versions of Alvin and the Chipmunks, less emphasis is placed on the original Bagdasarian Chipmunks. Although all of the original albums have been released to CD (save for *The Chipmunks See Doctor Dolittle*), many of the stray singles songs have not. Also, only three full *Alvin Show* episodes have been officially released, causing many to seek out unauthorized bootlegs to complete their collections.

Ross Jr. and wife Janice Karman continue to run The Chipmunks empire, but now their adult children Vanessa and Michael are working with them and are poised to eventually take over at whatever time Ross Jr. and Janice choose to retire.

Time will tell as to whether Ross Jr. and Janice will have a complete change of heart and release more of Bagdasarian's Chipmunks and solo recording legacy and more episodes of *The Alvin Show*, but one thing is for sure, Alvin and the Chipmunks will continue to endure.

Ad promoting the re-release of "The Chipmunk Song" single and the *Christmas With The Chipmunks* album as a two-record set on United Artists Records in *Record World*, November 30, 1974.

The 1975 Smokey Bear record picture sleeve front and back and label featuring the John Erwin version of The Chipmunks. Erwin is best known as the voice of He-Man and Morris the Cat.

 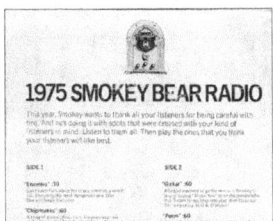 

1975 ad promoting the re-release of the two Chipmunk Christmas albums on Mistletoe Records from Springboard.

The first official Chipmunks compilation *The Very Best of The Chipmunks* (1976) from United Artists Records, successor to Liberty Records.

Article touting the Saturday morning return of *The Alvin Show* in *The Fort Lauderdale News*, March 31, 1979.

An updated history discussing the Bagdasarian heirs in *The Los Angeles Times*, April 10, 1980.

A four-page ad touting the return of The Chipmunks with *Chipmunk Punk* (1980).

One of many articles touting The Chipmunks comeback. This one from *The News Record*, August 10, 1982.

The old vs. new Chipmunks encounter.

Very rare "E.T. and Me" picture sleeve with artwork by Rick Detorie from 1982.

Ross Bagdasarian, Jr. and Janice Karman today.

The Very First Alvin Show was released onto DVD in 2009.

Later, it was re-released with two other Alvin Show episodes on DVD and Blu-Ray in 2015. Hopefully, the other 23 episodes will see release someday.

# POSTSCRIPT: TRIBUTES AND PARODIES

SIGNIFICANTLY, THERE HAVE BEEN many tributes to and parodies of The Chipmunks over the years, usually somewhat harsh and seemingly mean-spirited, but it all comes back to the love we have had for these characters since our youth. Here are some of the best:

Travesty Ltd. with their tracks "Rock Archives, Part One and Two" from the album *Teen Comedy Party* (1982). The comedy troupe, best known for the drug-related comedy track "Rock and Roll Doctor" does a fictional mini-documentary on what actually happened to The Chipmunks.

*Mighty Mouse: The New Adventures* (1987-1989) was a Saturday morning revival of the popular Terrytoons character from the 1940s by Ralph Bakshi (*Fritz the Cat, Lord of the Rings, American Pop*) and John Kricfalusi (*The Ren and Stimpy Show*). They come up with a set of familiar characters here named Elwee and the Tree Weasels with their hit song "Twitch and Writhe" in the episode called "Mighty's Benefit Plan". The David Seville character here is named Sandy Bottomfeeder.

Song parodist Bob Rivers performs "The Twisted Chipmunk Song" on his album *Chipmunks Roasting On An Open Fire* (2000). This one is an actual parody of "The Chipmunk Song" with much rougher lyrics.

Comedian Patton Oswalt skewers The Chipmunks on the track "My Christmas Memory" from his album *Feelin' Kinda Patton* (2004), where he discusses his happy childhood memories of listening to "The Chipmunk Song" and then slowing it down on the turntable so that The Chipmunks sound like some normal monotone guys singing this boring Christmas song being tormented by a demon from Hell screaming at them.

# DISCOGRAPHY:

(Ross Bagdasarian, Alfi & Harry, David Seville, The Chipmunks, The Bedbugs, Bruce & Dutch)

## ALBUMS:
1. *The Music of David Seville* - Liberty 3073 (1957)
2. *The Witch Doctor Presents David Seville...and his Friends* - Liberty 3092 (1958)
3. *Liberty Proudly Presents Stereo* - Liberty LST100 (June 1959) (two spoken bits)
4. *Let's All Sing With The Chipmunks* - Liberty 3132/7132 (1959) (*Billboard* #4)
5. *Sing Again With The Chipmunks* - Liberty 3159/7159 (1960) (*Billboard* #31)
6. *Around the World With The Chipmunks* - Liberty 3170/7170 (1961)
7. *The Alvin Show* - Liberty 3209/7209 (1961)
8. *The Chipmunk Songbook* - Liberty 3229/7229 (1962)
9. *Christmas With The Chipmunks* - Liberty 3256/7256 (1962) (*Billboard* #84)
10. *Christmas With The Chipmunks, Volume 2* - Liberty 3334/7334 (1963) (*Billboard* #9)
11. *The Chipmunks Sing The Beatles Hits* - Liberty 3388/7388 (1964) (*Billboard* #14)
12. *The Chipmunks Sing With Children* - Liberty 3405/7405 (1965)

13. *Chipmunks à Go-Go* - Liberty 3424/7424 (1965)
14. *The Mixed-Up World of Ross Bagdasarian* - Liberty 3451/7451 (1966)
15. *The Chipmunks See Doctor Dolittle* - Liberty/Sunset 5300 (1968)
16. *The Chipmunks Go to the Movies* - Liberty/Sunset 5312 (1969)
17. *A Summer Day's Delight* (Ross Bagdasarian) - Monarch Music RB 1-2 (1970)

## Posthumous Compilations:

1. *Christmas With The Chipmunks* - United Artists UA-LA352-E2 (2-LP repackage of *Christmas With The Chipmunks* and *Christmas With The Chipmunks Vol. 2*) (November 1974)
2. *Christmas With The Chipmunks* - Mistletoe (Springboard) MLP-1216 (1975)
3. *Christmas With The Chipmunks Volume 2* - Mistletoe (Springboard) MLP-1217 (1975)
4. *The Very Best of The Chipmunks* - United Artists UA-LA570-E (December 1976)
5. *Christmas With The Chipmunks* - Pickwick SPC-1034 (1980)
6. *The Twelve Days of Christmas With The Chipmunks* - Pickwick SPC-1035 (1980) (*Christmas With The Chipmunks, Volume 2* with new cover drawing.)
7. *Christmas With The Chipmunks* - Liberty LM-501071) (1982) (10-track version)
8. *The Chipmunks Sing The Beatles Hits* - Liberty LN-10177 (1982) (10-track version)
9. *Chipmunks à Go-Go* - Liberty LN-10178 (1982) (10-track version)
10. *20 All-Time Golden Greats* - EMI GO-2026 (1982) (UK only release)
11. *'Munk Rock* - EMI America (1985) (cassette only)
12. *Solid Gold Chipmunks-30th Anniversary Collection* - Buena Vista 62530 (1988) (one track only)

13. *The Chipmunks Greatest Hits* - Capitol/Curb Records (November 17, 1992)
14. *The Chipmunks 35th Birthday Party* - Chipmunk Records A24027 (1993) (three tracks only)
15. *The Chipmunks Sing Alongs* - Sony Wonder (May 4, 1993)
16. *Here's Looking at Me!* - Sony Wonder (February 1, 1994) (two tracks only)
17. *The Chipmunks Greatest Christmas Hits* - Capitol (September 14, 1999)
18. *Greatest Hits: Still Squeaky After All These Years* - Capitol 72435-21395-2-1 (September 21, 1999)
19. *Merry Christmas From The Chipmunks* - Capitol (September 16, 2003) (*Billboard* Kids Album #13)
20. *Christmas With The Chipmunks* - Capitol (September 12, 2006) (24-track version)
21. *Greatest Hits: Still Squeaky After All These Years* - Capitol (September 18, 2007) (expanded compilation from 1999 version)
22. *Christmas With The Chipmunks* - Capitol (2007) (complete 25-track version including the Canned Heat version of "The Chipmunk Song")
23. *Christmas With The Chipmunks* - Capitol (September 16, 2008) (20-track version) (*Billboard* #64)
24. *Christmas With The Chipmunks* - Capitol (August 30, 2010) (16-track version)
25. *Chipmunks Christmas* - Capitol (October 9, 2012) (*Billboard* #111) (16 of 18 tracks)
26. *The Music of David Seville* - Liberty Bell 23073 (January 29, 2013) (Italian bootleg)
27. *The Mixed-Up World of Ross Bagdasarian* - Liberty Bell 23074 (January 29, 2013) (Italian bootleg)

28. *All the Hits and Then Some* - Liberty Bell 23075 (January 29, 2013) (Italian bootleg)

## SINGLES:

1. Come On-a My House/Oh, Beauty (William Saroyan and Ross Bagdasarian/Ross Bagdasarian) - Coral 96054 (1951)
2. The Girl with the Tambourine/He Says 'Mm-Hmm' (Ross Bagdasarian) Coral 60597 (1951)
3. Let's Have a Merry, Merry Christmas/Hey Brother, Pour the Wine (Ross Bagdasarian) - Mercury 70254X45 (November 1953)
4. The Trouble With Harry/A Little Beauty (Alfi and Harry) - Liberty F-55008 (December 1955) (*Billboard* #44)
5. The Bold and the Brave/See a Teardrop Fall (Ross Bagdasarian) - Liberty F-55013 (1956)
6. Persian On Excursion/Word Game Song (Alfi and Harry) - Liberty F-55016 (April 1956)
7. Armen's Theme/Carousel in Rome (David Seville) - Liberty F55041 (November 1956) (*Billboard* #42)
8. The Donkey and the Schoolboy/The Gift (David Seville) - Liberty 55055 (February 1957)
9. Safari/Closing Time (Alfi and Harry) - Liberty F-55066 (May 1957)
10. Gotta Get To Your House/Camel Rock (David Seville) - Liberty F-55079 (June 1957) (*Billboard* #77)
11. Cecilia/Pretty Dark Eyes (David Seville) - Liberty F-55105 (September 1957)
12. Bagdad Express/Starlight, Starbright (David Seville) - Liberty F-55113 (November 1957)
13. Bonjour Tristesse/Dance From Bonjour Tristesse (David Seville) - Liberty F-55124 (February 1958)

14. Witch Doctor/Don't Whistle at Me Baby (David Seville) - Liberty F-55132 (March 1958) (*Billboard* #1)
15. The Bird On My Head/Hey There Moon (David Seville) - Liberty F-55140 (June 1958) (*Billboard* #34)
16. Little Brass Band/Take Five (David Seville) - Liberty F-55153 (August 1958) (*Billboard* #78)
17. The Mountain/Mr. Grape (David Seville) - Liberty F-55163 (October 1958)
18. The Chipmunk Song/Almost Good (The Chipmunks/David Seville) - Liberty F-55168 (November 17, 1958) (*Billboard* #1)
19. Alvin's Harmonica/Mediocre (The Chipmunks/David Seville) - Liberty F-55179 (February 20, 1959) (*Billboard* #3)
20. Judy/Maria From Madrid (David Seville) - Liberty F-55193 (April 1959) (*Billboard* #86)
21. Ragtime Cowboy Joe/Flip Side (The Chipmunks/David Seville) - Liberty F-55200 (June 1959) (*Billboard* #16)
22. Alvin's Orchestra/Copyright 1960 (The Chipmunks/David Seville) - Liberty F-55233 (January 1960) (*Billboard* #33)
23. Lotta Bull/???? (Ross Bagdasarian) - Liberty F-55239 (1960) (unreleased - b-side unknown)
24. Comin' Round The Mountain/Sing a Goofy Song (The Chipmunks) - Liberty F-55246 (April 1960)
25. The Chipmunk Song/Alvin's Harmonica (The Chipmunks) - Liberty F-55250 (April 1960) (*Billboard* #39/73)
26. Witch Doctor/Swanee River (The Chipmunks) - Liberty F-55272 (June 1960)
27. Lazy Lovers/One Finger Waltz (Ross Bagdasarian) - Liberty F-55275 (July 1960)
28. Alvin For President/Sack Time (The Chipmunks/David Seville) - Liberty F-55277 (August 1960) (*Billboard* #95)

29. Rudolph the Red-Nosed Reindeer/Spain (The Chipmunks) - Liberty F-55289 (December 1960) (*Billboard* #21)

30. Oh Judge, Your Honor, Dear Sir, Sweetheart/Freddy, Freddy (David Seville) - Liberty F-55314 (March 1961)

31. The Alvin Twist/I Wish I Could Speak French (The Chipmunks) - Liberty 55424 (February 1962) (*Billboard* #40)

32. America the Beautiful/My Wild Irish Rose (The Chipmunks) - Liberty 55452 (May 1962)

33. Armen's Theme/Russian Roulette (Dark Eyes) (Ross Bagdasarian) - Liberty 55462 (May 1962)

34. Witch Doctor/The Bird On My Head (David Seville) - Liberty 54520 (1963) (reissue)

35. Ragtime Cowboy Joe/Alvin's Orchestra (The Chipmunks) - Liberty 54521 (1963) (reissue)

36. The Chipmunk Song/Rudolph, the Red-Nosed Reindeer (The Chipmunks) - Liberty 55250/55289 (1963) (promo only)

37. Alvin's All Star Chipmunk Band/Old MacDonald Cha Cha Cha (The Chipmunks) - Liberty 55544 (1963)

38. Gotta Get To Your House/Cecilia (Ross Bagdasarian) - Liberty 55557 (February 1963)

39. Lucy, Lucy/Scalawags and Sinners (Ross Bagdasarian) - Liberty 55619 (September 1963)

40. Eefin' Alvin/Flip Side (The Chipmunks/David Seville) - Liberty 55632 (October 1963)

41. Wonderful Day/The Night Before Christmas (The Chipmunks) - Liberty 55635 (October 1963)

42. Yeah, Yeah/Lucy, Lucy (The Bedbugs) - Liberty 55679 (February 29, 1964)

43. Well, Happy Birthday Anyway (The Chipmunks) - Columbia Record Productions 50B9031 (1964)

44. Happy Birthday (The Chipmunks) - Columbia Record Productions 50B9032 (1964) (donkey)

45. Happy Birthday (The Chipmunks) - Columbia Record Productions 50B9033 (1964) (singing)

46. Because I Love You (The Chipmunks) - Columbia Record Productions 50B9040 (1964)

47. It Sure is Rough Being Sick (The Chipmunks) - Columbia Record Productions 50B9044 (1964)

48. Soaky the Fun Bath Sends Greetings from The Chipmunks - Columbia Record Productions (1964)

49. All My Loving/Do You Want to Know a Secret (The Chipmunks) - Liberty 55734 (October 1964)

50. Supercalifragilisticexpialidocious/Do-Re-Mi (The Chipmunks) - Liberty 55773 (March 1965)

51. Navel Maneuver/La Noche (Ross Bagdasarian) - Liberty 55810 (June 1965)

52. I'm Henry VIII, I Am/What's New, Pussycat? (The Chipmunks) - Liberty 55832 (September 1965)

53. Come On-a My House (remake)/Gotta Get To Your House (Ross Bagdasarian) - Liberty 55837 (October 1965)

54. Betcha Can't Kiss Me (Just One Time Baby)/Don't Lie To Me (You Know I Know) (Ike & Tina Turner (with The Chipmunks)/Ike & Tina Turner) - Innes 6666 (1966)

55. Sorry About That, Herb/Apple Picker (The Chipmunks) - Dot 16997 (February 1967)

56. Red Wine/The Walking Birds of Carnaby (Ross Bagdasarian) - Liberty 56004 (October 1967)

57. My Friend the Doctor/Talk to the Animals (The Chipmunks) - Sunset 61002 (January 1968)

58. The Song of Bruce & Dutch/I Remember Dillinger (Bruce & Dutch) - Liberty 56041 (June 1968)

59. Yallah/Navel Maneuver (Ross Bagdasarian) - Liberty 56043 (June 1968) (unreleased)

60. The Winds of Time/When I Look in Your Eyes (Ross Bagdasarian) - Liberty 56048 (June 1968)

61. The Christmas Blues/The Chipmunk Song (Canned Heat/The Chipmunks with Canned Heat) - Liberty 56079 (November 1968)

62. Jone - Cone - Phone/Spanish Pizza (Ross Bagdasarian) - Imperial 66379 (May 1969)

63. Chitty Chitty Bang Bang/Hushabye Mountain (The Chipmunks) - Sunset 61003 (September 1969)

64. You've Got Me on a Merry-Go-Round/You Better Open Your Eyes (Ross Bagdasarian) - Imperial 66414 (October 1969)

65. I Treasure Thee/Lie-Lie (Ross Bagdasarian) - Liberty 56165 (May 1970)

66. Holding You Now/Armen's Theme (remake) - Phillips 6006 096 (March 1971) (UK only release)

## Posthumous Singles:

1. The Chipmunk Song/Ragtime Cowboy Joe - United Artists XW056 (1973)

2. Alvin's Harmonica/Rudolph the Red-Nosed Reindeer - United Artists XW057 (1973)

3. Witch Doctor/The Bird On My Head (David Seville) - United Artists XW063 (1973)

4. The Chipmunk Song/Rudolph the Red-Nosed Reindeer - United Artists XW576-X (1974)

5. Alvin For President (1983) (one-sided soundsheet)

6. The Chipmunk Song/Frosty the Snowman - Capitol S7-17645 (1993)

7. The Chipmunk Song/Rudolph the Red-Nosed Reindeer - Collectables COL6197

## EPs:

1. *Kismet* (Ross Bagdasarian) - Mercury EP-1-3160 (1954) (two tracks only)
2. *Witch Doctor* (David Seville) - Liberty LSX-1003 (1958)
3. *Let's All Sing With The Chipmunks* - Liberty LSX-1007 (1960)
4. *Sing Again With The Chipmunks* - Liberty LSX-1008 (1961)
5. *The Chipmunk Songbook* - Liberty LSX-1015 (April 1962)
6. *Christmas With The Chipmunks* - Liberty LSX-1016 (1962)
7. *Christmas With The Chipmunks, Volume 2* - Liberty LSX-1017 (1963)
8. *Cooperative Forest Fire Prevention Campaign* (The Chipmunks) US Dept. of Agriculture Platter-20 (1964) (two tracks only)
9. *The Chipmunks Sing The Beatles Hits* - LIberty LSX-7388 (September 1964)

## Songs:

(WS = William Saroyan; RB = Ross Bagdasarian, Sr.; AH = Alfi and Harry; DS = David Seville; TC = The Chipmunks; TB = The Bedbugs; IT = Ike and Tina Turner; BD = Bruce and Dutch; CH = Canned Heat)

### 1934
Nuts to You

### 1951
Come On-a My House (WS and RB)
Oh, Beauty (RB)
The Girl with the Tambourine (RB)

### 1953
He Says 'Mm-Hmm' (RB)
What's the Use (RB)
Dot's Nice, Don'-a Fight (RB)

Y-y-y-yup (RB)
Shepherd Boy (RB)
Let's Have a Merry, Merry Christmas (RB)
Hey Brother, Pour the Wine (RB)

**1954**
Not Since Nineveh (RB)
Zubbediya (RB)

**1955**
The Trouble With Harry (AH)
A Little Beauty (AH)

**1956**
The Bold and the Brave (RB)
See a Teardrop Fall (RB)
Persian On Excursion (AH)
Word Game Song (AH)
Armen's Theme (DS)
Carousel in Rome (DS)

**1957**
The Donkey and the Schoolboy (DS)
The Gift (DS)
Safari (AH)
Closing Time (AH)
Gotta Get To Your House (DS)
Camel Rock (DS)
Cecilia (DS)
Pretty Dark Eyes (DS)
Bagdad Express (DS)
Starlight, Starbright (DS)

Amapola (DS)
Third Man Theme (DS)
Willow Weep For Me (DS)
Goofus (DS)

**1958**
Bonjour Tristesse (DS)
Dance From Bonjour Tristesse (DS)
Witch Doctor (DS)
Don't Whistle at Me Baby (DS)
The Bird On My Head (DS)
Hey There Moon (DS)
Little Brass Band (DS)
Take Five (DS)
Dinah (DS)
I Can't Give You Anything But Love (DS)
The Mountain (DS)
Mr. Grape (DS)
The Chipmunk Song (TC)
Almost Good (DS)

**1959**
Alvin's Harmonica (TC)
Mediocre (DS)
Judy (DS)
Maria From Madrid (DS)
Ragtime Cowboy Joe (TC)
Flip Side (DS)
Yankee Doodle (TC)
Chipmunk Fun (TC)
The Little Dog (TC)
Old MacDonald Cha Cha Cha (TC)

Three Blind-(Folded) Mice (TC)
Good Morning Song (TC)
Whistle While You Work (TC)
If You Love Me (Alouette) (TC)
Pop Goes the Weasel (TC)

**1960**
Alvin's Orchestra (TC)
Copyright 1960 (DS)
Lotta Bull (RB)
Comin' Round The Mountain (TC)
Sing a Goofy Song (TC)
Witch Doctor (Chipmunk Version) (TC)
Swanee River (TC)
Sing Again With The Chipmunks (TC)
Home On the Range (TC)
I Wish I Had a Horse (TC)
When Johnny Comes Marching Home (TC)
Swing Low Sweet Chariot (TC)
Working On the Railroad (TC)
Row Your Boat (TC)
Lazy Lovers (RB)
One Finger Waltz (RB)
Alvin For President (TC)
Sack Time (DS)
Rudolph the Red-Nosed Reindeer (TC)
Spain (TC)

**1961**
The Brave Chipmunks (TC)
Japanese Banana (TC)
I Wish I Could Speak French (TC)

Stuck in Arabia (TC)
August Dear (TC)
The Pidgin English Hula (TC)
Oh Gondaliero (TC)
Comin' Through the Rye (TC)
The Magic Mountain (TC)
Lily of Laguna (TC)
Oh Judge, Your Honor, Dear Sir, Sweetheart (DS)
Freddy, Freddy (DS)
The Alvin Show Theme (TC)
Mrs. Frumpington's Song (TC)
Crashcup's Work Theme - One Finger Waltz (TC)
What's for Dessert? Jell-O Song (TC)
Start Your Day a Little Bit Better Post Jingle (TC)
Jeanie with the Light Brown Hair (TC)
Clementine (TC)

**1962**
The Alvin Twist (TC)
America the Beautiful (TC)
My Wild Irish Rose (TC)
The Band Played On (TC)
Buffalo Gals (TC)
Funiculi, Funicula (TC)
Down in the Valley (TC)
Get Along Little Dogies (TC)
Twinkle, Twinkle, Little Star (TC)
On Top of Old Smokey (TC)
The Man On the Flying Trapeze (TC)
While Strolling Through the Park One Day (TC)
Polly Wolly Doodle (TC)
Bicycle Built For Two (TC)

Russian Roulette (Dark Eyes) (RB)
Here Comes Santa Claus (Right Down Santa Claus Lane) (TC)
Up On the House Top (TC)
Silver Bells (TC)
Jingle Bells (TC)
Over the River and Through the Woods (TC)
Santa Claus is Coming to Town (TC)
It's Beginning to Look a Lot Like Christmas (TC)
Frosty the Snowman (TC)
White Christmas (TC)
We Wish You a Merry Christmas (TC)

**1963**
Alvin's All Star Chipmunk Band (TC)
Lucy, Lucy (RB)
Scalawags and Sinners (RB)
Eefin' Alvin (TC)
Wonderful Day (TC)
The Night Before Christmas (TC)
Jingle Bell Rock (TC)
Deck the Halls (TC)
The Twelve Days of Christmas (TC)
Hang Up Your Stockin' (TC)
Have Yourself a Merry Little Christmas (TC)
Jolly Old Saint Nicholas (TC)
Christmas Time (Greensleeves) (TC)
All I Want For Christmas (is My Two Front Teeth) (TC)
O Christmas Tree (O Tannenbaum) (TC)
Here We Come a-Caroling (TC)

**1964**
Yeah, Yeah (TB)
Lucy, Lucy (TB)
Well, Happy Birthday Anyway (TC)
Happy Birthday (donkey) (TC)
Happy Birthday (singing) (TC)
Because I Love You (TC)
It Sure is Rough Being Sick (TC)
Soaky the Fun Bath Sends Greetings from The Chipmunks (TC)
Smokey's A-B-C's (TC)
All My Loving (TC)
Do You Want to Know a Secret (TC)
She Loves You (TC)
From Me to You (TC)
Love Me Do (TC)
Twist and Shout (TC)
A Hard Day's Night (TC)
P.S. I Love You (TC)
I Saw Her Standing There (TC)
Can't Buy Me Love (TC)
Please Please Me (TC)
I Want to Hold Your Hand (TC)

**1965**
Supercalifragilisticexpialidocious (TC)
Do-Re-Mi (TC)
Rag Mop (TC)
Me Too (Ho-Ho! Ha-Ha!) (TC)
Mister Sandman (TC)
Hello Dolly (TC)
Puff (the Magic Dragon) (TC)
Tonight You Belong to Me (TC)

Tea For Two (TC)
Que Sera Sera (TC)
Mississippi Mud (TC)
Down By the Old Mill Stream (TC)
Navel Maneuver (RB)
La Noche (RB)
I'm Henry VIII, I Am (TC)
What's New, Pussycat? (TC)
This Diamond Ring (TC)
Mr. Tambourine Man (TC)
Mrs. Brown You've Got a Lovely Daughter (TC)
I'm a Fool (TC)
Sunshine, Lollipops and Rainbows (TC)
The Race is On (TC)
King of the Road (TC)
Downtown (TC)
California Girls (TC)
The 'In' Crowd (TC)

**1966**
Betcha Can't Kiss Me (Just One Time Baby) (IT and TC)
The Prom (same as "Judy") (RB)
Come On-a My House (RB)

**1967**
Sorry About That, Herb (TC)
Apple Picker (TC)
Red Wine (RB)
The Walking Birds of Carnaby (RB)

## 1968
My Friend the Doctor (TC)
Talk to the Animals (TC)
Doctor Dolittle (TC)
When I Look in Your Eyes (TC)
Fabulous Places (TC)
I've Never Seen Anything Like it (TC)
Beautiful Things (TC)
The Song of Bruce & Dutch (BD)
I Remember Dillinger (BD)
Yallah (RB)
The Winds of Time (RB)
When I Look in Your Eyes (solo version) (RB)
Chitty Chitty Bang Bang (TC)
Hushabye Mountain (TC)
The Chipmunk Song (Canned Heat version) (CH and TC)

## 1969
We're Off to See the Wizard (The Wonderful Wizard of Oz) (TC)
The Bare Necessities (TC)
Chim Chim Cher-ee (TC)
Consider Yourself (TC)
You Two (TC)
The Roses of Success (TC)
Jone - Cone - Phone (RB)
Spanish Pizza (RB)
You've Got Me on a Merry-Go-Round (RB)
You Better Open Your Eyes (RB)

## 1970
I Treasure Thee (RB)
Lie-Lie (RB)

Armen's Theme (vocal version) (RB)
House of Romona (RB)
Be a Star (RB)
Holding You Now (RB)
The Vineyard (RB)
The Girl in the Ocean (RB)

## FILMOGRAPHY:

1. *The Greatest Show on Earth* (January 10, 1952) as Spectator (uncredited)
2. *Viva Zapata!* (February 7, 1952) as Officer (uncredited)
3. *The Stars Are Singing* (March 11, 1953) as Song Promoter (uncredited)
4. *Destination Gobi* (March 20, 1953) as Paul Sabatello
5. *The Girls of Pleasure Island* (April 1, 1953) as Marine (uncredited)
6. *Stalag 17* (July 1, 1953) as Singing Prisoner of War (uncredited)
7. *Alaska Seas* (January 27, 1954) as Joe, Jim's crewman
8. *Rear Window* (September 1, 1954) as The Songwriter
9. *The Ray Milland Show: Be Bop* (February 10, 1955) as Leroy Garrison
10. *The Pepsi-Cola Playhouse: The Boy With the Beautiful Mother* (May 29, 1955) as Father
11. *Big Town: The Big Fight* (June 20, 1955)
12. *Kismet* (December 23, 1955) as Fevvol (uncredited)
13. *Hot Blood* (March 1956) as Gas Station Attendant (uncredited)
14. *The Proud and Profane* (June 13, 1956) as Louie
15. *Three Violent People* (February 9, 1957) as Asuncion Ortega
16. *Heinz Studio 57: Explosion* (March 25, 1957)
17. *The Devil's Hairpin* (October 4, 1957) as Tani Ritter
18. *The Deep Six* (January 15, 1958) as Private Aaron Slobodjian
19. *The Ed Sullivan Show* (May 4, 1958)

20. *The Dick Clark Saturday Night Beech-Nut Show* (July 12, 1958)
21. *The Ed Sullivan Show* (December 21, 1958)
22. *The Dick Clark Saturday Night Beech-Nut Show* (January 3, 1959)
23. *The Ed Sullivan Show* (March 8, 1959)
24. *This is Your Life: Dick Clark* (June 24, 1959)
25. *Sunday Showcase: The First Annual Grammy Awards* (November 29, 1959)
26. *The Ed Sullivan Show* (December 13, 1959)
27. *The Ed Sullivan Show* (April 17, 1960)
28. *The Ed Sullivan Show* (September 25, 1960)
29. *CBS Fall Preview Special: Seven Wonderful Nights* (Fall 1961)
30. *The Alvin Show* (10/4/61-3/28/62) as Alvin, Simon, Theodore, Dave Seville, Sam Valiant
31. *The Tonight Show Starring Johnny Carson* (March 6, 1963)
32. *Mannix* (December 16, 1967) as Armenian merchant

## *The Alvin Show* Episodes:

| # | The Chipmunks | Musical Segment 1 | Clyde Crashcup | Musical Segment 2 |
|---|---|---|---|---|
| 1 1. | Stanley The Eagle 2. 10/4/61 | Oh Gondaliero 3.c. | Invents Baseball 4. | I Wish I Could Speak French 17.c.d. |
| 2 5. | Sam Valiant, Private Nose 6. 10/11/61 | August Dear 7.c. | Invents the Bathtub 8.d. | Alvin's Orchestra 18.b. |

| # | The Chipmunks | Musical Segment 1 | Clyde Crashcup | Musical Segment 2 |
|---|---|---|---|---|
| 3 9. | Squares 2.d. 10/18/61 | Swanee River 10.b. | Invents the Wife 11. | The Magic Mountain 17.c. |
| 4 12. | Ostrich 6. 10/25/61 | The Brave Chipmunks 13.c. | Invents the Baby 4. | Yankee Doodle Dandy 18.a. |
| 5 5. | Good Neighbor 2. 11/1/61 | The Little Dog 3.a. | Invents Electricity 8. | Old MacDonald (Cha Cha Cha) 17.a. |
| 6 14. | Fancy 6. 11/8/61 | Japanese Banana 7.c. | Invents Music 11. | When Johnny Comes Marching Home 18.b. |
| 7 9. | Alvin's Alter Ego 2. 11/15/61 | The Pidgin English Hula. 13.c | Invents the West 4. | Chipmunk Fun 17.a.d. |
| 8 5. | Sam Valiant, Real Estate 6. 11/22/61 | Working on the Railroad 10.b. | Invents the Stove 11. | Stuck in Arabia 18.c. |
| 9 14. | Camping Trip 6. 11/29/61 | Good Morning Song 15.a. | Invents Jokes 11. | I Wish I Had a Horse 17.b. |

| # | The Chipmunks | Musical Segment 1 | Clyde Crashcup | Musical Segment 2 |
|---|---|---|---|---|
| 10<br>9. | Overworked Alvin<br>2.<br>12/6/61 | Witch Doctor<br>7.b. | Invents Flight<br>4. | The Chipmunk Song<br>18.a. |
| 11<br>16. | Dude Ranch<br>2.<br>12/13/61 | Home on the Range<br>10.b. | Invents First Aid<br>11. | Alvin For President<br>17.f. |
| 12<br>1. | Jungle Rhythm<br>6.<br>12/20/61 | Lily of Laguna<br>7.c. | Invents Egypt<br>11. | Row Row Row Your Boat<br>18.b. |
| 13<br>9. | Bentley Van Rolls<br>2.<br>12/27/61 | Swing Low Sweet Chariot<br>13.b. | Invents Self-Preservation<br>4. | Comin' Thru the Rye<br>17.c. |
| 14<br>12. | Good Manners<br>6.<br>1/3/62 | Bicycle Built for Two<br>7.e. | Invents Physical Fitness<br>4. | Ragtime Cowboy Joe<br>18.a. |
| 15<br>5. | Little League<br>6.<br>1/10/62 | Buffalo Gals<br>10.e. | Invents the Chair<br>4. | While Strolling in the Park One Day<br>17.e. |
| 16<br>14. | Hillbilly Son<br>2.<br>1/17/62 | Spain<br>15.c. | Invents the Bed<br>11. | Pop Goes the Weasel<br>18.a. |
| 17<br>5. | Alvin's Cruise<br>6.<br>1/24/62 | Alvin's Harmonica<br>3.a. | Invents the Telephone<br>4. | If You Love Me (Alouette)<br>17.a. |

| # | The Chipmunks | Musical Segment 1 | Clyde Crashcup | Musical Segment 2 |
|---|---|---|---|---|
| 18<br>1. | Lovesick Dave<br>2.<br>1/31/62 | Coming 'Round the Mountain<br>7.b. | Invents the Time Machine<br>8. | Three Blind-Folded Mice<br>18. a. |
| 19<br>16. | Eagle In Love<br>6.<br>2/7/62 | Sing a Goofy Song<br>13.b. | Invents Do it Yourself<br>4. | Twinkle Twinkle Little Star<br>17.e. |
| 20<br>14. | Theodore's Dog<br>2.<br>2/14/62 | Clementine<br>3. (new) | Invents the Shoe<br>11. | Maria from Madrid<br>18.f. |
| 21<br>9. | Haunted House<br>2.<br>2/21/62 | Whistle While You Work<br>10.a. | Invents Glass<br>8. | My Wild Irish Rose<br>17.e. |
| 22<br>5. | Alvin's Studio<br>6.<br>2/28/62 | Jeanie with the Light Brown Hair<br>15.(new) | This is Your Life, Clyde Crashcup!<br>11. | The Band Played On<br>18.e. |
| 23<br>1. | The Whistler<br>2.<br>3/7/62 | The Alvin Twist<br>13.e. | Invents the Boat<br>4. | The Man on the Flying Trapeze<br>17.e. |
| 24<br>16. | Sir Alvin<br>6.<br>3/14/62 | Git Along Little Doggies<br>3.e. | Invents Crashcupland<br>8. | Down in the Valley<br>18.e. |
| 25<br>14. | Disc Jockey<br>2.<br>3/21/62 | Funiculi, Funicula<br>7.e. | Invents Birthdays<br>11. | Polly Wolly Doodle<br>17.e. |

| # | The Chipmunks | Musical Segment 1 | Clyde Crashcup | Musical Segment 2 |
|---|---|---|---|---|
| 26<br>9. | Eagle Music<br>10.<br>3/28/62 | On Top of Old Smokey<br>15.e. | Invents Self-Defense<br>8. | America the Beautiful<br>17.e. |

### Bumpers Legend:

1. Fortune Teller
2. Chalkboard
3. Archery
4. Clyde Intro by Alvin: Great Inventor
5. Balloons
6. Shadow Puppets
7. Car Crash
8. Clyde Intro: Message in Bottle
9. Dishes
10. Cowboys
11. Clyde Intro: Surgery TV
12. Wrecking Ball
13. TV Station Doors
14. Bull in China Shoppe
15. Submarine
16. Janitor
17. Outro: Clyde - Running Out of Time
18. Outro: Camera Crash

## Album Legend:
    a. *Let's All Sing With The Chipmunks*
    b. *Sing Again With The Chipmunks*
    c. *Around the World With The Chipmunks*
    d. *The Alvin Show*
    e. *The Chipmunks Songbook*
    f. single only

## Commercials:
1. Jell-A sponsor tag opening
2. Jell-A sponsor tag closing
3. Jell-O: What's for Dessert? Jell-O song
4. Jell-O: Seville's ode to Jell-O
5. Jell-O: Jell-O recipes
6. Post Treat-Pak sponsor tags at open and close
7. Post: Start Your Day a Little Bit Better
8. Post Alpha-Bits and Treat-Pak: Little Red Riding Hood
9. Post Sugar Crisp: Neighbor
10. Smokey Bear A-B-C's (not on *The Alvin Show*) (1964)
11. Soaky Toys (not on *The Alvin Show*) (1965)

## Animated Characters from *The Alvin Show*:
- Bentley Van Rolls III
- Billy Brown
- Chuck Wagon
- Clyde Crashcup
- Daisy Belle
- Dragon
- JP Lester
- Leonardo
- Miss Fancy

- Mrs. Frumpington
- Pictorial Crashcup
- R. B. Huston
- Reese
- Roger Marsell
- Sam Valiant
- Stanley the Eagle

## END CREDITS FROM *THE ALVIN SHOW*:

Produced by Format Films Inc.

Executive Producer: Herbert Klynn (and Alvin)

Associate Producer: Leo Salkin

Art Director: Jules Engel

Production Executive: Bud Getzler

Direction: Osmond Evans, Rudy Larriva, Alan Zaslove, Gil Turner, Hal Ambro

Story: Leo Salkin, Cal Howard, Bob Kurtz, Ed Nofziger, Dale Hale, Jan Strejan, Al Bertino, Jack Cosgriff, Bill Danch, Chris Jenkyns, Dick Kinney, Tedd Pierce

Animation: Ed Friedman, Bob Goe, Fred Grable, Chuck Harriton, Leroy Cross, Chuck Downs, Frank Braxton, Ken Hultgren, Stan Wilkins, Amby Paliwoda, Ruth Kissane, Ruben Apodaca, Dorris Collins, Jim Fletcher, Roy Abel, Hank Smith

Production Design: Sam Weiss, Vern Jorgensen, Ernie Nordli, Dale Barnhart, Cullen Houghtaling, Raymond Jacobs, Ray Aragon

Background: Rosemary O'Connor, Bob McIntosh, Boris Gorelick, Ervin Kaplan

Supervising Editor: Joe Siracusa

Voices: Ross Bagdasarian, Shepard Menken, June Foray, Bill Lee, Johnny Mann, Lee Patrick

Musical Director; Johnny Mann

Music: Ross Bagdasarian (and Alvin)

Production Manager: Ray Thursby

Production Associate: Nick Draklich

Ink and Paint: Vera McKinney

Checking: Paul Marron

Camera: Jack Eckes

Sound Engineers: Marne Fallis, Ted Keep

Recording: Glen Glenn Sound

A Presentation of Bagdasarian Film Corporation

CBS Television Network

## FORMAT PRODUCTIONS LOONEY TUNES:

1. Run, Run, Sweet Road Runner (8/21/65, with DePatie-Freleng Enterprises)
2. Tired and Feathered (9/18/65, with DePatie-Freleng Enterprises)
3. Boulder Wham! (10/9/65, with DePatie-Freleng Enterprises)
4. Just Plane Beep (10/30/65, with DePatie-Freleng Enterprises)
5. Hairied and Hurried (11/13/65, with DePatie-Freleng Enterprises)
6. Highway Runnery (12/11/65, with DePatie-Freleng Enterprises)
7. Chaser on the Rocks (12/25/65, with DePatie-Freleng Enterprises)
8. Shot and Bothered (1/8/66, with DePatie-Freleng Enterprises)
9. Out and Out Rout (1/29/66, with DePatie-Freleng Enterprises)
10. The Solid Tin Coyote (2/19/66, with DePatie-Freleng Enterprises)

11. Clippety Clobbered (3/12/66, with DePatie-Freleng Enterprises)
12. Quacker Tracker (4/29/67) (Transitional cartoon to Warner Bros.-7 Arts Animation)
13. The Music Mice-Tro (5/27/67) (Transitional cartoon to Warner Bros.-7 Arts Animation)
14. The Spy Swatter (6/24/67) (Transitional cartoon to Warner Bros.-7 Arts Animation)

## *THE LONE RANGER EPISODES:*

1. The Trickster / The Crack of Doom / The Human Dynamo (9/10/66)
2. Ghost Riders / Wrath of the Sun God / Day of the Dragon (9/17/66)
3. The Secret Army of General X / The Cat People / Night of the Vampire (9/24/66)
4. Bear Claw / The Hunter and the Hunted / Mephisto (10/1/66)
5. Revenge of the Mole / The Frog People / Terror in Toyland (10/8/66)
6. Black Mask of Revenge / The Sacrifice / Puppetmaster (10/15/66)
7. Valley of the Dead / Forest of Death / The Fly (10/22/66)
8. A Time to Die / Ghost Tribe of Commanche Flat / Attack of the Lilliputians (10/29/66)
9. Circus of Death / The Brave / Cult of the Black Widow (11/5/66)
10. El Conquistador / Snow Creature / The Prairie Pirate (11/12/66)
11. Man of Silver / Nightmare in Whispering Pine / Sabotage (11/19/66)
12. Mastermind / The Lost Tribe of Golden Giants / Monster of Scavenger Crossing (1/7/67)
13. The Black Panther / Thomas the Great / Island of the Black Widow (1/14/67)
14. Paddle Wheeling Pirates / A Day at Death's Head Pass / The Mad, Mad, Mad, Mad Scientist (9/9/67)
15. The Kid / Stone Hawk / Sky Raiders (9/16/67)

16. The Man From Pinkerton / Tonto and the Devil Spirits / The Deadly Glassman (9/23/67)
17. Black Knight / Taka / Fire Rain (9/30/67)
18. The Secret of Warlock / Wolfmaster / Death Hunt (10/7/67)
19. Terrible Tiny Tom / Fire Monster / The Iron Giant (10/14/67)
20. Town Tamers, Inc. / Curse of the Devil Doll / It Came From Below (10/21/67)
21. Black Arrow / The Rainmaker / Flight of the Hawk (10/28/67)
22. The Avenger / Battle at Barnaby's Bend / Puppetmaster's Revenge (11/4/67)
23. Reign of the Queen Bee / Kingdom of Terror / Quicksilver (11/11/67)
24. The Legend of Cherokee Smith / The Day the West Stood Still / Border Rats (11/18/67)
25. Lash and the Arrow / Spectre of Death / Mr. Happy (1/6/68)
26. Mr. Midas / Unknown / Unknown (1/13/68)

## FORMAT TV SERIES TITLES, SHORTS AND MOVIE TITLES:

1. *The Outlaws* (1960-1962)
2. *Icarus Montgolfier Wright* (1962) (Best Animated Short Film Academy Award nominee)
3. *I Spy* (1965-1968)
4. *Honey West* (1965-1966)
5. *The Glory Guys* (1965)
6. *Clambake* (1967)
7. *The Mothers-in-Law* (1967–1969)
8. *Hee Haw* (1969-1997)
9. *Curiosity Shop* (1971-1973)
10. *The Duck Factory* (1984)

# Musicians and singers appearing on Chipmunks and other Bagdasarian records:

## THE WRECKING CREW:

The Wrecking Crew was a group of Los Angeles-based session musicians who appeared as the backing band for hundreds of hit records by such individuals and groups as The Beach Boys, Sonny and Cher, The Turtles, The Mamas and the Papas, Herb Alpert, Jan and Dean, Dean Martin, The Righteous Brothers, Gary Lewis, Petula Clark, Ike and Tina Turner, Simon and Garfunkel, Frank Sinatra, The Monkees, Neil Diamond, The Carpenters, The Fifth Dimension, and of course, Ross Bagdasarian. A documentary about the group was made in 2008 and released to home video in 2015.

- Bill Aken - guitar
- Doug Bartenfeld - guitar
- Vinnie Bell - guitar
- Max Bennett - electric guitar, electric bass
- Chuck Berghofer - upright bass
- Hal Blaine - drums
- Jimmy Bond - upright bass
- Salvatore "Sonny" Bono - percussion
- Bud Brisbois - trumpet
- Dennis Budimer - guitar
- Allan Buetler - saxophone
- Larry Bunker - percussion
- James Burton - guitar
- Red Callender - upright bass, electric bass
- Glen Campbell - guitar
- Frank Capp - percussion

Al Casey - guitar
Roy Caton - trumpet
Gene Cipriano - saxophone
John Clauder - drums
David Cohen - guitar
Jerry Cole - guitar
Gary L. Coleman - percussion
Al De Lory - keyboards
Mike Deasy - guitar
Steve Douglas - saxophone
Gene Estes - percussion
Victor Feldman - percussion
Chuck Findley - trumpet
John Goldthwaite - guitar
Jim Gordon - drums
Bill Green - saxophone
René Hall - guitar
Ron Hicklin Singers - backup singers (see below)
Milt Holland - percussion
Jim Horn - saxophone, flute
Richard "Slyde" Hyde - trombone
Plas Johnson - saxophone
Carol Kaye - guitar, electric guitar, electric bass
Jackie Kelson - saxophone
Jim Keltner - drums
Barney Kessel - guitar
Larry Knechtel - electric guitar, electric bass, keyboards
John Lowe - saxophone
Lew McCreary - trombone

Mike Melvoin - keyboards

Jay Migliori - saxophone

Ollie Mitchell - trumpet

Tommy Morgan - harmonica ("Alvin's Harmonica"!)

Lou Morrell - guitar

Dick Nash - trombone

Jack Nitzsche - conductor, arranger

Joe Osborn - electric guitar, electric bass

Earl Palmer - drums

Don Peake - guitar

Bill Pitman - guitar, electric guitar, electric bass

Ray Pohlman - guitar, electric guitar, electric bass

Joe Porcaro - percussion, drums

Don Randi - keyboards

Malcolm Rebennack (Dr. John) - keyboards, guitar

Michel Rubini - keyboards

Lyle Ritz - upright bass

Howard Roberts - guitar

Irv Rubins - guitar

Leon Russell - keyboards

Louie Shelton - guitar

P. F. Sloan - guitar

Billy Strange - guitar

Tommy Tedesco - guitar

Nino Tempo - saxophone

Tony Terran - trumpet

Al Vescove - guitar

Julius Wechter - percussion

Bob West - electric bass

**ABNUCEALS EMUUKHA ELECTRIC SYMPHONY ORCHESTRA:** This was a group of Hollywood session musicians (some of whom were also in The Wrecking Crew) organized by Frank Zappa in 1967 to record music for his first solo album *Lumpy Gravy*. These musicians worked together in various combinations under the leadership of Ken Shroyer as far back as 1959, and this orchestra was the same one that played on "Alvin's Orchestra" in 1960. It was Zappa who gave the orchestra their name several years later.

Harold Ayres - violin

John Balkin - bass

Arnold Belnick - violin

Harold G. Bemko - cello

Chuck Berghofer - bass

Jimmy Bond - bass

Dennis Budimir - guitar

Frankie Capp - drums, Latin percussion

Don Christlieb - bassoon, contra bassoon

Gene Cipriano - oboe, flute, bass flute, E flat clarinet, bass clarinet, contra bass clarinet

Vincent DeRosa - French horn

Joseph DiFiore - viola

Jesse Ehrlich - cello

Alan Estes - percussion

Gene Estes - percussion, mallets, tympani, Latin percussion

Victor Feldman - percussion, mallets, tympani, Latin percussion

Bunk Gardner - flute, piccolo, clarinet, bassoon, bass, soprano, tenor saxes

James Getzoff - violin

Philip Goldberg - viola

John Guerin - drums

Jim Haynes - guitar

Harry Hyams - viola

Jules Jacob - oboe, English horn, flute, piccolo, tenor sax

Pete Jolly - piano, celeste, electric harpsichord

Raymond J. Kelley - cello

Jerome A. Kessler - cello

Alexander Koltun - violin

Bernard Kundell - violin

William Kurasch - violin

Mike Lang - keyboards, celeste, electric harpsichord

Leonard Malarsky - strings

Shelly Manne - drums

Lincoln Mayorga - piano, celeste, electric harpsichord piano, celeste, electric harpsichord

Arthur Maebe - French horn

Ted Nash - flute, bass flute, alto sax, contra b. clarinet, clarinet, bass clarinet

Richard Parisi (Perrisi) - French horn

Jerome J. Reisler - violin

Emil Richards - percussion, mallets, tympani, Latin percussion

Lyle Ritts (Ritz) - bass

Tony Rizzi - guitar

Johnny Rotella - flute, piccolo, saxophone, clarinet

Joseph Saxon - cello

Ralph Schaeffer - violin

Leonard Selic - viola

Ken Shroyer - tenor and bass trombone, bass trumpet (also formed the orchestra)

Paul Smith - piano, celeste, electric harpsichord

Tommy Tedesco - guitar, bells, bongos

Al Viola - guitar

Bob West - bass

Tibor Zelig - violin

Jimmy Zito - trumpet, flugelhorn, piccolo

## THE RON HICKLIN SINGERS:

Often they were not credited, or were credited under other names. For example, on the TV theme of *Love, American Style*, they were credited as The Charles Fox Singers.

The core group usually consisted of:

John Bahler, tenor

Tom Bahler, tenor

Ron Hicklin, lead tenor

Gene Morford, bass

Sally Stevens, soprano

Jackie Ward, alto

The core group was augmented with other vocalists such as:

Al Capps

Buzz Cason (Snuff Garrett's assistant in 1962)

Linda Dangcil

Stan Farber

Mitch Gordon

Jim Haas

Thurl Ravenscroft, bass (voice of Tony the Tiger)

Ron Rolla

Andra Willis

Bob Zwirn

**THE ELIGIBLES:**

These were the singers on *The Chipmunks Sing The Beatles Hits, The Chipmunks Sing for Children* (where they are pictured on the back cover), *Chipmunks à Go-Go, The Chipmunks See Doctor Dolittle* and *The Chipmunks go to the Movies,* plus the later *Chipmunk Punk* and *Urban Chipmunk.*

Probably their most famous musical contribution other than a few singles and albums and appearances on *Shindig* is singing the revised version of "The Ballad of *Gilligan's Island*" for the second and third season of the series.

They also released a few albums and singles under The Eligibles moniker.

Al Capps - first tenor
Stan Farber - first tenor
Ron Hicklin - second tenor
Ron Rolla - bass
Bob Zwirn - baritone, guitar, bass guitar, arranger

# BIBLIOGRAPHY:

Alexander, Shana, "Alvin! Composer's Yells at Son Inspire Another Chipmunk Hit", *Life* magazine, March 23, 1959

"Bagdasarian, Chipmunk Song Author, Dies", *The Courier-Journal*, January 18, 1972

"Bagdasarian, Father of Actor, Song Writer, Dies", *The Fresno Bee*, April 7, 1969

Bagdasarian, Jr., Ross, "Alvin and The Chipmunks Greatest Hits: Still Squeaky After All These Years", CD booklet, 1999

Barris, George and James Joseph, "I Build Cars for the Stars", *The Pantagraph*, October 15, 1967

Bianculli, David, "Chipmunks Return to TV and Saturday's Time Warp", *Fort Lauderdale News and Sun-Sentinel*, March 31, 1979

Campbell, Mary, "Cosby Relives His Funny Childhood", *The Kansas City Times*, August 20, 1966

"CBS Plans New Cartoon Series", *The Daily Capital News*, April 15, 1961

Childs, T Mike, *The Rocklopedia Fakebandica*, Thomas Dunne, November 2004

"Chipmunk Creator Dies", *Wilmington News-Journal*, January 18, 1972

Chipmunks Home Page, The

Chipmunks Wiki, The

Coleman, William, "A Platter for Grandma", *The Corpus Christi Caller-Times*, November 18, 1956

Cox, Stephen, "The Chipmunk Song" Turns 60: Secrets of a Holiday Novelty Smash", *The Hollywood Reporter*, December 18, 2018

"David Seville and Chipmunks Bring Fortune to Bagdasarian", *The Burlington Free Press*, April 1, 1959

"Deaths", *The Odessa American*, January 18, 1972

"Deaths Elsewhere", *The Akron Beacon Journal*, January 18, 1972

Edwards, David and Mike Callahan, "The Liberty Records Story", January 20, 2001

"Ex-Grape Grower Making Millions on Songs by Imaginary Chipmunks", *The Decatur Herald*, March 31, 1959

"Famed Cousins Follow Footlights", *Honolulu Star-Bulletin*, January 24, 1971

Fanning, Jim, "*The Lone Ranger*: The Forgotten CBS Classic", *Tulgey Wood*, July 3, 2013

Fife, Enid, "David Seville: Brings Alvin to TV", *TV Radio Mirror*, October 1961

Foray, June with Mark Evanier and Earl Kress, *Did You Grow Up With Me, Too?: The Autobiography of June Foray*, BearManor Media, 2009

Goldmark, Daniel and Yuval Taylor, *The Cartoon Music Book*, A Cappella, 2002

Grey, Jerry, "Music Executive Plans to Push 'Memphis Sound'", *The Lowell Sun*, August 20, 1977

James, Ed, "Frustrated Grape Grower Gains Fame in Witchy Tune", *Richmond Palladium-Item*, November 3, 1988

Jason, Johnny, "The Zany World of David Seville", *'Teen* magazine, January 1960

Johnson, Erskine, "Alvin Runs For President", *The Pittsburgh Press*, September 16, 1960

Lee, Lawrence and Barry Gifford, *Saroyan: A Biography*, Harper and Row, 1984

Lyon, Herb, "Tower Ticker", *Chicago Tribune*, February 10, 1967

"No Chipmunk Role This Time", *San Antonio Express*, October 8, 1967

"Obituary: Dies", *The Troy Record*, January 18, 1972

"Old Estate Program Aides Heirs", *The Los Angeles Times*, April 10, 1980

"Ross Bagdasarian, 52; Writer of Hit Song", *The Los Angeles Times*, January 18, 1972

Rutkoski, Rex, "Animal Darting Across Road Inspires Bagdasarian to Hits", *News Record*, August 10, 1982

Sanderson, Lucinda Ann and Michael J. Tawney, "Alvin and the Chipmunks: Ross Bagdasarian Remembered", *Mindrot* #12, November 1, 1978

Schelly, Bill, *John Stanley: Giving Life to Little Lulu*, Fantagraphics, 2017

"Seville Dies", *The Evening Independent*, January 19, 1972

Thomas, Bob, "Combine Chipmunks and The Beatles? David Seville Did", *The Daily Tribune*, September 9, 1964

Thompson, Steven Paul, "The Man Behind The Chipmunks", 1989

"Those Chipmunks Are in the Chips", *Detroit Free Press*, March 31, 1959

"3 Chipmunks Make Grape Grower Hottest Item in Record Business", *The Greenville News*, March 31, 1959

"Time of Life to be Performed Today, Thursday", Colorado Springs Gazette-Telegraph, November 18, 1970

Tralfaz, "Alvin Might Have Been a Rabbit", July 2, 2016

Turmel, Kitte, "Be Thankful For Life Itself", *The Times*, November 20, 1960

Turmel, Kitte, "Songwriter Offers Success Cues", *The Times*, June 18, 1961

Winters, Marty, "Ross Bagdasarian: The Man Who Would Be Chipmunk King", *Cool and Strange Music* #18, August-November 2000

Woo, William, "The Chirpy Guy Behind The Chipmunks", *St. Louis Post-Dispatch*, October 19, 1965

"Writer of 'Chipmunk Song' Dead", *The Indiana Gazette*, January 18, 1972

# INDEX

Aaron Slobodjian -14
ABC - 78
Abnuceals Emuukha Electric Symphony Orchestra, The - 87
Abrahams, Adam - 133
Abramson, Lester - 83
Academy Pictures - 138
"Achy Breaky Heart" - 314
Acorn Hunt Game - 109
AD Council - 250, 310
*A-Files: Alien Songs, The* - 314
Africa - 193
Air Force - 6
"Akh, Vavroos" (see "Oh, Beauty")
*Akron Beacon Journal, The* - 306
Alfi and Harry - 9-10, 12, 75
Aladdin Records - 34
*Alaska Seas* - 12, 14
Alexander, Shana - 56,79-80
Alfred E. Neuman - 90
*Alice in Wonderland* - 31
"All My Loving" - 252
"Aloha Oe" - 84
Alpha-Bits - 224-225
Alvin - ix, xi, 37, 55, 65-70, 73-77, 79-87, 89-91, 93-94, 101-102, 109-116, 119, 129-132, 140, 144, 148, 151, 174, 183-193, 195-197, 202-217, 222-239, 244-245, 247-248, 250-253, 255-258, 260-261, 265, 270-271, 274-296, 298-299, 301-303, 312-319, 321-325
*Alvin* (comic book) - 241, 245, 282-285, 310

*Alvin and his Pals in Merry Christmas with Clyde Crashcup and Leonardo* - 242, 286
Alvin and The Chipmunks (see Chipmunks, The)
Alvin and The Chipmunks (see *Alvin Show, The*)
Alvin and The Chipmunks (1983-1991 TV Series) - 198, 312-313
*Alvin and The Chipmunks: Chipwrecked* - 315
*Alvin and The Chipmunks: Chipwrecked: Music from the Motion Picture* - 315
*Alvin and The Chipmunks Meet Frankenstein* - 314
*Alvin and The Chipmunks Meet the Wolfman* - 314
*Alvin and The Chipmunks: Original Motion Picture Soundtrack* - 315
"Alvin and the Chipmunks: Ross Bagdasarian Remembered" - 57-58
*Alvin and The Chipmunks: The Road Chip* -316
*Alvin and The Chipmunks: The Road Chip: Original Motion Picture Soundtrack* - 316
*Alvin and The Chipmunks: The Squeakquel* - 315
*Alvin and The Chipmunks: The Squeakquel: Original Motion Picture Soundtrack* - 315
"Alvin! Composer's Yells at Son Inspire Another Chipmunk Hit" - 56-57
"Alvin For President" - 90-91, 126, 268
*Alvin For President* (comic book) - 241-242, 285
"Alvin Might Have Been a Rabbit" - 168
Alvin's Acorn - 73, 256-259, 294

"Alvin's All-Star Chipmunk Band" - 245, 289
"Alvin's Harmonica" - 79-86, 88, 115-119, 310
*Alvin's Lost Voice* - 142, 176
"Alvin's Orchestra" - 82, 87, 89-90, 101, 125-128
*Alvin Show, The* - x-xii, 72, 82, 85-86, 90-91, 94-95, 101-102, 129-133, 137, 140, 144-145, 151-154, 158-161, 167-170, 183-190, 192-195, 197-199, 201-239, 241-243, 260-261, 270, 274, 310-311, 313, 316, 319, 325
*Alvin Show, The* (LP) - ix, 195-197, 222, 243, 246, 274-276, 298
"Alvin Twist, The" - 242, 244, 249, 287
*ALVINNN!!! And the Chipmunks* (CD) - 315-316
*ALVINNN!!! And the Chipmunks* (TV) - 315-316
"Almost Good" - 76-77, 81
"Amapola" - 12
"Amazing Grace" - 247
"America the Beautiful" - 244
*American Bandstand* - 61, 71, 82, 86, 100, 108, 260
*American Pop* - 327
Andrina, Frank - 165
*Animalogic* - 163
*Antiques Roadshow* - 62
"Apple Picker" - 263
Aragon, Ray - 151
Archbishop Calfayan - 16
*Archie Show, The* - 310
Armen, Kay (Armenuhi Manoogian) - 3, 17
"Armen's Theme" - 4, 9-10, 22, 244, 273
Armenian-Americans - 1-5, 141, 263-264
Army - 6-7, 135
Arnaz, Desi - 65
Arnold, Mark - ix, xii
*Around the World With The Chipmunks* - ix, 91, 93-94, 132, 222, 243, 245, 298
Arwin Records - 33
Asuncion Ortega - 14

Atco Records - 262
Atlantic Records - 262
Austin Healey - 150
Avnet - 34

"Baby Love" - 261
"Back to Our Future" - 198
*Back to the Future* - 198
"Bagdad Express" - 11
Bagdasarian, Adam Serak - 15, 56-57, 66-69, 72, 75, 79-80, 314, 320
Bagdasarian, Armen (Armenouhi Kulhanjian) - 3, 6-7, 10, 16, 57, 61, 314, 320
Bagdasarian, Carol Askine - 15, 56-57, 71-72, 123, 200, 263-264, 273, 305, 314, 320
Bagdasarian, Dikran "Dick" - 69, 270, 301
Bagdasarian Enterprises (Bagdasarian Productions) - 95, 133, 195, 215-225, 251, 268-269, 311
Bagdasarian Film Corporation - 95
Bagdasarian, Harry Sisvan - 1
Bagdasarian, Michael - 316
Bagdasarian, Richard Sirak - 1, 262
Bagdasarian, Jr., Ross Dickran - xii, 1, 3-4, 6, 8-9, 55-60, 63-68, 72, 88, 91, 160, 184-187, 198, 251, 268, 272, 309-314, 316, 320, 324
Bagdasarian, Sr., Ross (Rostum Sipon Bagdasarian) (David Seville) - ix-xii, 1-11, 12-29, 31-32, 35-36, 46, 55-103, 115-132, 138-146, 148, 151, 157-160, 162, 166, 169-170, 183-197, 200, 202-216, 220, 222, 228, 230-231, 234-235, 238-239, 241-275, 277-279, 282-299, 301-304, 306-310, 312-318, 320, 322-323, 325, 327
Bagdasarian, Vanessa - 316
Baker, Ted - 136
Bakshi, Ralph - 327
Balboa, California - 149
Ball, Lucille - 65

"Band Played On, The" - 192
Barbour, Dave - 7
Barris Company, The - 73
Barris, George - 256-259, 294
Barrymore, John - 245
*Batman* - 256, 260, 294
Batmobile, The - 256, 294
"Baubles, Bangles and Beads" - 20
"Be a Star" - 273
Beach Boys, The - 33, 259
*Beany and Cecil* - 62, 189
"Bear Necessities, The" - 271
BearManor Media - 165
Beatles, The - ix, 249-254, 261, 266, 272
"Because I Love You" - 249
Bedbugs, The - 249
Bennett, Alvin "Al" - 34-35, 37, 55, 59, 73-74, 78, 314
Berlin, Irving - 74
Berry, Jan - 33-34
Besser, Joe - 183
"Betcha Can't Kiss Me (Just One Time Baby)" - 262
Betty Boop - 157
Beverly Hills, California - 5, 95, 273
"Bicycle Built For Two" - 244
Big Record Game, The - 73, 110
*Billboard* Magazine - 43, 50, 77-78, 263, 312-316
Billy Ward and the Dominoes - 31
Billy Ward's Orchestra and Chorus - 84
"Bird is the Word, The" - 33
"Bird On My Head, The" - 9, 61, 98-100, 246, 310
*Black Orpheus* - 142
Blaine, Cullen (see Houghtaling, Cullen Blaine)
Blocker, Dan - 255-256
Blondie - 311
Blue Cheer - 31
Blues Project, The - 269
Bluth, Toby - 312
"Bold and the Brave, The" - 10

"Bonjour Tristesse" - 11
Boris Badenov - 189
Bosustow, Steve - 133, 137-138
Braxton, Frank - 142
Brennan, Walter - 33
Brittany - 312
Broadway - 5, 8, 273
Brooks, Garth - 36
Brown Derby, The - 163
Brubeck, Dave - 62
Bruce and Dutch - 266
Bryson, Rhett - 61
"Bubble Bath" - 84
Buena Vista Home Video - 198
Bugs Bunny - 79
Bunin, Morey - 61-62, 86, 91, 98, 107-108
Bunin, Rachel - 62
Bunnyhoppers, The - 105
Burbank, California - 137
*Burlington Free Press* - 121
Burnette, Johnny - 33, 49
"Buy For Me the Rain" - 52

Cal Arts - 154
California - 165
"Call Me" - 311
Callahan, Mike - 9, 29, 34-36, 55
*Calvin and the Colonel* - 187
"Camel Rock" - 11, 23, 62
Campbell, Mary - 263
"Candy Man" - 52
Canned Heat - 35, 262, 269-270, 272, 300
Cannon, Hana - 137
Cannon, Robert "Bobe" - 134, 136-137, 143-144, 147
"Can't Take My Eyes Off You" - 272
Capitol Records - 36, 254, 268-269, 311
Capps, Al - 260
"Caravan" - 84
Carmichael, Hoagy - 159
"Carousel in Rome" - 10, 22
Carr, Vikki - 33
Carrey, Jim - 172
*Cartoon All-Stars to the Rescue* - 313

Cason, Buzz - 33, 260
Cates, George - 17
CBS - 138, 169-171, 183-184, 188, 197, 199, 241, 246, 261, 310
"Cecilia" - 11, 246
Chapel of the Pines Crematory - 273
Characters, The - ix
*Charlie Brown Christmas, A* - 138
Checker, Chubby - 242
Chevalier, Maurice - 93
Chicago, Illinois - 269
*Chicago Tribune, The* - 297
China - 91
Chinese - 266
Chip and Dale - 72, 84, 104, 141
Chipettes, The - 312-314
*Chipmunk Adventure, The* - 313
*Chipmunk Celebration, A* - 313
*Chipmunk Christmas, A* - 198, 311-312
"Chipmunk Fun" - 85, 197
*Chipmunk Punk* - 256, 309, 311-312, 321
Chipmunk Ranch, The - 66
*Chipmunk Reunion, A* - 313
*Chipmunk Rock* - 313
"Chipmunk Song, The" ("Christmas, Don't Be Late") - xi, 13-14, 32, 55, 60-61, 64-67, 70, 72, 74-79, 84-88, 94, 101-105, 115-116, 121, 222, 245, 248, 252-253, 259, 269-270, 300, 310, 317, 328
"The Chipmunk Song" Turns 60: Secrets of a Holiday Novelty Smash" - 252-254, 259
*Chipmunk Songbook, The* - 84, 222, 243-244, 288, 311
*Chipmunks à Go-Go* - 259, 295, 298
*Chipmunks and The Chipettes: Born to Rock, The* - 314
*Chipmunks Christmas* - 315
*Chipmunks Go Hollywood, The* - 313
*Chipmunks Go To the Movies, The* (LP) - 198, 271, 296, 301
*Chipmunks Go To the Movies, The* (TV series) - 313

*Chipmunks in Low Places* - 314
*Chipmunks' Merry Christmas, The* - 111
Chipmunks on 16 Speed, The - 259
*Chipmunks Roasting On An Open Fire* - 327
*Chipmunks Rock the House, The* - 314
*Chipmunks See Doctor Dolittle, The* - 264-266, 296, 299, 316
*Chipmunks Sing The Beatles Hits, The* - 84, 250-254, 256, 261, 292-293, 298
*Chipmunks Sing With Children, The* - 254-256, 272, 294
Chipmunks, The (Alvin and The Chipmunks) - ix-xii, 8, 14-15, 29, 35-37, 55, 60-62, 64-66, 68-70, 72-77, 82-89, 91-95, 101-119, 121-132, 138-140, 143, 168-170, 183-184, 187-193, 195-198, 202-214, 216, 222-223, 225, 228-229, 232, 235, 239, 241-266, 268-272, 274-303, 306-319, 321-323, 327-328
Chipmunks, The (TV series) - 313
*Chipmunks 35th Birthday Party, The* - 314
Chippers, The - 252
"Chitty Chitty Bang Bang" - 271, 302
*Chitty Chitty Bang Bang* - 271
"Christmas Blues" - 259, 300
"Christmas, Don't Be Late" (see "Chipmunk Song, The")
*Christmas With The Chipmunks* - 84, 94, 244, 248, 254, 261, 270, 288, 298, 300, 310, 317
*Christmas With The Chipmunks, Volume 2* - 244, 248, 254, 289, 298, 300, 310
Chouinard Art Institute - 134, 155
*Clambake* - 172
Clampett, Robert "Bob" - 62, 79, 86, 103, 134
Clark, Dick - 61-62, 71, 86, 100, 103, 259
Clarke, Grant - 83
"Clementine" - 243
Cleveland Board of Education - 166
Cleveland, Ohio - 134, 136, 165-166
Cleveland School of Art - 135
Clooney, Rosemary - 3-5, 7, 12, 17-18

"Closing Time" - 10
*Club Chipmunk: The Dance Mixes* - 314
*Clutch Cargo* - 159
Clyde Crashcup - 133, 138-139, 141, 158, 183, 186, 189, 194, 197-198, 216, 221, 239, 279, 286-287, 325
*Clyde Crashcup* (comic book) - 241-242, 286-287
*Clyde Crashcup and Leonardo* - 142, 176, 197-198
"C'mon Everybody" - 31
Cochran, Eddie - 11, 31, 48
Cole, Corny - 312
Colgate-Palmolive - 250
Colonna, Jerry - 31
*Colorado Springs Gazette Telegraph, The* - 305
Columbia Records - 3-4
Columbia Records Productions - 249
"Come On-a My House" - 1, 3-5, 7-8, 10-12, 17, 141, 256, 262, 313
"Comin' Through the Rye" - 84
"Coming 'Round the Mountain" - 88-91, 125, 196
Connors, Mike - 263-264
"Consider Yourself" - 271
*Cool and Strange Music* - 6, 8-10, 13, 58-59, 74-76, 84, 183-184, 262-263, 266
"Cooperative Forest Fire Prevention Campaign" - 250
"Copyright 1960" - 87, 91
Coral Records - 3, 8, 12
Corpus Christi Caller Times - 38
"Cosby Relives His Funny Childhood" - 263
Costanzo, Jack - 84
Costco - 165
"Count Me In" - 34-35
*Courier Journal, The* - 306
Cox, Stephen - 252, 256, 259
Cowboys, The - 273
Craig, Skip - 168
"Crashcup's Work Theme" - 90
"Crazy" - 32
Crickets, The - 33

Crippen, Fred - 138
Cross Country Game - 110
Cruise Director, The - 186
"Cry Me a River" - 30, 39
Culver City, California - 135
Cyrus, Billy Ray - 314

Daffy Duck - 170-171
*Daily Capital News* - 199
*Daily Tribune, The* - 251, 293
Daisy Bell - 183, 191
Damone, Vic - 8, 20
"Dance from Boujour Tristesse" - 11-12
Dancer, Prancer and Nervous - 94, 106
Danch, Bill - 164
Darin, Bobby - 264
David Seville (see Bagdasarian, Sr., Ross)
"David Seville: Brings Alvin to TV" - 5, 59
Davis, Mac - 247
Davis, Marc - 157
Davis, Jr., Sammy - 264-265
Dayton, Ohio - 135
"Dead Man's Curve" - 33
*Decatur Herald* - 121
"Deep Purple" - 31
*Deep Six, The* - 13-14, 28
DeLara, Phil - 265, 272, 296
Dell Comics - 142, 241-242, 282, 310
Denny, Martin - 11, 32, 49, 84
DePatie, David - 167
DePatie-Freleng Enterprises - xi, 165, 167, 170-171
*Destination Gobi* - 12-14, 26-27
Detorie, Rick - 323
*Detroit Free Press* - 121
Detroit, Michigan - 153
"Devil or Angel" - 32
*Devil's Hairpin, The* - 13-14
DiC - 313
Dick and Dee Dee - 33
*Dick Clark Beech-Nut Show, The* - 61, 79, 82, 100
Dietrich, Marlene - 12
"Dinah" - 62

Dino, Desi and Billy - 261
Dishonest John - 189
Disney, Walt (Walt Disney Productions) - 31, 72, 84, 104, 133-134, 136-137, 139, 141, 144, 147-148, 155-156, 158, 171, 187, 272
Disneyland Hotel - 171
"Do-Re-Mi" - 254, 294
"Do You Want to Know a Secret?" - 252, 292
*Doctor Dolittle* - 264-265, 271
Dodd, Ken - 34
Doherty, Bob - 255-256, 265
Dolphins, The - 273
Dolton Records - 34-35
*Dominion News, The* - 302
Don Swan Orchestra, The - 84
"Donkey and the Schoolboy, The" - 10-11, 62
Donley, Roger - 136, 153, 159, 161-162, 168
"Don't Lie To Me (You Know I Know)" - 262
"Don't Whistle at Me Baby" - 60
"Don't Worry, Be Happy" - 246
Doors, The - 266
Dot Records - 35, 263, 297
"Dot's Nice, Don'-a Fight" - 12
"Dover Boys, The" - 134
Dowling, Eddie - 2
Downs, Chuck - 165
Draklich, Nick - 95, 251
"Drag City" - 33
Dragon - 183, 191
*Dr. Demento Show, The* - 3, 6, 8-9, 63-64, 311
Dr. Seuss (see Geisel, Ted)
"Dreamin'" - 33
*Duck Factory, The* - 172
*Duel With the Witch Doctor* - 56, 58
Duga, Don - 155
Dumont, Margaret - 195
Dunn, John - 165

East Technical High School - 134
*Easter Chipmunk, The* - 313
Ed Sullivan Show, The - 60-62, 65, 73, 78-79, 81-82, 86-87, 91, 96-98, 107

Edwards, David - 9, 29, 34-36, 55
Edwards, Ralph - 163
"Eefin' Alvin" - 247, 262-263
"El Cumbanchero" - 84
*El Paso Herald Post* - 302
El Paso Symphony Orchestra - 166
El Paso, Texas - 166
Elektra Films - 138
Eligibles, The - 253-254, 256, 259-260
Elwee and the Tree Weasels - 327
EMI Records - 36
Emmy Awards - 151
*Emperor's Nightingale, The* - 138
Engel, Jules - 135, 137-138, 142, 154, 171, 173
England - 31
Epstein, Brian - 250
Era Productions, Inc. - 250, 291
Era Records - 29-30
Erwin, John - 310, 317
"E.T. and Me" - 323
*Evening Independent, The* - 306
*Evening Review, The* - 302
"Everybody Loves a Clown" - 35
Excelsior Records - 311, 321
*Exotica* - 32

Fabian - 71
Facebook - 163
Fanning, Jim - 171
Farber, Stan - 253, 260
Federal Records - 3
*Feelin' Kinda Patton* - 328
Fevvol - 14
Fields, Gracie - 30-31
Fife, Enid - 5, 59
Figments - 160
Filmfair - 158
*First Annual Grammy Awards, The* - 78
*First French Kiss: And Other Traumas* - 314
Flintstones, The - 159, 169, 187, 243
"Flip Side" - 82-83, 247
Florida - 5
Floyd, Chick - 84
Foodini - 62

"For Mama" - 51
Foray, June -141, 168, 183, 191, 193-194, 313
Ford, Greg - 170
Ford Mustang - 256
*Forgotten Fire* - 314
Format Films (Format Productions) - x-xii, 95, 134, 138-144, 153, 156, 158-159, 161, 164, 167-168, 170-174, 177, 187, 190, 199, 250, 291
*Fort Lauderdale News, The* - 319
Fort Worth, Texas - 166
*Four Color* - 242, 282
Four Seasons, The - 272-273
France - 29, 147
Francis and Associates (see Pate/Francis and Associates)
Francis and Manahan, Inc. - 244
Francis, Edwin - 259
Franklin, Aretha - 266
"Freddy, Freddy" - 94
Freeman, Ernie - 33
"Freeway Flyer" - 50
Freleng, Friz - 167, 170
*Fresno Bee Republican, The* - 301
Fresno, California - 1-3, 7, 13, 66, 263, 266, 301
Fresno High School - 1, 16
*Fritz the Cat* - 327
"From All Over the World" - 50
"Frumpington's Song" - 90
*Funny Company, The* - 152
"Funny How Time Slips Away" - 32

Gallo - 266
Gants, The - 34
Garcia, Russ - 84
Garrett, Thomas "Snuff" - 247, 259-260, 263
Gary Lewis and the Playboys - 34-35, 49
Gaye, Marvin - 266
Geisel, Ted (Dr. Seuss) - 134, 264
General Electric - 258
General Foods - 183
Gerald McBoing-Boing - 134, 143, 174

Germany - 29, 193
Gershman, Ed - 138
Getzler, Buddy - 142
Getzoff, James - 197
Gibbs, Georgia - 8, 20
"Gift, The" - 10, 62
Gifford, Barry - 4
*Gilligan's Island* - 260
*Girl Can't Help it, The* - 31
"Girl in the Ocean, The" - 273
"Girl Upstairs, The" - 30
"Girl With the Tambourine, The" - 8, 12
*Girls of Pleasure Island, The* - 14
Givens, Bob - 134
Glenn, John - 190
*Glory Days, The* - 172
Goffin, Gerry - 32
"Going Up the Country" - 269
Golden Books - 82, 111, 142
"Gonna Get Along Without Ya Now" - 22, 30
"Good Neighbor, The" - 183, 202-212
'Good Vibrations" - 255
"Goofus" - 12
"Gotta Get to Your House" - 9-11, 14, 23, 62, 246, 256
Gottfredson, Norm - 158
Graham, Don - 155
Grammy Awards - 60, 65, 75, 78, 86, 91, 120, 244, 247, 252, 255
Grasshoppers, The - 86, 105
Gray, Dobie - 261
Great Foodini - 61
*Greatest Show on Earth, The* - 14
Green, Jan Strejan - 149, 162-163
"Green-Eyed Lady" - 35
*Greenville News* - 121
Grier, Roosevelt "Rosie" - 33
Grinch, The - 248
Gross, Milt - 145
*Gunsmoke* - 197

Hal Roach Studios - 136
Hale, Dale - 158-165, 173-174

Hale, Nona - 163-164
Halmos, Gabor - 272
Hanna-Barbera - 90, 147, 159, 161, 165, 187
Hanna, William - 137
Hansen, Barry (Dr. Demento) - 3
"Happy Birthday" - 249-250
*Happy Days* - 260
"Happy Reindeer, The" - 94, 106
Harrison, Rex - 264
"Have Yourself a Merry Little Christmas" - 248
Hassinger, David - 197, 252, 259, 272
He-Man - 310, 317
"He Says 'Mm-Hmm'" - 8, 12
*Hee Haw* - 172, 181
Hee, Thornton "T." - 136, 138-139, 144-146, 149-150, 155-157, 164
Helburn, Theresa - 2
"Hello Dolly" - 254
"Hello Walls" - 32
"Here Comes Santa Claus" - 245
*Here's Looking at Me!* - 314
Herman's Hermits - 261
Heritage Auctions - 226-236
"Hey Brother, Pour the Wine" - 4, 8, 14, 19
"Hey There Moon" - 61
Heywood, Eddie - 33
Hicklin, Ron - 253-254, 256, 259-260
Hilberman, David - 133, 137
Hirsch, Al - 77-78
Hitchcock, Alfred - 9, 13, 25
Hite, Bob "The Bear" - 269-270
Hitler, Adolph - 29
"Holding You Now" - 273
Holly, Buddy - 33
Hollywood, California - 7, 14, 163, 166, 260
"Home On the Range" - 90, 192
*Honey West* - 172
*Honolulu Star Bulletin, The* - 305
*Hot Blood* - 14
Houghtaling, Cullen Blaine - 160, 175
"Hound Dog" - 78
"House of Romona" - 273

Howard, Cal - 144-146, 149-150, 157, 160, 163
Hubley, John - 138
Huckleberry Hound - 90, 302
Hurtz, Bill - 136
"Hushabye Mountain" - 271, 302
"I Can't Give You Anything But Love" - 62
"I Got Rhythm" - 84
*I Love the Chipmunks Valentine Special* - 313
"I Remember Dillinger" - 266
*I Spy* - 172
"I Treasure Thee" - 272
"I Wish I Could Speak French" - 91, 93, 193, 197, 242
"I Wish I Had a Horse" - 90
"I'm a Fool" - 261
"I'm Henry VIII, I Am" - 261
Ike and Tina Turner - 35, 262-263, 272
Imperial Records - 34-36, 45-46, 270
"In a Village Park" - 66, 69
"In Crowd, The" - 261
*In Living Color* - 172
*Indiana Gazette, The* - 306
Innes Records - 262
Innovations, The - 84
Iowa - 159
*Ironside* - 273
"It Sure Is Rough Being Sick" - 249
Italian - 4
Italy - 165

*Jack and Jill* - 177
Jack Rather Productions - 171
Jackson, Michael - 251
Jad Paul's Banjo Magic - 84
Jan and Dean - 33-35, 49-50
Japan - 91, 193
"Japanese Banana" - 63, 92-93, 193
Jason, Johnny - 82
Jay Ward Productions - xi, 138, 147, 153, 168, 187
Jeanette - 312
"Jeanie With the Light Brown Hair, The" - 243

Jell-O - 143-144, 183, 224-225, 272
Jenkyns, Chris - 147, 164
*Jetsons, The* - 260
Jimmy Joyce Singers, The - 254-256
John Buzon Trio, The - 84
John Gart Orchestra - 3
*John Stanley: Giving Life to Little Lulu* - 242
Johnny Mann Singers, The - 33
"Jone - Cone - Phone" - 270
Jones, Chuck - 134, 152, 157, 170, 313
Jones, George - 261
Jones, Jack - 261
Jones, Spike - 32, 85, 136, 153, 159, 162, 165-168
Jolson, Al - 86
Jordan, Henrietta "Hank" - 135, 138, 154-155
Jorgensen, Vern - 151
"Judy" - 9, 82, 262

*Kansas City Times, The* - 263, 297
Kaplan, Ervin - 165
Karman, Janice - xii, 311-313, 316, 324
Kaufman, Millard - 134
Kausler, Mark - 312
Keep, Theodore "Ted" - 37, 55, 74, 85-86, 89, 94
Kennedy, John F. - 90-91, 249
Kevin - 312
King, Carole - 32
*King Leonardo* - 278
King, Pete - 255-256, 265, 272
Kinks, The - ix
Kinney, Jack - 144, 160
*Kismet* - 8, 14, 20
Klynn, Herb - 134-140, 142-146, 152-157, 164-173
Klynn-Walker Studios - 135
KMET - 311
Knickerbocker Hotel - 260
Knotts, Don - 272
Knox, Buddy - 33
Kovacs, Ernie - 197
Kricfalusi, John - 327

Kulhanjian, Armenouhi (see Bagdasarian, Armen)
Kurtz and Friends - 153-154, 158
Kurtz, Bob - 138-158, 160, 164, 169, 175-176

La Guardia Airport - 5
"La Noche" - 256
Laboe, Art - 270
Laguna Beach, California - 149, 163
Laine, Frankie - 7, 77
Lantz, Walter - 157
Larriva, Rudy - 138, 140, 152, 164
Lauper, Cyndi - 251
"Lazy Lovers" - 90
Lee, Bill - 183, 194-195
Lee, Jason - 315
Lee, Lawrence - 4
Lee, Peggy - 7
Leon Schlesinger Productions - 134, 136
Leonardo - 139, 186, 194, 216, 221, 239, 279, 286-287, 325
*Let's All Sing With Jerry Colonna* - 31
*Let's All Sing With The Chipmunks* - ix, 73, 83-86, 89, 130, 169, 222, 246, 298
"Let's Have a Merry, Merry Christmas" - 8, 21, 74
Lewis, Gary - 34-35
Lewis, Jerry - 12, 34, 272
*Liberty Proudly Presents Stereo… the Visual Sound* - 84
Liberty Records - x, xii, 9-10, 14, 22-23, 29-53, 55, 58-60, 63, 69, 73-78, 83-84, 87, 91, 102, 118, 124, 128, 170, 184, 222, 239, 247, 251, 263-272, 287-289, 294, 300, 310, 318
"Liberty Records Story" - 9, 29, 34
"Lie-Lie" - 272-273
*Life* Magazine - 56-57, 66, 73, 217
Liss, Abe - 138
*Little Alvin and the Mini-Munks* (CD) - 314-315
*Little Alvin and the Mini-Munks* (TV) - 314
"Little Beauty, A" - 9-10

"Little Brass Band" - 9, 62
"Little Dog, The" - 85
"Little Eefin' Annie" - 247
Little Lulu - 242
"Little Old Lady From Pasadena, The" - 34
*Live in Person* - 50
Lock, Stock and Barrel - 146
London, England - 251
London, Julie - 10, 30, 38-39, 49. 84
Lone Ranger, The - 171
*Lone Ranger, The* - xi, 138, 143, 171, 177-180
Looney Tunes - 62, 170, 272
*Lord of the Rings* - 327
Los Angeles, California - 4, 7, 29, 34, 78, 159-160, 259, 269-270
*Los Angeles Times, The* - 306, 320
"Lotta Bull" - 87-88
"Louie, Louie" - 261
"Love Me Do" - 251
*Love's Old Sweet Song* - 2
"Lucy, Lucy" - 246, 249
*Lumpy Gravy* - 87

*Mad* Magazine - 90
Malverne Distributors - 77
Mancini, Henry - 30, 32
Mann, Johnny - 183
*Mannix* - 263, 273, 298
Manoogian, Armenuhi (see Armen, Kay)
March Hare - 31
Marchutz, Robert - 255
*Marge's Little Lulu* - 242
"Maria From Madrid" - 82
Mar-Kets, The - 33
Martin, Dean - 4, 12, 19
*Mary Poppins* - 249
McCoy, Van - 33
McDaniels, Gene - 33, 49
McFerrin, Bobby - 246
McIntyre, Mark - 9, 30, 62-63, 73
McKimson, Bob - 134
McKuen, Rod - 30
McPhatter, Clyde - 31

"Mediocre" - 80-81
*Meet The Beatles* - ix
Melendez, Bill - 138
Mendelson, Lee - 138
Menken, Shepard "Shep" - 141, 183, 194
Mercury Records - 8, 12, 21, 74, 78
Messick, Don - 183
Mexico - 193
"Michigan, The" - 149
Mickey Mouse - 79, 148
*Mighty Mouse: The New Adventures* - 327
"Mighty's Benefit Plan" - 327
Miles, Gary - 33
Miller, Marvin - 171
Miller, Mitch - 3-4, 83
*Mindrot* - 1, 5-6, 12-13, 57-58, 72, 186-196, 261-262
Minit Records - 34-35
Minneapolis, Minnesota - 76
Miss Croner - 312
Miss Smith - 312
Mistletoe Records - 310, 318
*Mixed-Up World of Bagdasarian, The* - 241, 246, 249, 256, 262-263, 297
Mogull, Artie - 36
Monarch Music Corporation - 95, 117, 266, 268, 273, 287
"Money Tree, The" - 22
Monkees, The - ix, 259, 272
*Monkees, The* - 260
Monro, Matt - 33, 51
Monty Python - 31
*Moose That Roared, The* - 168
Morford, Gene - 260
Morris the Cat - 310, 317
*Mothers-in-Law, The* - 172
"Mountain, The" - 62-63
"Mr. Grape" - 62-63
Mr. Magoo - 134, 145, 150, 164
Mr. Sweetheart - 191
"Mr. Tambourine Man" - 259
"Mrs. Brown, You've Got a Lovely Daughter" - 261

Mrs. Claus - 313
Mrs. Frumpington - 183, 186, 195-197
Mrs. Waterford - 313
MTM - 172
"Mule Train" - 77
Munstermobile, The - 256
Murakami, Jimmy - 138
Murakami-Wolf - 138, 147
Murphy, Marty - 163
*Music of David Seville, The* - 10-12, 23, 55
"My Christmas Memory" - 328
"My Friend the Doctor" - 264-265, 299
"My Girl" - 261
*My Name is Earl* - 315
"My Wild Irish Rose" - 244

Nahai Insurance Services - 95
Natwick, Grim - 157
"Navel Maneuver" - 256, 266
NBC - 167, 197-198, 311
Nelson, Ricky - 33
Nelson, Willie - 32
Nestle's Quik - 274
New Mexico - 3
New York - 2, 4, 7, 78, 269
*New Yorker, The* - 149
Newman, Alfred - 29
Newman, Herb - 29
Newman, Lionel - 29-30
Newman, Paul S. - 242
Newport Beach, California - 149
*News Record, The* - 322
Nickelodeon - 198
Nickelson, Sam - 158
"Night Before Christmas, The" - 248
Nitty Gritty Dirt Band, The - 35, 52
Nixon, Richard M. - 90-91
Noble, Nick - 33
Nofziger, Ed - 149, 160, 162-163
"Notre Dame Victory March" - 84
"Not Since Ninevah" - 8, 20
"Nuts To You" - 2, 15
Nutty Squirrels, The - 94, 106, 169, 183, 197
*Nutty Squirrels Present, The* - 183

"O Sole Mio" - 93
O'Connor, Rosemary - 151-152
*Ocean Blues, The* - 296
*Odessa American, The* - 306
"Oh, Beauty" ("Akh, Vavroos") - 3, 5, 12
"Oh Judge, Your Honor, Dear Sir, Sweetheart" - 94
Ohanian, Krekor (see Connors, Mike)
Ohio - 134
Ohio State University - 135
Ojai, California - 163
Oklahoma City, Oklahoma - 136
"Old MacDonald Cha Cha Cha" - 196, 245-246
*Oliver!* - 271
"On the Road Again" - 35
"On Top of Old Smokey" - 192, 244
"One Finger Waltz" - 90
Orange County, California - 149
Original Sound Records - 270
Ostrich, The - 186, 238
Oswalt, Patton - 328
Otis Art Institute - 147
"Over the River and Through the Woods" - 245
Owl Yearbook - 16

Paliwoda, Amby - 153
Palm Springs, California - 254
*Pantagraph Sun, The* - 256, 294
Pantomime Pictures - xi
"Papa Oom Mow Mow" - 33
Paramount Home Entertainment - 198
Paramount Pictures - 12, 263
"Part Where I Cry, The" - 32
Partch, Virgil - 149, 163
Pastor, Tony - 4
Pate/Francis and Associates - 86, 89, 94, 197
Patience and Prudence - 9, 22, 30, 38, 47
Patrick, Lee - 183
Paul Butterfield's Blues Band - 269
Paul Sabatello - 14
Paxton, Gary - 33
PBS - 62

Pell, Dave - 259
Perkins, Lee - 247
"Persian On Excursion" - 10
Peter Rabbit - 79
Philadelphia, Pennsylvania - 29
Philips Records - 273
Phoenix Records - 262
Pierce, Tedd - 160, 164
Pin the Tail on the Donkey - 249
Pink Panther, The - 170
*Pittsburgh Press, The* - 91, 127
Playboy - 163
Playhouse Pictures - 137-138
"Polly Wolly Doodle" - 151
"Pop Goes the Weasel" - 85
Popeye - 144
Post cereals - 183, 225
Pratt, Hawley - 159
Presley, Elvis - 71, 86, 260
"Pretty Dark Eyes" - 11, 62
Prima, Louis - 12
Proby, P.J. - 33
"Prom, The" - 82, 262
*Proud and Profane, The* - 13-14
"Puff (The Magic Dragon)" - 254
"Purple People Eater" - 61
Pushmi-Pullyu - 265, 299

"Que Sera Sera" - 254, 272
Quebec, Canada - 162
"Quiet Village" - 32

"Race is On, The" - 260-261
"Ragtime Cowboy Joe" - 81-85, 123-124, 247, 310
Ray Charles Singers - 3
Ray, Johnny - 12
RCA Records - 30, 32, 36, 259
*Rear Window* - 14, 25
*Record World* - 317
"Red Wine" - 263
Redding, Otis - 266
Regan, Russ - 94
Reggie Mantle - 310

*Ren and Stimpy Show, The* - 327
"Respect" - 261
Riddle, Jimmie - 247
Rivers, Bob - 327
Rivingtons, The - 33
Road Runner, The - 152-153, 170
"Rock and Roll Doctor" - 327
"Rock Archives, Part One and Two" - 327
*Rockin' Through the Decades* (CD) - 314
*Rockin' Through the Decades* (TV special) - 313
Rocky and Bullwinkle - 189
*Rocky and Bullwinkle and Friends Sound Effects Library, The* - 168
*Rocky and his Friends* - 168
Roger Ramjet - 138, 158
Rogers, Kenny - 36
Rolling Stones, The - ix
Rose Parade, The - 293
"Ross Bagdasarian: The Man Who Would Be Chipmunk King" - 6, 58
Rubinstein, Jerry - 36
Ruby-Spears - 313
"Rudolph, the Red-Nosed Reindeer" - 91, 94, 129, 222, 245, 310
"Russian Roulette (Dark Eyes)" - 244

"Sack Time" - 90
"Safari" - 10
Salkin, Leo - 138-141, 143, 145-146, 148, 150-151, 164
"Salta Perico" - 84
Sam Valiant - 183, 186, 189
"Samba de Orfeu" - 142
"Samoan Knife Dance" - 84
*San Antonio Express* - 298
San Bernardino, California - 134
Sanderson, Lucinda Ann - 1, 57-58, 80, 83, 187
Sandy Bottomfeeder - 327
Saperstein, Henry G. - 137
*Saroyan: A Biography* - 4, 16
Saroyan, Aaron - 16
Saroyan, Carol - 16

Saroyan, Lucy - 246, 264, 305
Saroyan, Verna "Verkin" - 3
Saroyan, William "Bill" - 3-5, 7, 11, 16-17, 141, 246, 263-264, 313
"Scalawags and Sinners" - 246
Scarry, Richard - 111
Schelly, Bill - 242
*School's Out for Summer* - 314
Schulz, Charles M. - 159
Scotland - 91, 193
Scott, Keith - 168
Schwartz, Zachary - 133
Secrest, Mike - 10
"See a Teardrop Fall" 10
Segall, Don - 241-242
*Sgt. Pepper's Lonely Heart Club Band* - 251
Seville, David (see Bagdasarian, Sr., Ross)
Seville, Spain - 6, 65
Shannon, Del - 34
Shaw, Dick - 145, 149-150, 157
Shaw!, Scott - xi
"Shepherd Boy" - 12
Sierra Wine Company (Corporation) - 1, 266, 269-270
Simon - ix, 37, 55, 66, 72-73, 76-77, 81, 84-86, 90, 101-102, 109-116, 129-132, 140, 183-188, 202-214, 216, 218, 222-223, 225, 228-229, 231-232, 235, 239, 245, 250, 253, 255, 274-296, 298-299, 301-303, 312, 317, 319, 321-323, 325
*Simpsons, The* - 243
Sinatra, Frank - 254
"Sing a Goofy Song" - 88-89, 125, 195
*Sing Again With The Chipmunks* - ix, 89-90, 131, 222, 298
Sing Along With Mitch - 83
*Sing Along With The Chipmunks* - 83, 131
"Sing As We Go" - 31
Siracusa, Joe - 136, 138, 144, 149-150, 152, 159, 161-162, 165-168, 176
"Sit On My Face" - 31
"Sittin' in the Balcony" - 31

Slatkin, Felix - 32
*Sleeping Beauty* - 171
Smith, Keely - 12
*Smile* - 255
Smokey Bear - 250, 291, 310, 317
"Smokey's A-B-C's" - 250, 291
*So Fine* - 262
"Soaky Soaks You Clean" - 250
Soaky, the Fun Bath - 73, 249-250, 272, 291
"Soaky the Fun Bath Sends Greetings from The Chipmunks" - 250, 291
Society for Quiet and Universal Appreciation of Refined Enterprises, The (SQARE's) - 196
Solazzi, Danny - ix-x
*Solid Gold Chipmunks: 30th Anniversary Collection* - 313-314
"Song of Bruce and Dutch, The" - 266
*Songs From Our TV Shows* - 313
Sonny and Cher - 259
"Sorry About That, Herb" - 263, 297
Sound Ideas - 168
Spain - 6
"Spain" - 91
"Spanish Pizza" - 270
Speedy Gonzales - 170-171
Spencer Hagen Orchestra, The - 84
Springboard Records - 310, 318
*St. Louis Post-Dispatch* - 295
*Stalag 17* - 14
Stanley, John - 241-242
Stanley Johnson Orchestra, The - 84
Stanley the Eagle - 186, 190
"Stardust" - 31
"Starlight, Starbright" - 11
*Stars are Singing, The* - 14, 18
Stewart, James - 14
*Still Squeaky After All These Years* - 55, 58, 60, 64, 184-187, 250-251, 272
Storyboard, Inc. - 138
Strange, Billy - 33
"Stranger in Paradise" - 20, 84

Streegen, Jan - 160
Studio Five - 86, 89, 94, 245, 252, 255
Studio City, California - 141, 149
Sugarloaf - 35-36, 53
Sullivan, Ed - 65
*Summer Day's Delight, A* - 1, 266, 270-271, 273, 304
"Summertime Blues" - 31
*Sunday Showcase* - 78
Sunset Records - 35, 252, 264-265, 294, 299, 301-302
"Sunshine, Lollipops and Rainbows" - 260
Super Bowl VI - 273
"Supercalifragilisticexpialidocious" - 254-255, 271-272, 294
*Supercar* - 278
"Surf City" - 33
"Surfin' Bird" - 33
"Swanee River" - 89
Sweden - 258
"Sweet Someone" - 84
Sweetheart Pool Company - 191
"Swing Low, Sweet Chariot" - 192
"'Swonderful" - 39

T-Bones, The - 34
"Take Five" - 62
"Take Good Care of My Baby" - 32
"Talk to the Animals" - 264-265, 299
Tani Ritter - 14
Target - 316
Tawney, Michael J. - 1, 57-58. 80, 83, 187
Taylor, Bob - 27
Taylor, Chuck - 311
Tarzana, California - 187
TBS - 198
"Tea For Two" - 254
*Teen Comedy Party* - 327
*'Teen Magazine* - 68-72, 82, 130
Tempo Productions - 137-138
Terrytoons - 327
Theatre Guild - 2
Theodore - ix, 37, 55, 66, 73-74, 76-77, 81, 84-86, 90, 101-102, 109-116,
129-132, 140, 183-188, 192-193, 195, 202-214, 216, 219, 222-223, 225, 228-229, 231-232, 235, 238-239, 245, 250, 253, 255, 274-296, 298-299, 301-303, 312-313, 317-319, 321-323, 325
Thermos - 274
*Think Pink! The DePatie-Freleng Story* - 165
"Third Man Theme" - 10, 12, 273
*Thirteen "Going on Eighteen"* - 242
"This Diamond Ring" - 34-35, 259, 261
*This is Your Life* - 62, 82, 86, 103
*Three Chipmunks, The* - 242, 282
*Three Violent People* - 14
"Tiger Rag" - 84
*Time For Beany* - 62, 103
*Time of Your Life, The* - 2-5, 305
*Times, The* - 199
Tolegian, Manuel - 16
"Tomorrow" - 323
"Tongue in Cheek" - 36
*Tonight Show Starring Johnny Carson, The* - 246
"Tonight You Belong to Me" - 30
Tonto - 171
*Top Cat* - 187
Torrence, Dean - 33
Townsend, Ed - 33
*Tralfaz* - 168
Transamerica Corporation - 35-36
Trashmen, The - 33
Travesty Ltd. - 327
*Trick or Treason* - 313
Tripp, Irving - 242
"Trouble With Harry, The" - 9
Troup, Bobby - 30
*Troy Record, The* - 306
*Truth or Consequences* - 163-164
TTV - xi
Turkey - 3
Turner, Gil - 164
Turner, Ike and Tina (see Ike and Tina Turner)
Turtles, The - 272

*TV Guide* - 173
*TV Radio Mirror* - 5-7, 13-14, 59, 73, 169
TV Spots - xi, 139, 155-156, 158
"Twelve Days of Christmas, The" - 248
20th Century Fox - 12, 29, 264
"Twenty Flight Rock" - 31
Twinkies - 65
"Twinkle, Twinkle, Little Star" - 244
"Twist and Shout" - 252
"Twist, The" - 242
"Twisted Chipmunk Song, The" - 327
"Twitch and Writhe" - 327

"Uh Oh" - 94
Uncle Sam - 6
*Undeniable* - 315
United Artists Records - 35-36, 310-311, 317-318
Universal Music Group (UMe) - 36
Universal Studios - 30
University Brass Band - 84
Up On the Housetop - 245
UPA (United Productions of America) - xi, 133-138, 143, 147, 154-157, 167-168, 171, 174
*Urban Chipmunk* - 256, 312
US Department of Agriculture - 250, 263

Valli, Frankie - 272
Van Dyke, Dick - 249
*Variety* - 199
Vee, Bobby - 10, 32-33, 35, 48
*Very Best of The Chipmunks, The* - 311, 317
*Very First Alvin Show, The* - 325
*Very Merry Chipmunk, A* - 314
Viacom Enterprises - 198
Vietnam - 270
"Vineyard, The" - 273
Vining, Steve - 311
*Viva Zapata!* - 14

"Walk Away" - 51
"Walking Birds of Carnaby, The" - 263
Wallington, Jimmy - 84
Walt Disney Productions (see Disney, Walt)

Warner Bros. - xi, 103, 134, 136, 148, 152, 170-171, 272
Waronker, Simon "Si" - 29-30, 34, 37, 55, 59-60, 73-74, 76, 315
Watts, California - 260
"We Wish You a Merry Christmas" - 245
*We're the Chipmunks (Music From the TV Show)* - 315
Weinerville - 198
Weiss, Sam - 151, 160, 164-165
"Well, Happy Birthday Anyway" - 249
"What's New, Pussycat?" - 259, 261
"What's the Use" - 12, 14
"When I Look in Your Eyes" - 266
"When Irish Eyes Are Smiling" - 2
*When Magoo Flew: The Rise and Fall of Animation Studio UPA* - 133-134
*When You Wish Upon a Chipmunk* - 314
Whistler's Mother - 190
"White Christmas" - 74-75
Who, The - 31
Widmark, Richard - 27
*Wild Wild West, The* - 171
Wilkins, Stan - 147
Williams, Sam - 6
"Willow Weep for Me" - 12
*Wilmington News Journal, The* - 306
Wilson, Brian - 33
Wilson, Jackie - 31
"Winds of Time, The" - 266
Winters, Jonathan - 256
Winters, Marty - 6, 58-59, 84
"Wipe Out" - 261
"Witch Doctor" - 13-14, 32, 55-64, 68, 70, 74, 87, 89, 91, 96-98, 121, 196-197, 310
*Witch Doctor Presents David Seville ... and Friends, The* - 10-11, 60-63, 96
*Wizard of Oz, The* - 271
Wolf, Fred - 138, 147
Womack, Bobby - 35
"Wonderful Day" - 248, 250
"Wonderful Figures" - 78
Woodward, Woody - 265

Woody the Chipmunk - 252
Woolery, Adrian "Ade" - 137-138
"Word Game Song" - 10
World War II - 65, 135
Wrather, Bonita Granville - 171
Wrather, Jack - 171
Wrecking Crew, The - 259
*Wrecking Crew!, The* - 78, 259

XKE Jaguar - 159

"Yakety Eef" - 247
"Yalleh" - 266
"Yankee Doodle Dandy" - 85-86
"Yeah, Yeah" - 249
"Yellow Rose of Texas, The" - 260
"Yesterday and You" - 10
Yogi Bear - 302

"You Better Open Your Eyes" - 270-271
Young, Ralph - 166
"You're Sixteen" - 33
"You've Got Me on a Merry-Go-Round" - 270-271
Yuro, Timi - 33, 49
Yosemite - 74
YouTube - 247
"Y-y-y-yup" - 12

Zappa, Frank - 87
Zaslove, Alan - 136-138, 147, 151, 154, 156-157, 160
Zentner, Si - 32, 49
"Zubbediya" - 8, 20
Zwirn, Bob - 260

# ABOUT THE AUTHOR:

MARK ARNOLD IS AN animation, comic book and pop music historian with books on Harvey Comics, TTV (Underdog), Cracked Magazine, The Beatles, Disney, DFE (Pink Panther), Dennis the Menace, The Monkees to his credit. He is currently working on a Monkees solo book and a TTV Scrapbook and eventually a book on Marvel's Crazy Magazine. He lives in Springfield, Oregon.